D1453542

Warfare in Atlantic Africa, 1500–1800

Warfare in Atlantic Africa, 1500–1800

John K. Thornton

Millersville University

For my father, Robert L. Thornton for all his support through
the years

First published 1999 in the UK and the USA
by UCL Press
11 New Fetter Lane, London EC4P 4EE

The name of University College London (UCL) is a registered trade mark
used by UCL Press with the consent of the owner.

UCL Press in an imprint of the Taylor & Francis Group

© 1999 John K. Thornton

Typeset in Bembo by Best-set Typesetter Ltd.
Printed and bound in Great Britain by TJ International, Padstow Cornwall

British Library Cataloguing in Publication Data
A catalogue record for this book is available from the British Library

Library of Congress Cataloging in Publication Data
A catalogue record for this book has been requested

ISBN 1-85728-392-9 (Hbk)
ISBN 1-85728-393-7 (Pbk)

Contents

Maps

1. *The Gold Coast, 1500–1800*

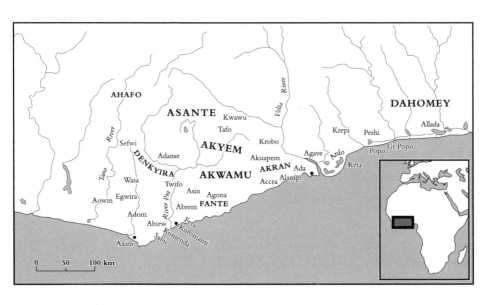

2. *The Gap of Benin and Niger Delta, 1500–1800*

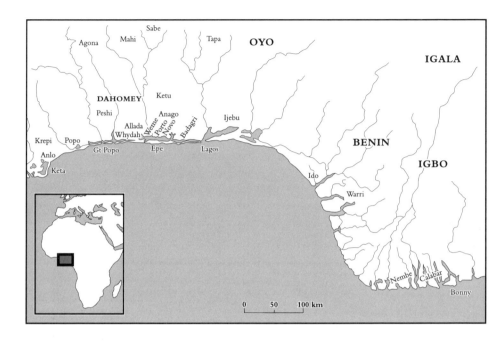

MAPS

3. West Central Africa, 1500–1800

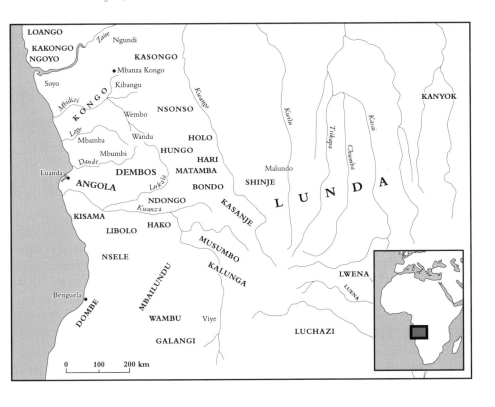

4. Senegambia, Sierra Leone and the Western Sudan, 1500–1800

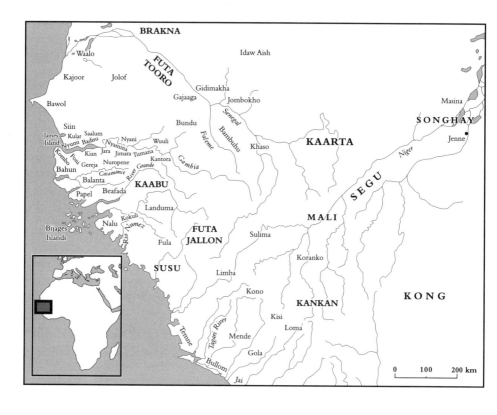

5. Battle of Mbwila, 29 October 1665
   (Shaded units are Portuguese, unshaded are Kongo)

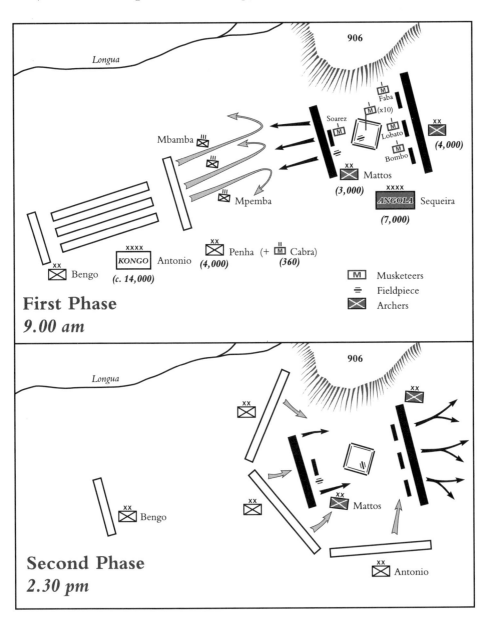

6. *Battle of Tondibi, 1591*
   (Shaded units are Moroccan, unshaded are Songhay)

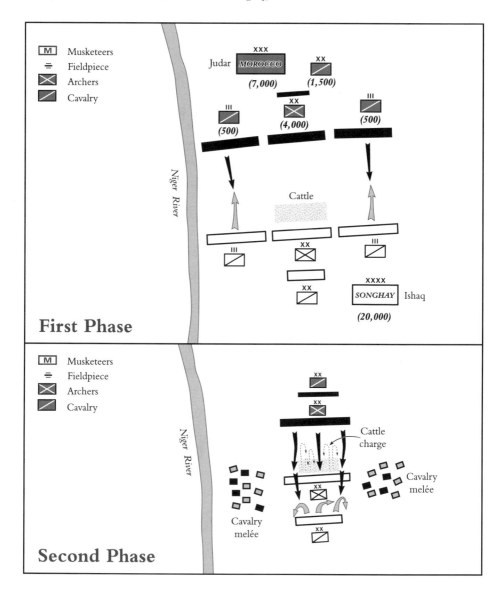

Preface

Although I was born into a military family, and served in the United States Air Force myself during the Vietnam era, it was not until after I completed my PhD in 1979 that I took a serious interest in military history. In 1980, Hans Schmidt, then a colleague at the University of Zambia, lent me his copy of John Keegan's *Face of Battle*, and awakened my interest in military history. The interest was further shaped through many conversations with Jay Luvaas, when we were colleagues at Allegheny College, 1981–3. It was largely because of these influences that I decided, while preparing an edition of Cavazzi's history of Queen Njinga, that I would study that famous Angolan queen as a military leader. The result was my brief study, "The Art of War in Angola", published in 1988, the work which eventually brought me into contact with the series editor Jeremy Black, who persuaded me to extend my interest in the military history of Angola to other parts of Africa.

Because African military historiography is fairly underdeveloped, I found it necessary to attempt this work largely through direct consultation of the relevant primary sources. Obviously, given the large number of such sources available, I have not been able to be comprehensive in this search, and although readers will see a wide variety of sources cited, both published and unpublished, archival and manuscript, these are not the result of a systematic search of the archives. Rather they represent a range of material that I have been able to locate, often through following footnotes of other authors, and to copy or consult.

This work has benefited from the research of many previous scholars, who not only guided me through the general histories of the regions of their specialities but, through their footnotes, allowed me to locate primary sources. Many of the sources, especially the archival sources, were located by following up footnotes in other work, for the Dutch and Danish materials by ordering relevant reels of microfilm from the microfilm collection at Northwestern University. For the French archival material I would like to thank Donna Eveleth, who at my request located documents in the various Parisian archives and forwarded transcriptions of them to me by e-mail – a remarkable new way to do research! She also supplied me with xerox copies of other documents and without her help I would never have been able to sort out the many unpublished French references. I would like to extend special thanks to various student assistants, Amber Kerkhoff, Christine Eenhorn and Femke Kitslaar, who helped me locate, reproduce and transcribe Dutch documents from microfilm.

I would like to thank the interlibrary loan department at Millersville University for their support in locating and borrowing a wide variety of material that was often hard to find. I have also received financial support from Millersville University Faculty Development, whose research grants allowed me to travel to Portugal and France in 1990, England in 1996, and to Brazil in 1998. Student helpers were also paid thanks to Millersville's work study program.

I owe a great debt to Jeremy Black, who not only encouraged me to undertake the project, but also provided me with a careful reading of the manuscript and some interesting discussions by mail and in person when he visited Millersville in 1997. Final thanks go, as always, to Linda Heywood, whose endless discussions of African history have continually shaped my thought and work.

Introduction

African War and World History

African Invisibility

The distinguished military historian John Keegan draws a fascinating map of the world in his *History of Warfare*, a thoughtful and generally well informed review of world military history. Intended to illustrate areas where climatic and population factors make war possible and impossible, the map is interesting for its depiction of Africa. The only areas in Africa where Keegan regards wars as being possible form a thin band along the north and west African coast, extending as far as Cameroon; and South Africa plus another thin band up the east African coast including the Horn of Africa and Ethiopia.[1] Historians of Africa could not help but be amazed by such a map – for it renders war impossible in the whole of the savannas of both west and central Africa. It leaves out the empires of the western Sudan, or the southern Nile valley. It asserts that war was impossible in Angola, apparently ignoring the long and complex wars of the seventeenth and eighteenth centuries, including extended campaigns, armies numbering in the tens of thousands, and battles, such as the battle of Mbwila in 1665, that are well described by contemporaries.[2] Angola, moreover, has been the scene much more recently of fairly large pitched battles: the siege of Cuito Cuanavale in 1988 between forces of the Angolan government and the rebel UNITA movement and its South African allies employed tens of thousands of soldiers, many tanks, aircraft and considerable artillery.[3]

This is not to pick on Keegan, whose point in drawing this map – that geographical and climatological factors prevent war from being waged everywhere – is well taken, and remains true even if its specific manifestation in Africa is clearly poorly researched. But the map does highlight the fact that Africa is largely ignored in world and comparative history, and also that

1

African military history is still in its infancy, with perhaps the exception of the history of South African wars such as the Zulu war of 1879 or the Anglo-Boer Wars (1881, 1897–1902), both well within Keegan's field of vision.[4] Furthermore, although one can easily remark that Africa is often left out or dealt with in a very unsophisticated manner in the literature of comparative history, military historians are often less inclined than their colleagues in other subspecialities to engage in an easy Eurocentrism. As any reader of popular military history magazines is readily aware, there is a willingness of such magazines and their readers to be quite receptive to articles on a wide range of regions, cultures and time periods. The idea that military history is universal, that war may be fought according to set laws which can be illustrated and discovered in many times and places, and the respect that some non-Western armies are accorded for their courage, tenacity, and sometimes even victory over Western armies (as in Vietnam) all contribute to this willingness of the discipline to see beyond the history and culture of Europe and its extensions. But this willingness has not yet reached to Africa in any systematic way.

Early writing on African military history was often by anthropologists, and subsumed under the category of "primitive war", of which Hugh Turney-High's 1949 pioneering work was a model.[5] While Turney-High presented comparative examples from widely dispersed societies, he included a number of African examples in his sample, which was organized thematically rather than regionally or temporally. Although he made occasional references to ancient and medieval European fighting in his book, these were not sustained, and for the most part, Turney-High seems to have accepted that African societies were primitive because this was their conventional designation, rather than as a result of careful study of their structures outside of the military.

Alongside ideas that Africa was primitive, in the specialized sense that this term was used in anthropology, African wars are often described as "tribal", perhaps simply another way of expressing the same ideas. Neil Whitehead has developed a theory that proposes a connection between European contact and the intensification and redirection of war to meet this new challenge among tribal people, grounded in his own research in the Carib region of South America. In a collection of essays dedicated to elaborating the concept, Robin Law sought to apply this theory to African societies engaged in the slave trade, but was not wholly supportive of Whitehead's approach, at least.[6]

Law's uneasiness with the concept of tribal war is perhaps a product of his own role in the development of a new and quite different African history from that of the older anthropologists. The new history has been available to historians of the world ever since Africa's rediscovery for professional histo-

2

rians in the 1960s. This historical work has transformed our conceptions about African tribalism, primitivism and development. Among other things, it has shown that most of Atlantic Africa had long ago passed the threshold of "civilized war", at least if war is to follow society.[7] The new scholarship on African history has included its wars, though, with a few notable exceptions, such as Ray Kea, Robin Law, and Robert Smith,[8] this has not generally included specifically military history. In part this may be because the young historians who pioneered the new African history in the 1960s and 1970s were frequently not shaped by military experience themselves – indeed many were responding to the anti-war sentiments engendered in the United States and Europe by the Vietnam war, which made them avoid the study of war and its suspect associations with militarism.

Nor was the problem simply Western anti-militarism discouraging historians from those regions, for the topic was also bypassed by African historians active after independence. African military men, many of whom rose to positions of power and authority in the coup-ridden 1960s, also neglected this historical field. The fact that modern African armies arose in the colonial period, created more or less from scratch by the conquering Europeans or by guerrilla leaders fighting against Europe at an even more recent time, meant that they had little tradition extending back to precolonial times. Their accoutrements, uniforms, ceremonies and memories reach to Europe more than to Africa, and their modern training still tends to be overseas, at least for its scholarly and historic elements. As a result the scholarly soldier, employed perhaps at a military academy, is generally absent in Africa, and so, therefore, is the careful study of the more distant military past. While modern African nationalism frequently seeks to evoke the past, and especially the precolonial and traditional past, this stricture does not really include the military, whose past in the colonial era is too darkly shadowed by their history as imperialist collaborators, and for whatever reasons African military men have not sought to rediscover a precolonial ideology and iconography for themselves.

Despite these obvious obstacles to the writing of military history for Africa, the historic blindness towards Africa is still curious. Warfare in Atlantic Africa, after all, was one of the primary means of the enslavement of literally millions of Africans and their transportation to America between the fifteenth and nineteenth centuries, the largest intercontinental migration in human history until the Industrial Revolution transformed migration altogether. Anyone who chose to interview slaves in America about their enslavement in this period, like the Moravian missionary Georg Christian Oldendorp working in the Virgin Islands in the 1760s, quickly came to this conclusion.[9]

Given the world historic significance of the slave trade, one might reasonably expect that these African wars would have been the subject of extensive scrutiny and research, and yet for the most part they have not been. An earlier generation was content to dismiss African wars as tribal wars that needed no special explanation, or whose explanation defied the logic of those civilized wars that were the proper subject of military history. Perhaps, too, the fact that pre-colonial African wars, especially in the period of the slave trade, are sometimes seen as simply slave raids, has inhibited attempts to study them as wars. Some historians of the slave trade have tended to treat these military events as "raids", often more akin to hunting expeditions than wars. Thus when Henry Gemery and Jan Hogendorn wrote an economic study of the slave trade they suggested that the introduction of firearms reduced the cost of slaves by making slave raiding easier.[10] The same sort of logic was applied by Patrick Manning in his study of the demography of the slave trade. Manning described the event that resulted in the enslavement of Africans as a "raid" and imagined that such raids could be repeated regularly by one group on a victim population, while recognizing that in the long range sometimes roles could be changed or even reversed. The model, interestingly enough, assumes that the raiders suffer no casualties in their attack, though mortality in capture is assumed for the raided group, reflecting, unconsciously perhaps, that these were wars of an unusual type.[11] Such work was typically theoretical, without connecting the model to any actual war, even as an example or a source for data, and likewise, quantitative work on the slave trade has rarely tried to match real wars to exports in any systematic way.

On the other hand, the historiography of the slave trade is highly controversial and this in turn has affected the study of war. When Philip Curtin published his landmark study of the economy of the slave trade era in Senegambia in 1975, he suggested that enslavement might follow one of two models. Either it was an economic model, in which people were enslaved and wars fought largely in response to the possibilities of profit (the slave raid model), or it was a political model, in which wars were fought for political reasons and people were enslaved more or less as an afterthought.[12] Curtin's contention that the political model might be dominant, however, brought a sustained attack from Boubacar Barry, who sought to show that the economic model worked better, or rather that African warfare was much more a response to the demands of the slave trade.[13] When Paul Lovejoy tried to assess the demographic cost of the slave trade, for example, all casualties and dislocations caused by wars – "slave trading wars" – were added into the cost factors, obviously assuming that these wars had a motive rooted in the slave trade.[14] On the whole, the field has tended more towards Barry's position than Curtin's and the economic model of war – African wars as slave raids – has tended to prevail, with a concomitant reluctance to grant war much status or close study.

Theories of War

Since African wars have not been closely studied except through the slave trade, and even then only a few scholars, such as Kea and Law, have studied them as military historians would study them, they have also been subject to a great deal of casual determinism. This is particularly true with regard to the role of Europeans in promoting African wars and supplying African armies. Thus, the relationship between war and the slave trade might be seen as one or another "cycle", such as the "gun–slave cycle" or the "horse–slave cycle". In the gun–slave cycle, first advanced in the eighteenth century by Abolitionists, the European monopoly on guns plays a central role. By channelling guns to powers willing to cooperate with them, European buyers guaranteed that slaves would be captured because guns gave their clients the opportunity to make war successfully, and slaves were a natural outcome of war. Captives of the wars became the means to pay for the weapons that prosecuted them successfully. Those who opposed the slave trade were effectively cut off, for without guns they became victims of their neighbours who cooperated and thus obtained guns. They were either destroyed by their neighbours or forced to give in to traders' demands and obtain guns, to be paid for by slaves.[15]

The other cycle, more recently advanced, proposed that horses provided the same sort of military dynamics, when ecological and epidemiological conditions favoured it. Thus, Robin Law has suggested that the horse-breeding nomads of the Sahara were able to monopolize high-quality cavalry mounts for the armies to their south, where climatic and ecological conditions made breeding of the best horses impossible. By doing this, the Saharans managed to force the southerners into wars to pay for the horses. The same process repeated itself farther south, where the Oyo empire, growing up far from the Sahara, still relied on imports controlled by their northern neighbours to fight their wars and needed slaves to pay for the horses.[16]

Ultimately, verification of such hypotheses can only advance when African wars, whatever their causes or motivations, are seriously and carefully studied, using the original primary sources in the way that Kea and Law have opened up. Although some studies have done this for some times and places, there is still a substantial amount of work to do. Whatever can be said about motives, moreover, it is important to see just how those African wars that we can document were fought, and we must seek to answer basic questions about weapons, strategy and tactics, organization and logistics for Africa as for any other part of the world.

Those scholars who have attempted to approach this issue have been intrigued by questions raised in the late 1960s by Jack Goody, whose anthropologically inspired meditations on African war have been a starting point for much of the work that followed. Goody began with the contention that in Africa, with low population densities and inefficient technology, control of the "means of destruction" was more important than control over "means of production" and thus placed armies firmly in the panoply of state and political development. From there he made distinctions in the types of social organization that armies generated: cavalry forces in the savannah regions of west Africa tended towards a sort of decentralized military oligarchy (though not feudalism), because mounts were expensive and only a limited number of people could afford them. Armies in forested regions, on the other hand, used bows as their principal weapon, which necessarily created much more democratic organizations, since bows were owned by everyone and used in hunting. Finally, he argued that the introduction of firearms by Europeans gave the forest rulers the opportunity to strengthen their authority by concentrating the imported weapons, thus leading to the rise of highly centralized forest kingdoms such as Asante and Dahomey in the eighteenth century.[17] Goody's work was based on a fairly superficial reading of the documentary record; a much more careful reading and description of west African fighting by Robert Smith in 1976 demolished many of his analytically exciting but undemonstrable positions about the distinctions between bow-using and horse-riding regions and the impact of the use of firearms.[18]

Although few are interested any longer in the examination or testing of Goody's specific conclusions, the idea that social organization and military technology have jointly shaped both African politics and its warfare is still widespread in the study of African military history, as it is in military history in general. Thus, the question of how cavalry was organized and how horses were obtained has been of great importance in some areas, and the role of firearms in transforming warfare has been much discussed in others. Contrasts between savannah cavalries and forest infantries continued to be made as well, if for other reasons than those developed by Goody.[19]

European Models

The study of African military history can fit into a growing literature of comparative history that has emerged in the last decade and has come to re-evaluate earlier generalizations about the military history of the past four hundred years. In part, this literature has traced in greater detail the change of military organization and technology in western Europe, often under the rubric of the "military revolution", a term first coined in 1956 by Michael

Roberts and more recently modified and generalized by Geoffrey Parker.[20] In this scheme a series of changes, both technological and organizational, sets the agenda for modernization. Starting with the effective use of gunpowder for artillery, which ended the era of castles, and handheld firearms, which ended that of armoured cavalry, the military revolution saw changes in the relationship of infantry to cavalry, and with it the social standing of the principal arms. No longer did the armoured and noble knight hold sway over the battlefield: wars were decided by sweating, dirty commoners, even riff-raff, in the increasing masses of infantry. Permanent, paid soldiers replaced feudal infantry levies and the private forces of nobles, and bureaucratization and fiscalization of the military necessarily followed.[21] Keegan, whose version of this tale is less triumphalist and more nuanced, notes that the final stages of the revolution produced the huge, conscripted, standardized armies of post-Napoleonic Europe, whose greatest pride, inspired by Clausewitz and already being nourished in the armies of the eighteenth century, was their ability to take casualties in ghastly and horrifying numbers.[22]

This paradigm of military history is often taken as being universal, or at least world historic rather than simply European in orientation, largely because it coincided with European expansion and conquest, or because in many areas, but especially in south and west Asia, it was imitated by local powers. Other military systems and cultures are judged effective and important to the degree that they conform to this pattern.[23] Although the general tendency in this literature has been to ignore Africa (even Angola, where a conquest was attempted), it has been generally assumed that Africans were behind in these developments, not possessing the requisite social or political resources, perhaps because of their continuing label as "primitive" societies. Keegan, for example, invokes a widely held belief when he explains that African kingdoms survived during the Age of Expansion through being "protected by their disease barrier".[24] Disease has been invoked as an explanation of why the Portuguese failed to conquer a significant African power in Angola, the one place in Africa where serious and sustained conflict between European-led and trained forces and African forces took place.[25] Frequently, when Africa is brought in, it has been fitted into this scheme through the cycles, especially the gun–slave cycle.

Military backwardness has been assumed as a parallel to economic backwardness, itself a product of Africa's divergent economic pattern. This allows the apparent modernization of the adaptation of guns into armies to be put aside because its connection to the slave trade makes it appear to be a result of European-directed actions: this allows sixteenth- to eighteenth-century Africa's military history to be seen as an aspect of the remarkable capacity of Europeans to "underdevelop" Africa without occupying it.[26]

The idea of the military revolution, like that of modern economies, has assumed the primacy and uniqueness of a single pattern and, as with the course of economic progress, the European model is viewed as both the norm and the necessity. But while economic proficiency has been measured by the achievement of such ultimate goals as increased life expectancy, lower infant mortality, higher per capita income[27] and so on, the same attention to ultimate goals has not always applied to armies.

Armies are successful if they win. That is, armies succeed if they achieve the objectives set for them by their commanders and political superiors. Victory in operational contexts is easy to judge, since it is not difficult to fix objectives and determine whether they have been met. But armies also function as elements of society, and here military effectiveness is harder to judge, especially if it is tied up in assumptions about other aspects of development.

Military historians have assumed, more often than historians of economics, that the ultimate social goal is centralization, even though, in the United States at least, a prevailing mythology that irregular American militias allied to decentralized and democratic government defeated regular forces counters it to some degree. This is one reason why military systems that support the rise of centralization are seen as advancing in a developmental sequence. Thus, in European history one finds that the development of regular armies and the replacement of untrained feudal levies and aristocratic cavalries are seen as a step forward, both in promoting and reflecting centralization and in operational effectiveness. John Lynn's study of Western "Styles of War", including the way in which a larger social reorganization is affected by and affects the organization and maintenance of armies, is one such scheme.[28] On the other hand, Keegan's summary of various types of army organization, whether recruited by mass levy, from ethnically special groups, from mercenaries or other private forces, by militia call-up, or by employing slaves, probably should not be arranged in any evolutionary sequence,[29] and indeed, the evidence on African military organization presented below is testimony against any such attempt. African armies and military effectiveness are often assessed, not by the success that their commanders enjoyed in their own regions of operations, but against the standard of the approximation to the European model, especially difficult in Africa, where there were virtually no direct encounters outside of Angola. In Angola, the fact that Europeans were not particularly successful, and largely adopted African organization and technique, certainly does not support the idea that African armies that did not follow European models of organization were less effective. Above all else, however, the ease with which Africa was conquered by European-led forces of locally recruited African soldiers in the late nineteenth century has supported the belief that the military backwardness that this event illustrates was a permanent condition of Africa (even though the military transformations of the Industrial Revolution are not fully considered in the assessment).

Very often operational effectiveness is also equated to this developmental scheme: for example, the fact that the army of Dahomey impressed observers as being well-drilled and hence like a European army often gave it an aura of success and even invincibility that it did not enjoy in real life.[30] Thus armies with many regular soldiers should defeat those that lack regulars, since having large numbers of regulars is a sign of development. Presumably this is because regulars are more disciplined or better fighters than the non-professionals. The development of regular armies may well have the advantage of giving sustained training and coherence to professionals and thus produce a more effective body of soldiers, at least for the volley fire tactics of European armies that relied on drill to produce rapidity of loading and comradely cohesion while taking casualties. But regular soldiers also perform a social function which might be just as important, in that they are loyal to the state that pays and maintains them, and in time this same state comes to have a monopoly over the deployment of arms. By performing this function they contribute to centralized power. Such characteristics might make them more desirable even than forces that are superior from the point of view of operational effectiveness.

Skill in the handling of weapons and individual virtuosity might be the hallmark of the highly trained noble warrior, in sixteenth-century Kongo or in feudal Europe, and such troops might be well controlled by a state through professionalization (as in Kongo), or might be able to put military effectiveness in a programme of decentralized power and decision making (as in feudal Europe). Before embarking on any developmental approach to African warfare, one must consider both the military and social aspects of the deployment of armies and avoid quick judgments based on closeness to the trajectory of Europe.

Military Technology

Obviously a technological determinism follows that of organizational development, and forces us to abandon the paradigm based wholly on the experience of European forces with their complex historical evolution. The superiority of firearms to other types of missile weapons in fighting with armoured cavalry, well established on European battlefields during the Military Revolution, might not be so obvious in other military traditions and environments. Cycles such as the gun–slave cycle are predicated on the idea that a force using firearms will be able to defeat equal or even larger forces that lack these weapons. Yet, Malone's study of the use of firearms by Native Americans in New England showed that tactical use of the weapons was important also, and explains why Native Americans sought flintlocks many years before they were in general use in Europe, as accuracy and undetectability were crucial in their methods of fighting.[31]

In fact, there is a complicated logic of missile weapons that needs to be considered. Goody, in his argument that bow weapons were democratic because they were universal, overlooks the substantially different requirements of archery for hunting from military archery. Hunters are interested in accuracy first and foremost, a bit less in range, and not much at all in penetrating power. Most hunted animals are not armoured, although a certain penetrating power is necessary, and once one reaches killing range no further development is necessary. Range helps a hunter only in that it allows a poor stalker to shoot from farther away, but the gains in range may not be helpful enough to warrant improving bows to achieve it and, not surprisingly, hunting bows often seemed quite flimsy. Moreover, ultimately more powerful bows also require more powerful archers to use them, and hunters might not be capable of or interested in achieving the additional strength.

War is different. Range is always important in war because, unlike animals, humans shoot back and there is a very important gain in having long-range missile weapons that allow one side to shoot while out of the way of return fire. Likewise, the introduction of any armour makes penetrating power an element in the equation. As a result, the most powerful bows have been developed for war, and have had little extra utility in hunting. The pressure of military competition may well be the spur that drives archers to undergo the lifelong physical training required to use more powerful bows. Archaeologists can still identify archers in skeletal populations by the unusual bone density of the bow arm created through constant stress. Both the crossbow and the musket were designed to gain more power than could be delivered by ordinary human muscle, even the best trained and conditioned.

Missile weapon development in Europe was driven in large measure by the need to counteract armour, so that weapons of great penetrating power were needed. Those who equipped armies were prepared to give up the higher rate of fire of archery in exchange for the certain penetrating power of muskets, once a workable design had been developed in the late fifteenth century. Furthermore, muskets required little skill to use, and most training was simply to ensure that the weapon was fired rapidly, and not necessarily accurately.

African armies did not devote as much attention to armour, although they certainly did use some sort of body protection (especially shields) in most

10

areas. As a result, powerful missile weapons were less important. Many African armies relied heavily on shock tactics rather than missiles to win the day, and these in turn required the use of the *arme blanche* (hand-to-hand weapons) such as swords, battleaxes, or stabbing spears, rather than missiles, which were loosed only in the opening part of engagements. Firearms, because of limitations on range and especially on rate of fire, were no more effective in halting the charge of an army prepared to take casualties from missile weapons and intending to fight hand-to-hand than archers would be, especially if the fighters are not armoured. In both Europe and Africa, the slow rate of fire made firearms most attractive if they could be employed by large armies, so that sheer numbers could compensate for the rate of fire. Certainly, firearms would not allow a small force to defeat a much larger one, especially if the larger force were psychologically conditioned to deal with firearms and were prepared to take casualties before they closed.

Archers using poisoned arrows, fairly widespread in Africa, added another dimension: the important penetrating power of musketry, which outweighed its fairly slow rate of fire (its superior range being often offset by lack of accuracy), was much less important in a setting where any wound was potentially fatal. The earliest European–African military contests, waged on the Senegambian coast in the mid-fifteenth century, clearly reveal the superiority of poisoned arrows to the armour that Portuguese marines wore in the period, for the Portuguese accounts of the encounters constantly reveal the fear they had of poisoned archery. Given the musket's general inaccuracy, musketry was most effective when masses of troops confronted each other, and less effective when soldiers advanced in dispersed order (as they often did in Africa) or in environments such as rainforest.

Unarmoured African cavalry seem to have found firearms less important, as seems to have been the case in Senegambia, where battlefield combinations of infantry and cavalry were quite different to those in Europe. It is easy to imagine that the tight formations of eighteenth-century European armies, along with their insistence on marching, dress and cover, and drill, provided an absolute superiority on the battlefield, without considering that they were the product of an evolution in conjunction with cavalry. As long as large numbers of cavalry were on the field, infantry could not afford to straggle or leave gaps. The bayonet on the musket allowed the pikemen of older periods, also developed in partial defence against cavalry, to be retained. Once committed to tight formations by the cavalry, infantry tactics evolved into the kind of mass firing and bayonet charging that was the norm in European warfare of the time. Thus, for military observers of the eighteenth century, and often the modern historians who read their works, the organizational and tactical necessities of European armies were not just the specific adaptations of two arms to each other in a particular type of miltary environment, but the only or most effective way to organize men to fight.

Yet in much of Africa cavalry was impossible because of ecological factors (such as the coastal regions or the densely forested zones) or epidemiological factors (which kept horses from operating in central Africa). Without cavalry the logic of combat operations is completely thrown open. In much of Africa infantry did not have to close ranks and did not require pikes or other anti-cavalry weapons. As a result they tended to fight in open order, sometimes in order to enhance the individual skill of fighters, in other cases simply to make missile weapon strikes slower or less effective by requiring their users to aim at their targets. Of course, concentration in a strategic sense was still important and so the apparent straggling of African fighting formations – engendering constant comments by European observers that African armies fought without order – was only apparent. Generals still had to move troops together and to concentrate them in the battlefield if they expected to be effective, and did so. But it has been very easy for this apparent disorder to be seen as ineffectiveness, though in Angola where Europeans expecting to be able to use cavalry and to be able to engage in outright slaughter of African armies found out that in head-to-head combat, the true test of military effectiveness, African soldiers and African tactics had a firm foundation that could not be ignored.[32]

Increasingly historians of world military history are challenging the idea that military systems that did not follow the European model were developmentally backward or operationally inferior. A series of publications in the last decade have begun to delineate questions along these lines for warfare in North America, in India, Southeast Asia and China.[33] Some work has also questioned the paradigm for Africa, and the present study will continue to do so.

Atlantic Africa as a Region

In the chapters that follow, I will attempt a more detailed examination of the way in which Atlantic Africans conducted war in the period of 1500–1800, seeking to understand warfare as it has usually been approached by military historians, though with an eye to the questions that have been addressed specifically to this region. Any attempt to do this, however, must overcome certain difficulties. Although it is plausible to unite Atlantic Africa through its contact with Europe and through its common participation in the slave trade, these external contacts are the only unifying thread. In fact, Atlantic Africa can be seen as remarkably diverse. According to my own research, we can name

and locate at least 150 sovereign polities about which we can make meaningful military generalizations within this region in 1600.[34] There were undoubtedly more, for a map of the political geography of Atlantic Africa contains
significant blank areas which were occupied and undoubtedly politically
organized, but about which we have less information. We can take only some
solace in considering that those states which were outside European notice
(and hence are unknown to us) were also outside the zone whose unity shapes
the present work.

Each of these entities was sovereign, possessed its own government and
constitution, and deployed its own military organization and sent it into
battle. Potentially, therefore, we might have the unenviable task of describing
150 types of war or military organization. However, as it is impossible for a
single polity to make any but a civil war by itself and military interactions
shape all engaged parties, these 150 states formed distinct regional military
cultures.

When Robert Smith began his survey of precolonial west Africa in 1976,
he chose to adopt a thematic approach to the problem of dealing with the
complexity created by these many different states.[35] In effect, this choice of
approach assumed that west Africa formed its own, more or less uniform,
military culture. Thus, in spite of the many polities and wars, Smith had
relatively little problem in discussing an issue by amassing data from many
different areas. Of course, this work in practice does not conform to the
model of a single military culture, for Smith recognizes that forest, river and
savannah promoted fighting on foot, from boats and from horseback.
Similarly, he saw that these different ecologies necessarily shaped the way that
infantries fought in each of them, so that a regional dimension necessarily
crept back in.

Another possibility is to take a regional approach, and assume that converg-
ing systems of communication, trade and politics made states within a region
defined by these systems fight each other regularly. All armies that fought in
such a region would necessarily have to accommodate all the other armed
forces of the region and in this way a common regional style of fighting would
have to develop. Such an approach runs the risk of being repetitive, as there
are certainly some commonalities in African history and culture, but it
promises to tease out a greater variety of African military experience.

To flesh out a regional approach one must develop a number of geographical issues. The first of these is to define Atlantic Africa in a meaningful way.
This can be done by defining it in terms of the slave trade, that is, by arguing
that the region that supplied the slave trade forms a natural geographic region.
Two works help to make that definition: in 1627 Alonso de Sandoval, a Jesuit
priest ministering to slaves arriving in Cartagena, wrote a treatise on African

geography that probably defined comprehensively the origins of the people he was meeting.[36] In 1777 Oldendorp wrote a similar work on African geography that also relied on the testimony of a wide variety of African slaves, selected precisely because of the variety of their languages for linguistic work.[37]

Atlantic Africa as defined in these two works included a broad stretch of the western Sudan, essentially as defined by the coast from modern Liberia to Senegal and the system of rivers that arose from the Futa Jallon mountains in modern Guinea-Conakry (Niger, Senegal, Gambia, as well as many smaller ones). However, as few slaves came from the Niger once one passes the great bend of the river near Timbuktu until its lower reaches in modern southern Nigeria, the area east of the great bend will not be considered. The region also included the coasts of modern Ghana, Benin, Togo, Nigeria and Cameroon, and interior stretches that can best be defined by the southern limits of the savannah that lay inland from the great coastal forest. The last portion is west central Africa, defined also by riverine systems, of the Zaïre system west of the Lualuaba, the Kwanza system and the Kunene system. These rivers, the highland areas that formed their demarcations, and the transportation networks that used them provide us with the first and broadest definition of Atlantic Africa.[38]

A second geographical issue concerns specific terrain at a regional level. We can distinguish four zones that are militarily significant in Africa. First, there are the broad savannahs of the western Sudan, ideal for the use of cavalry and ruled by horse soldiers and their infantry accompaniment. Second are the extensive savannahs of central Africa, where because of disease cavalry could not survive; these were the land where infantry reigned supreme and even reconnaissance had to be done on foot. Thirdly, there is the great tropical rainforest of west Africa, impossible for horses and thus infantry country, but also so tangled by trees and undergrowth (for most of it was secondary forest even in the sixteenth century) that warfare was channelled into fairly fixed locations and a war of ambush and position was often important. Finally, there were the river valleys and coastal regions where boats and marines played an important role in moving troops and manoeuvre.

Taking the larger regions and combining them with the special military environments of Atlantic Africa, one can delineate what might be called military-diplomatic regions, that is, areas in which the political organizations within the region had more interactions among themselves than with those lying around them. I have defined African military-diplomatic regions based on geographical criteria as well as frequency of interactions between participants. Broadly, I have divided Atlantic Africa into three regions formed in part by European traders' designations: Upper Guinea, Lower Guinea and Angola (West Central Africa). Upper Guinea covers the region integrated by the rivers which flow northward and westward from the Futa Jallon and is cut off, in my 1600 map, from Lower Guinea by a band of unknown territory in modern-day Côte d'Ivoire and Burkina Faso. Lower Guinea then forms the coast and its hinterland as far as rivers flow from modern Ghana to Cameroon, and Angola the whole of west central Africa, from the coast of Gabon to Angola.

I have further subdivided Lower Guinea into two parts, although, unlike the divisions between Upper and Lower Guinea and between west Africa and Angola, this division is not created by a military no man's land where fighting was not connected to the Atlantic. It is for that reason not a very clean one. The western end, the trader's Gold Coast, dominated by people of the Akan group, is the land of forest warfare with a special method of fighting created by that environment. The eastern end, on the other hand, is characterized by open country backing into a complex coastal system of rivers, swamps and lagoons where entirely different methods of fighting were employed. But the border between the two, the region around the Volta River known in the eighteenth century as "Krepi" country, had characteristics of forest and of coastal marine warfare. There were frequent incursions across the boundary and it was not sharply delineated, but war on the Gold Coast side was sufficiently different to make it appropriate to divide this long coast into two separate regions.

Within all of Atlantic Africa war was overwhelmingly the business of state, even if individual armed forces might be private mercenary bodies (such as those raised by wealthy merchants on the Gold Coast) or independent bodies moved by religous cults (such as the Imbangala in Angola or the Sumbas in Sierra Leone). Atlantic Africa was a land of states, if we use the term state to mean a permanent institution that claims jurisdiction over people and sovereignty over defined areas of land, creates and enforces laws, mediates and if necessary settles disputes and collects revenue. Declaring war, calling up armies, and maintaining or controlling the forces so deployed were the business of state, and made war in Africa quite unlike the spontaneous and shortlived affairs often associated in anthropological literature, or Hollywood depictions, with primitive wars.

What made Atlantic African states interesting was their small size and corresponding large number. There were, of course, some large political units – kingdoms like Kongo, Oyo, Benin, or Ndongo covering thousands, even hundreds of thousands of square kilometres and ruling several hundred thousand and even millions of inhabitants, but probably more than half of the people in Atlantic Africa lived in polities that measured around 50 kilometres across and had only a few thousand inhabitants, comparable in size to an American county or perhaps to a parish in older European political organizations.[39] Such an organization often meant that wars were complex, involving frequent alliances, for example. It also meant that the total size of the polity was small, so that mercenary groups or private armies might play a more significant role than in areas with larger states. But the precise play of state and private forces of this sort was determined by the exact political landscape of any given region at any time, and these are outlined in detail in the chapters that follow.

People as Property

Although the organization of African societies by states may make African history come closer than that of some areas to the Clausewitzian model of war as a continuation of politics, there is one feature of African law that differs from that of Europe and has military implications. This feature is that African law, in all the polities about which we have any information, did not recognize land as private property. This legal variation had a number of important implications. Because land was not viewed as a source of revenue, only rights over people counted, which made state institutions critically important and control over the state crucial on the one hand, and also gave special impetus to slavery as an institution for private, revenue-producing wealth. Indeed, ownership of slaves in Africa was virtually equivalent to owning land in western Europe or China.[40]

The lack of landed property also made considerable physical mobility possible in Africa. Without title to a particular plot of land to tie them down, and with relatively little investment in land, peasants could move on their own, or be forcibly moved, with relatively little disruption. In addition, the custom in much of Africa of building relatively impermanent but easily replaceable structures for houses, which were moved when being rebuilt, benefited from the absence of ties to land and perhaps helped keep the legal custom vital. By destroying housing frequently and rebuilding quickly, populations in tropical zones could avoid the difficulties of sanitation in the climate, as well as limit the health problems of long-term occupation of single places. Of course, some locations were more fixed than others – cities anchored in one place by political necessity, religious significance, or strategic importance formed one element fixing population. São Salvador, the capital of Kongo, was such a town. Anchored by the cathedral, tombs of the dead kings, and other religious relics, it was fought over, occupied and reoccupied time and time again by the frequently quite mobile population of Kongo.[41] Indeed, fortification played a significant role in the length of time an area might be occupied, but many African fortifications were themselves not very permanent.

The mobility of population meant that wars conducted to remove people from an opponent might have the same impact as those aimed at conquest would elsewhere, by increasing the assessible population under one state's jurisdiction, but without the administrative costs. Enslavement and transportation of people was easier than conquest; it was also easier to enrich one's small state by increasing its population in this way. It also meant that armies along with their families and support might be moved from one place to another more or less permanently, as is attested, for example, in Kongo in the seventeenth-century civil wars, in the Gold Coast and regions around Dahomey. Indeed, refugee armies from Gold Coast wars fairly filled up the region around the Volta, while refugee royal houses and their troops occupied lands along the coast, thwarting Dahomey's plans for conquest in the eighteenth century.

The differences in political and economic structure between Africa and Europe thus make careful study of the original sources of military history important. African armies no longer fight wars as their ancestors did; guerrilla wars waged in the 1960s and 1970s and more conventional wars waged in Uganda, Zaïre, Angola and Biafra have followed models from the West or at least from outside Africa. Anthropological observation, if it was ever a guide to the more distant past, is impossible in this field at least.

The Sources

The full study of African war, like the study of African history in general, is greatly hampered by the source material available to historians. Aside from the Islamic region of west Africa and Christian central Africa, there were no local written documents. Even in these areas, local sources are not particularly numerous and often have limited scope and topic. The Arabic-language chronicles written in the seventeenth and eighteenth centuries on the Niger bend region provide military details of life there, and are invaluable sources of military history from an African perspective. They are also unique, for even in Senegambia, which also had a stratum of literate people, there is no equivalent military record.

The records of Christian central Africa are even less helpful. Most of the Kongolese records, royal letters almost entirely, contain only the scantiest of military details, while the documents generated by local rulers in the "Dembos" region are equally enigmatic and incomplete. The whole panoply of the Angolan wars of the seventeenth century are described in tolerable detail, though only from the Portuguese point of view.

Oral traditions recorded or set in writing in the late-nineteenth and twentieth centuries, while sometimes helpful for political history and occasionally for the mention or contextualization of wars, cannot give us any reliable information on the actual conduct of war. Battles in such sources, such as the dramatic description of the battle of Krina in the "Epic of Sundiata", Mali's legendary thirteenth-century king, are full of anachronism and storyteller's heroics, and cannot be considered trustworthy for details of organization of armies, battlefield manoeuvres, or losses.

In the end, therefore, we are left with European documentation. For much of Africa, Europeans are at least neutral witnesses, since they might write impartially of conflicts in which they were not directly involved. But at the same time, this very neutrality limits their interest and the fullness of their reports. Occasionally we learn of large-scale battles involving tens of thousands of combatants and of major political significance, from a few lines in a factor's report. Since Europeans did have some interest in warfare, if for no other reason than because it was an important source of slaves, we do occasionally have an account of "typical" military affairs. Such accounts often inform the reader how an army formed up, what equipment it carried, how it proceeded to battle, and general information on tactics. Obviously, such reports are invaluable for the reconstruction of African military history, and indeed, they are the lifeblood of this and any other study of African warfare.

But in addition to these generalized descriptions, one also needs descriptions of real-life operations. A few of these are found in the Arabic documents of the Niger bend, a few more in the campaign diaries of the Angolan armies led by Portugal (or in chronicles based on them), or in accounts of Europeans who for one reason or another accompanied an African army into action (often because a detachment of Europeans had been engaged in the war). Smaller and less informative chunks of information may give operational details as well of actions between two African armies where no European presence was noted. On the whole, however, very few African wars are documented with any sort of fullness; certainly even for the operations of European-commanded armies in Angola, accounts fall well short of the detail found in seventeenth- and eighteenth-century European wars. Much as we may wish to, we are unlikely to be able to evoke the feel of battle in seventeenth-century Africa the way Keegan has done for medieval and early modern Europe.

Chapter One

Cavalries of the Savannah

The core of the northern half of west Africa was a broad open savannah, gradually giving way to the scrubby semi-arid lands of the Sahel as one moved north, until eventually one came to the vast expanse of the Sahara desert. The savannah region and part of the Sahel were penetrated by two great rivers – the Senegal on the west and the looping Niger on the east, as well as a host of shorter rivers that all emerged from the highlands of Futa Jallon in the south and found their way to the sea. The rivers brought water to the tricky and variable climates of the Sahel and the bend of the Niger passed through land that might otherwise have been desert. Even further south, where rainfall was adequate for full time agriculture, the rivers and streams provided a vast transportation network that not only allowed irrigation but permitted the concentration of agricultural resources over larger areas and underwrote chains of towns and, on the Niger, thriving significant cities. As one neared the coast, especially the coast around the Gambia and south of it, the network of rivers thickened and combined with forests to became a complex riverine environment of creeks, estuaries and small rivers, promoting a unique flora of a semi-flooded environment. This environmental break also provided a significant break in the nature of warfare and separates the Guinea coast south of the Gambia from the great savannah and desert to its north and east.

Desert, savannah and river created three environments for politics and warfare. The desert's thin population, unfavourable conditions for agriculture, and open country made it a land of cattle-, horse- and camel-raising nomads and hence pre-eminently of cavalries. In the savannah and Sahel environments, with denser populations of peasants living along rivers or in villages favoured with sufficient water, leaders raised infantry as well as cavalry, though they still strove to use cavalries to master their flat and open country. On the larger rivers, like the Niger, boats might make navies that added a third branch of service to the armies of those places.[1]

War and Politics: Background

These military forces were commanded by leaders of a wide variety of political organizations, which were determined partly by the environment and partly by a long political history stretching back to before the time of Christ. Perhaps the greatest political contrast was between the extensive and powerful empires of the western Sudan anchored in the basins of the Niger, Senegal and Gambia rivers, and the nomads of the desert. The two bordered on each other, and warfare was endemic, though often small in scale, along that border.

In the desert, there was no permanent political organization of any scale. Although Antonio Malafante, listening to people from the desert in the oasis of Tuat in 1447, believed that they were ruled by "kings",[2] in fact, military capacities and control were largely personal, deriving from the wealth and status of individual people. As Alvise da Mosto, an Italian visitor to the coast of Senegal, noted in 1455, in the desert the richest had the largest following and the poorest the least, and it was wealth rather than lordly obedience that induced supporters to come.[3] It was probably this perceived status that created leadership and determined policy even though formal organization was tribal, and certain families were the source, no doubt, of the desert "kings" who were expected to lead them.[4] This was a constant feature of the desert culture, for the same sort of leadership by the richest with their following of clients and others following prestige was still a factor in the late seventeenth century,[5] and was re-affirmed by late eighteenth-century sources which show that desert military strength still relied on voluntary enlistment of free people with their own equipment.[6] Thus, the desert was more or less permanently led by people whose military power and prestige was largely achieved through their own merits with followers who waxed and waned according to success.

The rule of Malafante's kings, while probably real enough at any given moment, was temporary in the longer run and always subject to challenge, hence his contention that they often had great wars among themselves. Da Mosto thought that wars occupied them in 13 out of every 15 years.[7] These internal wars might shift wealth quickly and end the power of a strong man in an instant; the French traveller de la Courbe noted in 1685 that "the stronger make sudden irruptions on the land of the weaker to pillage and take up all they meet, then retire until their victim finds an opportunity for revenge".[8] A cycle of raid and revenge, a constant recirculation of wealth, slaves and followers formed an endless constant of desert life in this period.

At the same time, this cycle of raiding within the desert was complemented by routine military incursions on the Sahel and savannah regions to the south, usually to raid, and capture slaves, which João Fernandes, a Portuguese visitor of 1446, noted were sold to north Africa.[9] At times, however, raiding might be met with more permanent relationships of tribute taking and influence, especially if there was weak or divided authority in the Sahel and savannah. Such nomad demands did not involve direct government, more often tribute taking and even raiding without interference, but not day-to-day decision making. When Malafante was visiting Tuat in the mid-fifteenth century, he learned the nomads who "live in tents like Arabs" were masters of the desert and "all the towns of blacks that border them".[10]

The fifteenth century was a time of division in the Sudan, when the Empire of Mali had declined and the new power of Songhay had not yet ascended. The consolidation of the kingdom of Jolof in the late fifteenth century, followed by the establishment of Songhay's control over the Niger bend after 1464 and then the implantation of a powerful Fulbe state on the upper Senegal, ended the period of nomad domination. But the nomads returned to power in the eighteenth century when civil war weakened the powers who dominated the Sahel and, by century's end, they were calling the tune on the Niger and the Senegal as they had in the fifteenth century.

The great savannah with its rivers was the political opposite of the desert. There rule was firmly in the hands of hierarchically organized states which were of varying size and strength. The building block of the region was a small, regional polity of great durability, typically though not always (the lower Senegal valley was a notable exception)[11] anchored by a large settlement (often called a town or city in European languages and Arabic) and ruled by a well established family. From these basic blocks the savannah rulers sometimes built large empires that united dozens of these units under a single rule, often anchored on the rich resources and transportation potential of a river valley. Large armies under a permanent chain of command could be raised from these states and warfare typically involved expeditions to expand the empire, or punitive actions to ensure the loyalty of the incorporated smaller polities.

The empire of Mali, which was at its height in the mid to late fourteenth century, controlled virtually all the lands west of the Niger bend in the valleys of the Niger, Senegal and Gambia.[12] When empires weakened, these smaller units broke away and became independent, perhaps integrated into more modest regional powers, or dominated by desert nomads. Malafante spoke of a division of the "land of the blacks" (as the Sahel and savannah were known to the desert people and north Africans) into "civitates" and "castra" and described the then shrunken empire of Mali as possessing nine of them at the time. In this time of division, the desert nomads had established their particular sort authority over many of the independent northern towns such as Timbuktu and Es-Souk.[13]

The last part of the fifteenth century witnessed the rise of Songhay, from east of the Niger bend, expanding along the Niger around the bend and down into the heartland of Mali, which was raided sporadically but not conquered. Songhay's grasp reached eastwards, but was never established on the Senegal river, where it was met by a newly established Fulbe dynasty of Koli Tengala, who died in 1512 fighting Songhay forces. The Fulbe state (in Futa Tooro), in turn, bordered on a newly emerging kingdom of Jolof that dominated the lower river and the coast.[14]

This situation changed in turn when the kingdom of Jolof broke up following a succession dispute in the mid-sixteenth century, and Songhay was subjected to a successful attack from Morocco culminating in the battle of Tondibi in 1591. As a result, although Songhay power was broken, the Moroccan army that arrived was unable to assert itself effectively outside the Niger bend region and smaller polities re-emerged.[15] As Jolof declined in power, the Fulbe of the middle Senegal expanded both east and west, taking over the whole of the Senegal and extending their power eastward almost to the Niger by the early seventeenth century to form the Empire of the "Great Fulo".[16]

By the end of the seventeenth century, however, the situation had changed again. No great power dominated the Sahel, the Great Fulo was confined to the middle Senegal region of Futa Tooro and was soon to be divided by civil war, while the lower Senegal was contested almost constantly between Waalo, Kajoor and Bawol, three states that had once been provinces of the kingdom of Jolof and had thrown off the rule of the Great Fulo. The Moroccan Pashalik of Timbuktu replaced Songhay as a great power for a time, but in the middle of the eighteenth century the Pashas entered into a long-lasting civil war that sapped its influence. Mali had undergone a last decline as a great power after it failed to take Jenne in 1599, but was partially replaced as the dominant power on the upper Niger in the early to mid-eighteenth century by the Empire of Segu in the upper Niger region. None of the new regional powers – the Moroccan Pashalik anchored at Timbuktu on the Niger bend, the Empire of Segu, or Futa Tooro – provided the sort of overarching authority that the great empires had done in earlier centuries.

As a result, the eighteenth century was a great period of military conflict. Civil wars disturbed several of the regions, sometimes matching rival pretenders to the throne, sometimes between states, and sometimes the two types of conflict merged, with pretenders seeking assistance from nearby rival states, as took place frequently in Waalo, Kajoor and Bawol along the lower Senegal valley, and in Futa Tooro and Gajaaga along the middle valley. This situation gave great advantages to the nomads of the desert, and they intervened freely in the civil wars and inter-state struggles to their south, sometimes as invited participants by the losers, sometimes on their own when they sensed that no one could mount an effective resistance to them. After 1722 the situation was confused by the attempt of the ruler of Morocco to use the desert nomads to his advantage. He dispatched his own nomadic troops to intervene, but as his predecessors in the sixteenth century had learned from their adventure in the middle Niger, these Moroccan cavalry, known locally as "Ormans", followed their own course, fitting into the prevailing nomadic culture and participating in the affairs of those further south.[17]

Civil wars between rival branches of the ruling body established a similar dynamic on the middle Niger, when the Moroccan Pashalik was routinely divided by rivalries that were often exploited by the nomads of the nearby desert. As on the Senegal, the nomads sometimes invaded by invitation of the rivals, sometimes on their own. On rare occasions, Moroccan forces penetrated the desert in hopes of using the nomads' own rivalries to punish them.[18]

Further south along the Niger, however, a much more powerful and centralized Segu empire emerged at the start of the eighteenth century to dominate the region and in time to extend its power northward towards the Senegal, where it encountered another regional power in the state of Khasso. Segu, and a rival dynasty established on the lower Senegal in Kaarta, and Kaarta's neighbour Khasso contested control of the region between themselves for most of the eighteenth century, while raiding the upper valley to such a degree that the people of Khasso were called the "black Ormans" in imitation of the Moroccan troops of the desert.[19]

Europeans visited this coast from the sea for the first time in the middle decades of the fifteenth century, and after a few trial raids on coastal populations were resoundingly defeated in the 1450s by naval forces from Mali's Gambian states, and Great Jolof's Saalum and Siin using their shallow-draught watercraft to attack Portuguese parties seeking to land in longboats. As a result of these losses, the king of Portugal dispatched his courtier Diogo Gomes in 1456 to patch up relations with the people of the region, and by 1462 Portugal had negotiated a relationship of peaceful trade throughout the area. European presence in the region was confined to the offshore Cape Verde islands, which grew as colonial societies on previously uninhabited islands. In later periods, they occupied a few more islands along the coast which were more secure trading posts than colonies. They also were allowed to build and maintain trading posts along the coast in which they exercised limited but generally effective sovereignty, and sometimes erected fortifications.

Although no longer interested in raiding the coast, Europeans took a keen interest in the complex politics of their African neighbours, and sought to use their own naval capacities to shape these politics as much as possible to their advantage, to exclude their European rivals, and to enhance their own trade. Beginning with the abortive attempt to assist a defeated candidate to Great Jolof's throne to power in 1488,[20] Europeans sought to influence Africa's politics by judicious alliance with one or another state or rival. From the beginning of their establishment in Senegal in the late seventeenth century, the French sought to intervene and meddle whenever the opportunity presented itself in the politics of Kajoor, Bawol and Waalo during their many interstate wars and civil wars, often through supplying weapons or commercial credits, sometimes co-operating with the desert nomads and Ormans in the process.[21]

For most of the eighteenth century the French company manned a fleet and held several small forts along the Senegal River from which they played an occasional role in the local politics along the river. While this chain of forts was sometimes described as a French colonial settlement, in fact, the forts were even less secure than the coastal ports had been. They held them at the sufferance of a number of African allies, whose decision not to support them forced a French withdrawal.[22]

The pattern of civil war, military intervention, and occasional foreign intrigue that plagued most of the Senegal valley during the late seventeenth and early eighteenth centuries took its toll on the common people. From time to time they supported Islamic movements of purification, of which the prototype was Nasr al-Din's *Tubenan* movement of 1673–77. Although Nasr al-Din's origins in the desert and his alliance with nomadic elements could have alienated him from many Muslims in the Senegal, his preaching against the tyranny of the rulers and against the slave trade to Europe made him popular and his movement swept all before it until his death and the opportunistic behaviour of his nomad allies put an end to its popular support. It was probably the ideas behind the movement that fired another powerful Islamic reform in Futa Tooro in 1776 led by Abd al-Kadir, which was more successful. Like its predecessor, Abd al-Kadir's movement enjoyed popular support and opposed the export slave trade, civil war, and the sponsoring of nomadic invasions. But by the 1790s Futa Tooro had lost this revolutionary zeal and was more or less like its predecessors.

Weapons and Tactics

The armed forces of Upper Guinea varied gradually from north to south depending on the degree to which horses were available and cavalries could be fielded on the one hand, and the degree to which watercraft and waterways favoured the employment on the other. Thus as one moved southward from the desert, where there were no waterways and all fighters rode on horseback, one met a land of cavalry mixed with infantry and notable rivers like the Niger and Senegal. Going further south still into the savannah, the infantry component gradually became larger, and as one approached the coast, watercraft counted for a larger part of military thinking until one reached the coast at the Gambia and further south.

In addition to this geographical gradient, there was a temporal one that witnessed the introduction of gunpowder, an entirely new weapon that threatened to shake up timehonoured means of waging war. Gunpowder weapons first played a role in the coastal waters when an Italian navigator fired his bombard (a primitive cannon) at startled Gambian marines in 1456. In 1591 Moroccans with muskets arrived on the Niger to overthrow the Songhay Empire, confident that this weapon would give them a military edge that would compensate for their inferior numbers. From these beginnings muskets and artillery moved more and more into African warfare, especially after the development of flintlocks in the 1680s made for a weapon more suitable to Africa. Here the temporal gradient also becomes a geographical one and moves northward from the coast, just reaching the inland areas away from coast or Niger by the end of the period.

Cavalries were all armed more or less the same way, whether in the desert, where all armed men were riders, or in the cavalry of the mixed armies of the Sahel and savannah. They rode in simple saddles without stirrups in the fifteenth century, though by the seventeenth century they had taken to using stirrups.[23] They carried a shield made of hides "which lets no point through" which for most horsemen was their only defence in the fifteenth century, although Mali soldiers (probably cavalry) wore leather helmets at about that time.[24] Later, in Songhay the hide shields were augmented, but probably only for the elite, by chain mail armour and helmets. Askiya al-Hajj realized that his general was planning rebellion in 1584 when he was stripped following his arrest and found to be wearing the mailed armour beneath his outer clothes.[25] In the 1588 civil war, the Askiya was wearing a cuirass of iron, and another soldier was saved when a javelin glanced off his helmet.[26] The quilted armour of the central Sudan, justly famous and still displayed today, was already in use in the sixteenth century when a force of armoured horsemen from Katsina overcame a raiding party from Songhay in 1553 but spared their lives because of their brave efforts.[27] However such armour seems to have been confined to the Hausa states and Borno, although by the mid-sixteenth century cavalry of Jolof on the Atlantic coast had added cloth armour to protect their bodies, wrapping it around their chests and abdomen so that "no weapon can pierce them", when previously the shield had been their only defence.[28]

Offensive weapons of the cavalry included a lance, a sword, often of scimitar-shape, and several javelins.[29] On the coast, there were some mounted archers, and the Fulbe were best known in this regard.[30] But most cavalry, at least in the Senegal and Niger valleys, carried 10–20 javelins in a quiver, and threw them with great speed and skill, as fast as a musket ball, according to a seventeenth-century writer.[31] These weapons were a source of great pride – there were a good many stories and legends about Askiya Dawud's (1537–9) sabre, for example. In 1529 Askiya Musa revealed his quiver of poisoned javelins, saying as a threat, "these are the sun, and you are the shade. When they suffer pain they will rush to you, and then I will forgive them." Javelins were considered valuable enough to be heritable property.[32] During the 1588 civil war in Songhay, two principal fighters, the Kurmina-fari and the rebel Balma'a, engaged in single combat with javelins from horseback; the fight was decided when the Kurmina-fari managed to transfix his opponent with a mighty throw.[33] These weapons required great skill to use well, and no doubt considerable training, from boyhood, according to the mid-seventeenth-century Cape Verdean Lemos Coelho.[34]

The care, training and breeding of horses, as well as the equestrian skills of their riders, also required considerable expense and effort. Jolof horses were so well trained that they followed their owners around like dogs. The riders performed tricks and feats of equestrian skill, such as leaping on and off galloping horses, and retrieving lances from the ground without dismounting, clicking their heels together from the back of a charging mount, or reaching from horseback to erase the horses' hoofprints with their shields.[35]

The whole of the region presented serious barriers to the development of this equestrian tradition. The disease environment did not favour horse breeding, although a small local breed had been developed. Heavier and faster mounts were always imported and typically did not live long in the region. The demand for horses was filled by desert nomads, who lived in a better environment, and by imports from north Africa, although for much of the sixteenth century the Portuguese also brought in horses.[36]

The armies of the Sahel and savannah were large and composed of cavalry and infantry, though it is difficult to assess the ratio. Chroniclers from the area were so enamoured of cavalry that they often gave only its strength, confining themselves to describing infantry as limitless or infinite, while the European observers, listening to secondhand reports of parties likely to wish to exaggerate, gave huge numbers that are difficult to credit. These sources report a ratio of ten infantry to every horseman, but the ratios were certainly higher in the coastal areas where horses were harder to get and maintain (as well as use effectively).[37] By this standard, a kingdom like sixteenth-century Jolof could muster several thousand cavalry for an important war, and thus perhaps tens of thousands of infantry.[38] The Sudanese chronicles, using contemporary sources, gave Songhay's partially deployed army as between 12,500 and 18,000 cavalry and 9,700 to 30,000 infantry at the decisive battle of Tondibi against Moroccan invaders in 1591, a puzzling discrepancy which perhaps reflects differing views about potential forces versus those actually deployed.[39] The forces of the smaller states that succeeded Jolof had cavalries in the hundreds and infantries in the low thousands.[40]

Infantry forces also typically carried shields and had no other armour. Infantries were numerous, if somewhat disparaged in the cavalry cultures of the savannah and Sahel; a seventeenth-century visitor to Jolof noted the esteem of the cavalry "because they never fought on foot".[41] Their armament differed little whether they were employed as infantry in a cavalry battle or on their own, or fought from boats as a marine infantry in the rivers and creeks of the coast in regions that lay to the south. The infantry that the Portuguese first encountered on reaching Senegambia in 1445 carried a tough leather-covered shield, a javelin or a lance, and perhaps a sword or long knife, and frequently used a bow and arrows, weapons that they would continue to use until well into the next century.[42] The arrows loosed from these bows were small and weak, typically with a barbed head, but they carried a deadly poison that put more fear into the Portuguese than any other weapon in their armoury, and probably convinced them to stop raiding.[43]

The tactics with which these weapons were deployed varied according to the balance between infantry and cavalry. Cavalry tactics were uniform throughout the whole region. Perhaps because they could not breed or buy large horses in sufficient numbers, cavalry focused their attention more on delivering missile weapons than on home charges, though certainly these were performed. Engagements often began with showers of arrows or javelins: for example, when the forces of Sunni Ali were attacking Jenne in 1480, a "battle of arrows" began the engagement, which lasted for some hours.[44] In Jolof, towards the end of the sixteenth century, horsemen first threw their javelins, which had barbed points, and then closed in using a lance or sabre.[45] The opening phases of the major battle of the Songhay civil war in 1588 involved the Askiya's cavalry attacking a Tuareg force "like a swarm of locusts".[46] When the Moroccan force that invaded Songhay in 1591 met the desert cavalry, they were attacked with "little javelins that they usually carry" before being dispersed with gunfire.[47] The significance of personal agility in this sort of encounter was revealed by the story of Emmanuel, leader of a town in Bawol, who, during Bawol's revolt from Kajoor in 1686, was surrounded by men who peppered him with arrows, and was only able to save himself by adroit use of his shield.[48]

On the other hand, infantry did play an active role in the battles of areas with strong cavalry traditions as a steadying force. In one incident which is supposed to show the cowardice of Askiya Bunkan (1531–6), his infantry commander refused to stop playing "Sudanic chess" as an enemy force advanced, then, at the appropriate moment, attacked and broke their ranks. Returning to the Askiya, he said, "Now they have reached you, do what you like with them," so the cavalry chased down the broken opponent after the infantry victory.[49]

The infantry of late-sixteenth-century Jolof was possibly typical of the infantry found in Songhay and the Fulbe states as well. They were drawn up in formation, no doubt because only by forming up could infantry forces survive on a battlefield with cavalry. These formations "in squadrons and lines" had shield-bearing infantry in the front ranks and on the flanks, with archers behind shooting over them.[50] Such formations were typical of coastal armies as a whole in the sixteenth century.

The battle of Tondibi, fought in early March 1591 between the Songhay army and the invaders from Morocco, shows us a bit about how infantry and cavalry operated together in Songhay and perhaps can serve as a model for elsewhere as well. However, it might not be entirely typical since the Moroccans brought different methods of fighting and were equipped with firearms. Nevertheless, since Songhay took the initiative in the battle, it reveals how a savannah army fought. As the Songhay army advanced with infantry massed in the centre and cavalry on the wings, the two flanking wings of Moroccan cavalry attacked from both sides, resulting in a melée. At this point, the Songhay drove some 1,000 cattle into the Moroccan centre with the idea of breaking their lines. The infantry then advanced behind the cattle, but the discharge of the Moroccan guns turned back the stampede and disrupted the Songhay lines instead. The Moroccan infantry then advanced to follow up, and were met by determined arrow strikes from a group of 90 elite Songhay soldiers who had tied their calves to their ankles to make it impossible to flee, and thus encouraged the others to fight on. Nevertheless, the Moroccan infantry overcame these soldiers and also repelled a counterattack of Songhay cavalry that had been held in reserve. At that point the Songhay retreated, their rear covered by a few detachments that sacrificed themselves to allow an orderly withdrawal. The Moroccans did not follow the Songhay army up but carried the field.[51]

To the infantry and cavalry forces of the savannah and Sahel, Sudanese armies added watercraft on the rivers and along the coast, and their victories over the Portuguese gave them a permanent influence in the future of Senegambia. These watercraft were designed for use in the shallow waters of the coast and estuaries, and were much better suited to the environment than the Portuguese seagoing vessels. When the Portuguese sought to land marine forces by longboat, African navies were able to bring up larger forces by their own craft and stunned the invaders in a series of victories, which allowed people from Senegambia southwards to dictate their relationship with Portugal.

Originally all the craft were powered by paddles or oars, but by the eighteenth century watercraft in Senegambia were powered by sail, sometimes two sails, though basic construction had not changed.[52] Watercraft were also crucial for the movement of larger armies on rivers like the Niger. When one of the Moroccan army units stationed on the Niger was moved into battle in 1730, 62 boats carried 455 fusiliers, while another 40 salt boats commandeered into service for this task carried an additional 320.[53] At times real battles were fought on Sudanese rivers, such as the one waged on the Niger by two groups of partisans in the struggle over the Moroccan Pashilik in 1723, but such naval battles were probably always rare.[54]

The Europeans produced larger watercraft which might enter into the rivers such as the Gambia from the sea or, like those vessels constructed by the French for the Senegal in the late seventeenth century, be built locally and deployed from their posts on the river. The French also hoped to use their shipbuilding skills locally to gain commercial advantage on the Senegal, and these could have military applications as well. Such craft might be large, transporting often over 100 soldiers drawn especially from Christian Africans. However, conducting assault landings against prepared enemies was still a problem, as one such boat carrying 200 marines discovered in 1686 when it was defeated by a land force of some 500.[55] Indeed, their crews were used far more often for defensive purposes than as a projection of French power.

In addition to the mobile forces of cavalry, infantry and marines, there were fairly substantial efforts made at fortifications, though these were not uniform throughout. Most visitors to the Senegal area, for example, were struck by the absence of fortifications, where open villages were as vulnerable in the fifteenth century as they remained in the seventeenth.[56] This was also true in some inland areas. For example, the terrain in Bambuhu allowed its residents to flee to the hills and broken country, their usual recourse when attacked, but not to construct fortifications even well into the eighteenth century.[57] It was perhaps the absence of local fortification traditions that led Jannequin de

Rochefort, visiting Senegal in 1638, to think that the construction of earthworks with artillery would render 60 French defenders invulnerable against 6,000 attackers.[58] Indeed, the French were probably the first to construct fortifications along the Senegal river. Fort St Joseph was fortified, for example, when a marauding force of some 12,000 nomads under Moroccan command invaded the region and occupied Futa Tooro in 1719.[59] Later, the need to protect other stretches of the river from raiders from Khasso made the rulers of Futa Tooro more amenable to French overtures to construct the posts of their Senegal River system after 1727.[60] In the eyes of one official writing in 1734, without the guns of Fort St Joseph as a refuge, the kingdom of Gajaaga might be abandoned as Futa Tooro had been, because of nomadic raids.[61] It is not surprising then, that one of the first forts built on the Senegal by local people was constructed around 1744 by Guiabé, an enemy of those who had encouraged the French to build their forts and now used their protection.[62] Wooden fortifications were subsequently constructed elsewhere, for example, in military camps constructed in Kajoor by Farabakanda, a slave who became a rebel ruler of parts of the country in the 1770s.[63]

Much of the rest of the savannah areas had a tradition of fortifications, however. When Sunni Ali attacked Jenne around 1480, its ruler built a "tata" or mud brick fortification to protect himself and thwarted attempts to storm the town.[64] Similar fortifications were notable in the Niger region. The Moroccans, perhaps expecting to meet such fortifications, brought artillery across the desert with them. The guns from Timbuktu were brought, in 1715, to bombard the town of Cheibi.[65] Indeed, even within Timbuktu itself, as a result of factional fighting among the army, leaders constructed fortified residences with towers after a particularly difficult struggle in 1716, to allow the gunners greater height.[66] One of the most famous of these was that of the qadi al-hajj Milad, from whose towers one could see all the city, which was a refuge for a disappointed faction leader in 1745.[67] The fortifications of clay and stone that Mungo Park met in the Faleme region and throughout the land of Kaarta as well when he passed in 1796–7 may have relied on a Sudanic tradition as did those of the Niger, but they may just as well have been from the European tradition, introduced at the start of the century. In any case, many of these works were loopholed and constructed for fighting with gunpowder weapons, perhaps suggesting a more recent design.[68]

Park also reveals the extent to which counterworks might be used to attack a fortified place. At Sai, he was told that in about 1782 the king of Segu had constructed a complex network of trenches complete with square towers at regular intervals some 200 metres from the town walls during his successful siege of the town.[69] Doubtless, sieges of other places at other times might involve works as complex.

The slow and uneven arrival of gunpowder weapons had a profound impact on the way wars were waged throughout Upper Guinea, but it is also easy to overestimate the decisiveness of these new weapons as they were taken up. Once reliable flintlock muskets arrived in the last decades of the seventeenth century, African leaders began gradually adapting them to their own ways of fighting, and changing their ways of fighting to accommodate the characteristics of the new weapons. On the whole, however, armies of the savannah never became as fully attached to these weapons as armies in other parts of Africa such as the Gold Coast or Angola, perhaps because the employment of cavalry rendered them less useful and decisive.

Firearms were introduced by Europeans in the seventeenth century, although they were not quickly deployed by the rulers of the country. The weapons soon worked their way inland, for by the 1680s, the Fulbe, rulers at that point of Futa Tooro and lands to its south, were equipping a few soldiers with them.[70]

Even after the new weapons arrived in the region, they did not wholly replace older weapons, so that, at least in the Senegambia region, one could find that about half the 3,000 infantry regularly employed in Waalo carried firearms by 1734, a ratio that seems to have continued until the end of the century.[71] In the farther interior, along the Niger River, for example, firearms were less uniformly used, perhaps because of the distance from European or north African sources, although this may have been supplemented by a local industry – the local gunpowder that Park saw in 1797 was probably the result of a longer tradition.[72] For a long time the Moroccan invaders who replaced Songhay on the Niger bend after 1591, soon known locally as the "Arma" or "shooters", had a virtual monopoly on these weapons, maintaining contacts with Morocco to that end, while their immediate neighbours to the south often lacked guns entirely. The contrast was so sharp that as late as 1716 the "Bambara" leader of Deba was wrongly supposed to have defied the Pasha of Timbuktu by saying, "If you are a man, I am a man, if you have people with you, I have people with me. If you have guns, I have a bow and poisoned arrows. By God we will give you absolutely nothing [in obedience and tribute]."[73]

Although the Moroccan musketeers crossing the desert in 1591 travelled mounted, they fought as infantry; the use of firearms by purely cavalry forces, such as those of the desert, was slower and had to await the technical possibilities of the flintlock, probably in the early eighteenth century, for use by mounted men. Thus, the people in the western part of the Sahara began importing firearms at about the time that the Senegambian trade was bringing them to the Sahel and savannah areas. As early as 1685 one could meet Arab cavalry operating in the desert all armed with firearms imported from Morocco as their principal weapon; the French were prepared to sell them further weapons through their post at Arguin on the desert coast.[74] However, according to Park, by the end of the eighteenth century a double-barrelled gun had more or less completely replaced bows and javelins among nomadic forces in the western part of the region.[75] If the cavalry were equipped with firearms, their infantry forces, typically drawn from subordinated towns, were more likely to bear javelins and bows and muskets.[76]

Guns were more slowly adopted in the eastern end of the desert zone near the Niger. At the battle of Aghendel in 1726, Tuareg cavalry greeted an Arma force with a storm of javelins.[77] But it was perhaps the sabre and cavalry charge that counted more tactically than the musketeer infantry, which may explain the relative slowness of Tuaregs to take to firearms. In a pitched battle waged on 23 May 1737, the assembled Arma army of Timbuktu confronted a large Tuareg force. The Tuaregs rose at dawn and assembled themselves in formation, then launched a charge against the Moroccans, who were deployed in two wings with an advance guard of cavalry. The musketeers managed two volleys into the Tuareg ranks, but were unable to stop them, and in the melée that followed the Arma were broken and fled in disorder, suffering heavy casualties.[78]

Guns might not upset the balance of power even when borne by cavalry. The Bambaras, for example, who were equipped with only "poisoned arrows and sabres", still managed to defeat Moroccan-backed cavalry armies from the western desert with substantial numbers of firearms three times in the first two decades of the eighteenth century.[79] At about the same time, the people of Khasso, feared as attackers all along the Senegal, were also armed entirely with bows and poisoned arrows even as late as 1729.[80]

Firearms changed the ways wars were fought as they supplemented the poisoned arrows of earlier times. The tighter infantry formations and shields gave way to looser formations that could still resist cavalry, perhaps with firepower. Thus, in the later eighteenth century, the infantry of Kajoor and Bawol was deployed in a single, not very orderly line, with cavalry in the rear. The general or king was then with a reserve, entirely of infantry, farther back and only deployed if needed. The infantry advanced at will, by platoons, probing enemy lines for weakness, in a system which the French observer Doumet, writing in 1769, thought was "without order and without art". As the infantry advanced they fired their weapons, but rarely went so far as to engage their enemies hand to hand, relying on manoeuvre and firepower to break their opponents.[81]

In more purely infantry areas, and especially those where the lack of exports limited the number of firearms available, the tactics might be much less formal. The villages of the many states that made up the region of Bambuhu in the 1720s, for example, were typically placed on hills or mountain foothills, and their tactics were those of placing ambushes at key points and rarely standing up to large forces or cavalry.[82]

Operations

Throughout the period formal large-scale military operations co-existed with much smaller, sometimes not centrally directed lesser operations. The two depended on each other, for the smaller operations were often preparation for larger ones, or perhaps a substitute in situations where one country did not wish to risk larger engagements. Geoffroy de Villeneuve, who collected information in the late 1780s for the Abolitionist cause and tended to see all African warfare as simply an extension of the slave trade, called these smaller operations "Little Pillage" as opposed to formal wars, which he designated "Great Pillage". Often these little wars involved the nomads, operating on their own, or more often called in by participants in larger struggles and civil wars.

More local raiding was extremely common in the kingdoms of the former Jolof Empire, to weaken enemies and to capture slaves. Such raids involved assembling an appropriate force of foot and horse, depending on the size of the place to be raided. Then a careful secret journey was conducted, ensuring that the attackers would arrive at night, and sometimes travelling several days to ensure surprise. The village was surrounded and then attacked at dawn, "when the women have risen to pound millet but the men are still sleeping inside". In one such raid in 1785, the ruler of Kajoor used 3,000 infantry and 1,000 cavalry to attack a village and netted 30 slaves, the proceeds of the sale of which went to discharge a debt he owed to a nomadic king for some horses.[83]

Farther west, Park made similar observations about the region between the Faleme and Niger which he crossed in 1797. He distinguished two types of war, *killi*, which were large-scale, open and declared wars, in which people were enslaved when victorious armies swept through the countryside; and *tegria*, smaller scale raids that were undeclared, surprise operations designed to weaken enemies and particularly to settle old scores. Park witnessed such a war in 1797, when Mansong of Segu invaded Kaarta, and the smaller army of its king, Daisi, had to retire to a fortified town, leaving the country unprotected. Mansong invested the town and then split the remainder of his forces into smaller commands which systematically went through the country gathering up the people to enslave. During this time Mansong's forces sometimes captured as many as 900 people in a single day. In a short time Kaarta became "a scene of desolation". Park also was a near witness of the second type of war at Kamalia, when a troop of 500 horsemen from Fuladu fell unexpectedly on three villages a little south of him and carried off all the people. Such events often were avenged within a few days or months by the injured parties, at least to the best of their ability.[84]

Virtually all the armies south of the desert relied on the uncertain loyalties, and sometimes the propensity to raid, of the desert nomads, augmented as they were in the eighteenth century by the "Ormans" from Morocco. This tendency to call in outside help to assist their own armies, or on occasion simply to raid and thereby weaken their opponents, contributed to the wretched condition that much of the area sank to. When a major struggle broke out in Timbuktu between various military factions, Tuaregs from the desert and Bambaras from the south were both invited in by various groups as a way to augment their numbers, and in this case these groups also pillaged and advanced their own cause.[85] It was through invitation of the ruler of Futa Tooro in 1722 that a party of 200–250 Ormans, along with an equal number of Arabs from Futa, invaded Waalo, and then made their way through the country and into Galam, carrying off a large number of cattle and people (especially women) despite the attempts of the major powers in the country to bring them in. A second, smaller invasion was defeated at a high cost, but the episode allowed Futa Tooro to harass its enemy without cost to itself or even a direct declaration of war.[86]

In a raid on Galam in 1724, for example, the Moroccan leader Gaedy, after having made a false march to confuse his potential victims, crossed the Senegal river with 8,000–9,000 troops under his command from the "Moorish bank" into the south on 4 June. Dividing his forces in two, he completely encircled and ravaged seven small towns and their neighbouring villages over a two-day period, systematically rounding up cattle and people to enslave. The main forces that might have defended the country were deployed south of the area for a war with Bambuhu, and when the soldiers returned to their devastated land, the people of Bambuhu renewed their attack.[87]

Mansong of Segu, also, when he found that he could not break the army of Daisi in a siege, sought help from the Moors of the desert, sending an embassy to them. Likewise, when Daisi had driven off the Segu forces, his disloyal subjects, afraid of his vengeance, united against him, and sought to increase their numbers by appeal to the Moors.[88]

Organization

The powerful states of the Sudan, such as Songhay, built their armies around a core of full-time soldiers. Askiya Muhammad (1492–1529) took over an army composed in large measure of levies from allied or conquered provinces, and developed a permanent guard army, or, as al-Sa'di, a chronicler, put it, he "distinguished between the civilian and the army unlike Sunni Ali [1464–92] when everyone was a soldier".[89] Muhammad's attitude towards the traditionally independent cavalries could be cynical. In a costly action against Borgu in 1506 a great many of these soldiers fell, and Muhammad's brother said wistfully, "You have annihilated Songhay" to which he replied, that in fact he had "given life to Songhay," as they would have given "no peace in Songhay while they are with us." Indeed, he confessed "we brought them to this place so that they might perish here and we should be rid of them."[90]

In addition to a sizable royal guard, there were substantial regional armies under the command of officers, typically drawn from the Askiya's own family and serving at his pleasure. The use of family members ensured loyalty to a strong Askiya, but was also the source of endless intrigue, as family members who were also generals might plot to use their forces to overthrow the ruler.[91] The most important regional army was that commanded by a general entitled the Kurmina-fari. It was less numerous than the royal army, for in 1537 when Askiya Bunkan, having been deposed by Isma'il, fled with some followers to the general entitled the Kurmina-fari, the latter advised him not to resist, as an augmentation to the royal army of 1,700 cavalry now made it too strong.[92] Likewise, in a nearly successful attempt to overthrow Askiya Bana in 1588, the Kurmina-fari raised somewhere between 4,600 and 6,000 cavalry and "infantry without number" but faced a royal army that numbered 30,000 and was able to envelop it completely with its numbers.[93] These permanent forces, mostly cavalry, were strictly subordinate to the Askiya, for during his reign (1549–83) the Askiya Dawud introduced the custom of inheriting all the property of the soldiers, saying they were his slaves, whereas before he only inherited their horse and weapons.[94] Provisioning these professional armies was an important imperial task, but one that ensured a loyal army, and there were royal estates or villages whose tribute went to support specific army units all along the Niger.[95] To these armies under central control were added local armies raised and commanded by the rulers of the lesser states who had accepted subordination to Songhay and could be called up by the Askiya. Thus, two Tuareg nomadic leaders, with 12,000 cavalry each, waged a war against the desert nomads on behalf of Askiya Dawud in 1570, while the regional forces from several provinces in the western part of the empire joined in the revolt against Askiya Bana in 1588.[96]

Fifteenth- or sixteenth-century Mali seems to have had a similar organization, for al-Sa'di, a local chronicler who lived in Timbuktu, wrote of it in 1655 that the former king of Mali had two great commanders in the south and in the north, each of whom had a number of officers and troops under his command.[97]

The Moroccan forces who occupied the Niger bend after defeating Songhay were organized into several "divisions" based on the ethnic or regional divisions among the Moroccan force that invaded in 1591. By the eighteenth century the Marrakesh and Fez divisions dominated the country. In theory they were paid professionals, living in barracks in the city of Timbuktu or other places, so that in 1738 the Pasha Sa'id, hard pressed to make an expedition, had to tax merchants of Timbuktu to pay soldiers their salaries.[98] Although the Pasha could appoint the captains over them, the military class as a whole greatly limited the powers of Pashas, and each other, through near constant feuds and struggles. Pashas held power often briefly, and were deposed and reinstated in the labyrinthine politics of the Pashalik. In this situation, disciplined and loyal troops were not drawn from the formal army, but from other sources, especially the personal slaves (*legha*) of the Pasha and the various *qa'ids*, or lower commanders.

At least one Pasha, Mansour (1712 and 1716–19), sought to use his personal slaves to build a loyal force independent of the military structure to which the soldiers were incorporated. In fact, he was only able to appoint one local commander during his tenure in office, which was long by the standards of the Pashalik.[99] Other military leaders, *qa'ids*, also had their own slaves[100] and military forces. For internecine fighting among the great men of the city and for outside expeditions troops were also raised by making alliances with other groups, Bambara from the south, Fulbe from the west, or Tuareg from the north, who served in their own units. This took place during the civil war in Timbuktu of 1716,[101] or a similar conflict outside the city in 1726, in which two rival Tuareg groups each allied with a different rival Moroccan commander.[102] In undertaking an expedition against the Tuareg in 1718 or 1719, Pasha Mansour remarked that, as a general practice, in undertaking such an effort, the Moroccans should never number more than ten per cent of the forces, an indicator of the extent of involvement of professional soldiers in large-scale campaigns against external enemies.[103] Indeed, the number of professional soldiers must have been quite small, and so they were an inadequate assurance of a dependent military force even had they been loyal. The possibility of detaching 50 from one command to assure the safety of another was considered a great hardship in 1738;[104] often in the internal struggles of the city a dozen or twenty seemed a large number.[105] In a full deployment of 1730 to attack its rivals, the Division of Fez counted 775 musketeers, but was accompanied by an "innumerable mass, defying all estimation" of other troops armed with bows and javelins, certainly making up the bulk of the effective troops.[106]

Late fifteenth- and early sixteenth-century military forces in the Wolof kingdoms, then under the rule of the Empire of Jolof, were composed of small personal guards perhaps like that of Kajoor, of 15 cavalry and 150 foot soldiers that came to greet visiting dignitaries.[107] However, they could command much larger armies for major wars, probably recruited by raising levies on the population and winning the assistance of the "great men" of the country, who controlled their own military establishments.

In the early seventeenth century, after the break-up of Great Jolof into Waalo and Kajoor and the neighbouring kingdoms of Saalum and Siin, the kings had a system of regiments that were specially housed and commanded by *Jarafas* or commanders, who could be summoned for war. They inherited their military calling and served especially as infantry.[108] At almost the same time, however, the sovereign of Bawol actually had to face a revolt because he was making too many mass levies on the people to support his wars.[109]

The size of the army called out by mass levies was limited, however, by logistical considerations. In a war around 1638, troops from Brak on campaign had no supplies and ravaged the countryside to support themselves.[110] In the late seventeenth century, on the other hand, the king of Kajoor did not have any standing or regular troops, but the people did answer the summons to battle, given out by the king's provincial governors, who also collected his revenues.[111] This summons was described in detail by Chambonneau, the French governor in the mid-1670s, as involving beating a drum late at night; then within 15 days an army would be assembled at a predesignated point, raised first from the villages under their own leaders and then from the heads of provinces. Soldiers were required to provide their own arms, and they attempted to provide a supply train managed by horses and camels supplied by the conscripts. Even the horses that the army used were the property of the riders,[112] who were presumably from among the entourage maintained by the aristocratic lords, or from the royal guard.

This sort of organization was still prevalent in the 1760s. The Brak, for example, had a personal guard of some 200 infantry; the rest of his army was raised by officials, who were his personal slaves, from the rest of the country through levy, in which the levied soldiers supplied their own arms, sometimes of low quality. Such troops were not well disciplined or equipped, although there were elite units among them. The governors and other officials had relatively small forces themselves, though taken together in the royal army they could be a notable force.[113]

In 1686, a certain *alcalde*, or administrative official, of Bawol, was also the commander of his own troop of cavalry, making up an entourage.[114] These personal entourages were especially important during the many episodes of civil war that bothered all the Wolof states in the eighteenth century. For example, Beeco Maalikhuri, a provincial governor opposed to King Yerim Mbanyik in 1724, maintained himself in opposition with 300 armed men, his personal entourage, which managed to hold its own, thanks to help from neighbouring countries.[115] During a civil war in Bawol, between Ma Haoua and his nephew Maisa Bige in 1748, the deposed nephew raised his own troops to fight.[116] The forces of these various officials numbered several thousand "picked troops", allied with one or another would-be king who was able to maintain their loyalty (in theory as their master, kings should have unquestioned loyalty; in practice due to the divided sovereignty he had to negotiate it). They engaged in constant warfare, either pillaging the lands of their rivals, or entering into international intrigue which might bring foreign armies into the country, from the desert or from nearby kingdoms.[117] These nobles, called *lamanes*, were in fact hereditary rulers of their areas by 1785 and possessed permanent forces near their residences and the right to summon others for their armies. But they were not paid soldiers, except that they were allowed to share in the pillage of the country they attacked, and thus their service was something of a tax obligation and contributed to their rapaciousness.[118] Farakaba, a former slave, or rather an official of Kajoor, who rebelled against his ruler in the 1770s, formed a permanent armed force "in his pay" which he bivouacked in fortified locations around the area he controlled. This large dependent force of 4,000, which he commanded more directly than most governors seem to have, rendered him unbeatable. Indeed, in the 1770s his approach was considered a model by other rulers, some of whom sought to reorganize their forces along this model of smaller but more dependent units.[119]

In other parts of the Senegal valley in the eighteenth century, where power was much more decentralized, each little polity raised its own forces from within its limits, probably in much the same way as the larger states did. Thus Bambuhu, reported in 1725 to be divided into 24 "kingdoms", some of which were "monarchies" and others "republics", would have as many armed forces raised from its citizens. They were frequently at war with each other, and fought locally through sorties and ambushes with small forces, poorly equipped and rarely mounted.[120] This same situation seems to have prevailed in the lands of the former great empire, such as Galam and Gajaaga, where rival branches of the Bathily clan claimed control over various local polities with their own armed forces, and *marabouts* or religous leaders had their own settlements from which they also raised forces to fight their neighbours and to repel invasions from nomads on the one side and from Kasan on the other.[121] In 1744 one of the local rulers gave the French envoy David a group of 40 cavalry and 60 infantry, all "well armed" to accompany him to Bambuk. While he undoubtedly could command many more, his was clearly a small but well equipped force raised from his subjects and retainers. Elsewhere, such leaders were said to be able to gather 300–400 troops if needed.[122]

Mungo Park learned a great deal about the organization of the Bambara kingdom of Kaarta and Segu while visiting the region in 1797, and the observations probably would be true for earlier times. When threatened by Mansong of Segu, King Daisi wrote messages to each of his great men asking them to come to help him, but also allowing them to retire and remain neutral. Should they retire he would not hold it against them unless they supported his enemies, in which case he said that they had "broken the key to their hut" and would not be re-admitted. Although this mobilization produced only 4,000 men to face Mansong's 9,000, they were "very spirited" and could be counted on.[123] Clearly, troops were commanded much more by local than by central forces, and armies were raised by negotiation.

Conclusion

Whether large in scale or small, raised by conscription or entreaty, the armies of the broad savannahs were dominated by cavalry. Although many, in fact most, soldiers were organized in infantry units, it was the horsemen who determined the battle. But cavalry armies did not determine social structure, for the horsemen might be the independent Moors of the desert, who resisted all attempts to make a centralized society of them, or the backbone of highly disciplined armies such as those of the empire of Mali or even the latterday Segu kingdom. One must resist the temptation to see the large imperial tradition of the western Sudan as a product of their reliance on cavalry.

The predominance of cavalry may well have blunted the impact that the importation of firearms could make in the region. Certainly firearms made only slow progress as an infantry weapon in the region, and even at the very end of the period were still only unevenly deployed. In many parts of the world, the advent of the musket put an end to cavalry, but none of our sources suggest that this happened in the savannah region. This history must also cause us to reconsider the contention, often asserted, that the advent of musket-using Moroccan soldiers in Songhay, and their victory at Tondibi, was a turning point. The subsequent history of the Moroccans does not suggest that they had any longlasting military superiority because of their weapons, and the future even then still lay with the riders of Segu, or even the nomads of the desert.

Chapter Two

War in the Rivers: Senegambia and Sierra Leone

The Gambia River forms a convenient border from a military point of view between the savannah region of northern Upper Guinea and the areas further south. Geographically, the region was centred in the Futa Jallon, an upland area that was the origin of the Niger, Senegal and Gambia rivers, as well as most of the rivers that flowed along the coast right through Sierra Leone. North and east of Futa Jallon was the land of the western Sudan, flat and available for cavalry, cut by rivers that attracted dense settlements that were connected by watercraft. South and west of Futa Jallon the often watery environment and thick vegetation made the keeping of horses impractical, and the wooded countryside made cavalry warfare less attractive. Here infantry armies shared the military culture with marine forces that could exploit the network of water routes for mobility and surprise.

The Political Background

This geography co-existed with quite different politics to those in the northern regions. Although much of this area, and especially the Gambia corridor, fell into the Empire of Mali at its fourteenth-century height, the dramas of centralization and nomad intrusion were not played out in this area as they were farther north. The world of the savannah intruded into the southern part of Upper Guinea on its northern and eastern boundaries, but it was more an influential than a dominant presence.

In the sixteenth century, the Kingdom of Jolof, with its core in the Senegal valley and its cavalry armies, claimed to control Siin and Saalum on the coast and along the north bank of the Gambia, but its control was contested by local forces. Likewise, Mali had made its claims to the Gambia region at an even earlier period, and these claims along the river itself seem to have been stronger and better enforced, if we are to believe the earliest witnesses. Moreover, even when Mali's power was eclipsed in the mid to late sixteenth century, the Empire of Kaabu, a successor state, continued to exercise control in the region and to form a sort of regional centre. But militarily Kaabu was not a savannah cavalry state in the same way that the archetypical Mali had been – while it was a part of the Mandinka world culturally, politically and militarily it was more integrated into the coastal world.

South of the Gambia was the land of small, usually effectively independent little states in the Casamance, the "Rivers of Guinea" (modern Guinea-Conakry and Guinea-Bissau), and Sierra Leone coasts. In Sierra Leone, early and detailed accounts speak of the "land of the Sapes" as being divided into numerous kingdoms, constantly at war, but greatly integrated commercially by their water network that made for large and active markets and considerable regional trade, even in basic commodities.

In the middle of the sixteenth century, Mande-speaking armies claiming a connection with Mali, known as Sumbas or Manes, invaded and consolidated their control on Sierra Leone at the southernmost reach of the coast. These armies appear to have moved in from the savannah of southern Mali, if their traditions of the early seventeenth century are taken literally, perhaps for a time actually making some connection to the then moribund empire, following a corridor down what is modern Liberia and southern Sierra Leone. From there these warriors, renowned as cannibals and organized in mercilessly cruel military bands, conquered and destroyed the Sapes as they moved northwards up the coast. By the late sixteenth century, they reached the area of the "Rivers", where they met their match at the hands of the Limbas and the Jalungas.

In the seventeenth century older patterns re-asserted themselves in Sierra Leone and perhaps everywhere. Malian or unified Mane control waned and disappeared. Independent Siin and Saalum regained authority once lost to Jolof along the Gambia River and coast of their region. A chain of states of Malinke origin covered the length of the Gambia, while in the interior the kingdom of Kaabu formed the most powerful and coherent of the post-Malian states, while lesser states continued to rule over the coast.

Warfare in this region was largely a matter of interstate wars, or raids conducted by the various naval forces in the area, including the decentralized but powerful naval forces of the Bijagos islands – never a part of Mali but soon to become the nemesis of the coast. Indeed, the marine raiders from many of the riverine areas functioned militarily in the same way that the nomadic raiders did in the savannah and Sahel, except that they seem always to have been under some sort of state control, albeit that of a small state.

The Portuguese reached the Gambia soon after their first visits to west Africa in the 1450s, and by 1462 they were visiting the Sierra Leone coast. For much of their exploration in the southern end of the region they arrived as peaceful traders, having learned from their earlier experience on the Gambia and northwards of the effectiveness of coastal navies. Indeed, in Sierra Leone the Portuguese found themselves sometimes the victims of attacks, for the "Bulloms" of that coast tried to attack passing ships.[1] Aside from a failed raid on the Bijagos Islands in 1535, which re-affirmed African naval superiority in their own coastal waters, the Portuguese did not seek again either to raid or to impose their will.[2] Other European powers subsequently inserted themselves into the coastal mix – the Dutch in the late sixteenth century, followed by English and French, and including a brief mid-seventeenth-century attempt by the Duke of Courland (modern Latvia) to establish posts on the Gambia. Although Africans allowed all these Europeans to establish posts, and even to fortify them, the forts did not become the bases for long-term domination, though they did become centres for European naval forces. The English had a modest presence from their fortified island (James Island) in the Gambia, sometimes using their small fleet as raiders, more often in assistance to those African rulers who they thought might favour them in exchange.[3]

In the early eighteenth century, the Islamic revolution that had swept the savannah regions farther north following Nasr al-Din's movement took root in the southern interior. In 1727/8, Muslims of the region agreed to lead a movement to conquer Futa Jallon, convert the non-Muslims, and purify its Islam. They fought long and largely undocumented wars to achieve this goal, and after the decisive battle of Talansan in 1747/8 they established a new state. But it was not terribly secure, for a revolt among those who had been enslaved in 1755 disturbed the region. In 1766/7 a civil war broke out after the death of Ibrahima Sambegu, who was styled the Karamoko Alfa, the charismatic founder of the movement. When powers outside Futa Jallon sought to intervene, another charismatic leader named Ibrahima Sori managed to unite the forces against the enemy and had soon carried the war far beyond Futa Jallon. Its impact was felt at the coast and especially through the slave trade right into the 1790s.[4]

Weapons and Tactics

The armed forces in the southern part of Upper Guinea bordered on the cavalry-using regions, and shared with their neighbours most of the infantry and cavalry traditions of the great savannah regions, even though this sharing was more symbolic than real, as horses were limited and the country did not support large-scale cavalry warfare. As one moved farther south, into the riverine regions of the Casamance, the "Rivers of Guinea", and then to Sierra Leone, both horses and cavalry traditions weakened, but never really failed, giving this region a military tradition that differed quite substantially from those of regions like the Gold Coast or Angola where there had never been any cavalry.

If the cavalry tradition waned, however, the infantry and especially the marine elements of armies were far more important. Boatbuilding traditions were well established in this area, and everywhere the marines shared pride of place with the foot soldiers on land. In many respects, in fact, the marine element had some of the elements of the nomadic tradition, especially since, like the nomads, the coastal and riverine people were organized in small polities and raiding was important.

Observers tended to lump the military and weapons traditions of the Gambia in with those of Senegal, perhaps because the Gambians were speakers of Mandinka and thus united culturally in so many other ways with the people of the savannah. Infantries carried the same weapons: lances, javelins, swords and of course, bows and arrows. They used the same tactics and fought in the same sort of fortifications as farther north. The most important variant was simply that there was less of a role played by cavalry, and so the infantry tradition prevailed. Along with the emphasis on infantry, the people of the Gambia and south continued the long tradition of using poisoned missile weapons.

It was the archery emphasis which highlighted Sierra Leone, the farthest area from the savannah traditions. Combatants from all over Sierra Leone carried so many of these poisoned arrows into battle in the 1550s and 1560s that they required two quivers to carry them all.[5] When the English sea rover John Hawkins arrived in 1568 in Sierra Leone, he tried to seize coastal people by landing parties from his ships. But, like the Portuguese before him, Hawkins paid the price, for he lost a number of his men to poisoned arrows, and learned like his Iberian predecessors to respect the archers of the coast.[6]

André Thevet, who visited the Siin and Saalum area in about 1555, also noted one addition to the armoury of that region that seems to have been lacking farther north, a club of hard wood which was armed with sharp animal and fish teeth. This weapon was also much used farther south. A century later a visitor noted that these clubs were thrown with great speed and accuracy by Flup soldiers south of the Gambia, who managed to wipe out an attacking Portuguese force with them in the 1650s.[7]

Farther south, in Casamance and along the coast as far as Sierra Leone, soldiers carried fine large swords as well as arrows and javelins, and Sierra

Leoneans also bore shields covered with elephant hide.[8] The people around the Bijagos islands and the Manes (or Sumbas) who invaded Sierra Leone in the mid-sixteenth century made their shields out of wickerwork, which, when wet, were proof against various missile weapons, while using long two-handed pikes as their most important offensive weapons. But if Bijagos were committed to pikes, their frequent opponents, Beefadas, routinely used only archery, including a complex mixture of arrowheads, many poisoned.[9]

The impact of firearms was as slow and uneven in the southern part of the Upper Guinea coast as it was in the savannahs north of it. Initially they were weapons only of Europeans, and Portuguese and English musketeers served as mercenaries in the armies of Sierra Leone during the Mane invasion period of the mid to late sixteenth century, sometimes on opposing sides.[10] Their weapons, while valued, were not much imitated and people of the region do not seem to have taken a strong interest in developing their own corps of musketeers.

It was only in the later part of the seventeenth century, about the time that the flintlock musket became available, that Africans sought to obtain their own supplies and raise their own corps of musketeers. Muskets imported from Europe began to appear in the armies of the Gambia and Casamance in the 1670s as infantry weapons.[11] In fact, the king of Casamance defeated an English naval attack with continuous musket fire in about 1685.[12] In 1726 one extensive Gambian war involving "most of the countries bordering the river" occasioned, according to British traders, "vast demands for arms and gunpowder".[13]

But the spread of firearms did not wholly replace older missile weapons. When Francis Moore visited the Gambia in the 1731, he took pains to praise the Fulbe of the region for their military prowess. Their weapons included some guns, but they were still primarily armed with lance, assagai, short cutlass, and bow and arrows, and most of the Mandinkas of the riverine towns carried similar weapons and few guns in his day.[14] The poisoned arrows of earlier years were also still very much in use at the time: a man in Niumi showed the Englishman a "vast number" of them, each daubed in poison that was so "rank that it is only needed to draw blood to kill".[15] Likewise, a French visitor to the Gambia as late as 1763 felt that guns were primarily confined to elite and guards units, and were certainly not available to all infantry.[16]

Farther south it was much the same story in the Sierra Leone area. Nicholas Villault saw some musketeers in the armies of Sierra Leone in 1667, while people in the Cape Mesurado area south of Sierra Leone were familiar with firearms and confident they could deal with them when Gröben visited in 1682.[17] English traders dealing along the whole Sierra Leone coast in 1718 noted a substantial demand for gunpowder weapons and munitions.[18] But, as farther north, these weapons did not displace older ones. Nicholas Owen, writing about the area in 1750, described their weapons as including bows and arrows and clubs as well as guns.[19]

Nevertheless, firearms were desired everywhere, and it was probably inability to obtain them rather than a rejection of their military utility that caused them to be scarce in inland areas like Futa Jallon in the eighteenth century. In 1758 "Furry Do", the king of Futa Jallon, brought down a force of 5,000 men armed only with bows and arrows, and managed to subject many of the petty kingdoms of Sierra Leone to his rule and religion. But he appreciated guns, for he sold slaves to obtain guns and powder whenever possible.[20] In 1786, Matthews noted that the people of the coast had wholly "laid aside their national weapons for the sabre and gun"; by this time, the inland countries, including Futa Jallon, still used the bow, spear and dart, an opinion repeated by Thomas Winterbottom a few years later.[21] When James Watt visited Futa Jallon in 1794, guns were still rare and carried only by people in leadership positions, but Susus, near neighbours who had better coastal access, were almost all equipped with guns.[22] The leaders of Futa were anxious to obtain more supplies of muskets and artillery, and prepared to sell slaves in large numbers to acquire them to protect themselves against their enemies.[23]

Tactics and military formations underwent a substantial evolution as firearms became important. Initially, most armies in the southern part of Upper Guinea fought in tight formations and used discipline that impressed early European visitors. Undoubtedly the presence of cavalry traditions, and the maintenance of some horsemen south of the Gambia as well, went to create this situation. The Sumbas who invaded Sierra Leone organized their infantry into tight formations, perhaps because they developed their art of war in Mali (from which they claimed to originate), where cavalry was important. According to sailors of the Hawkins expedition in 1565, armies formed up with shield bearers in front, who also had a two-headed javelin for offensive fighting, supported by three archers standing behind each shield bearer. After a phase of using missile weapons, the onset was given with a terrible cry and hand-to-hand fighting followed.[24] The infantry formations created by this required drill, for when the Susus and Manes commanded by Xerebogo lined up to fight in the mid-sixteenth-century war, the Susu soldiers managed to stay in step helped by bells on horses, while resisting flanking attacks.[25]

Infantry tactics changed where gunpowder weapons were employed, though less so in the southern areas than in the savannah areas. The new tactics there, as in the savannah, involved more open formations and manoeuvre. Both Matthews and Winterbottom noted that local people laughed at them when told of European mass formations where large numbers of troops were exposed to hostile fire. Their manner of fighting, according to both visitors, was more like that of Native North Americans, skulking behind trees, firing at will from cover, and keeping in small units.[26]

These sort of tactics are illustrated well by Joseph Hawkins' description of a war between "Ebo" and "Galla" in the Rio Pongo area in 1795,[27] where warfare was often a matter of ambush. Facing an attack by Galla through a narrow defile, the ruler of Ebo disposed his army in three bodies, one to meet the Galla in the pass, and two others deployed in shallow ranks on his flanks. When pressed hard, the first body withdrew, feigning a retreat which drew the Galla into an envelopment by the remaining Ebo divisions. Although losses were heavy the Galla managed to extricate themselves from this and retreated to their own camp, followed by the whole Ebo army, who thought they had carried the day. But they met one last burst of determined resistance which cost them greatly before they eventually overcame this opposition and stormed the Galla camp. The surviving Galla were able to withdraw, pursued hotly for two days.[28]

Just as armies of the savannah and Sahel relied on a mix of infantry and cavalry to achieve their military objectives, the armies of the coastal region relied heavily on boats, and their own special art of war reflected this background. Coastal people's boats were critical for the deployment of their marine infantry, whose fighting techniques, described above, were fairly uniform. Early Portuguese reports speak of boats that generally carried only three to six marines, but at least some substantially larger craft also appeared, such as the two vessels carrying 38 fighting men each in the Gambia that Diogo Gomes met, or another with 30 that da Mosto encountered in the same area in the mid-fifteenth century.[29] On the other hand, the large trees of the region farther south, below the Gambia and into Sierra Leone, allowed larger boats, some of which, according to early sixteenth-century witnesses, could carry as many as 50 or 60 and even 120 people; these were made according to an ancient design from hollowed logs, and along the Sierra Leone coast had attempted attacking European ships in the earliest phases of their encounter.[30] By the late sixteenth century, larger canoes on the Gambia were protected from musket fire by thick wooden screens over the prow, and had attacked and captured French and Portuguese launches operating on the river.[31]

The larger warcraft of the early sixteenth century, said to hold as many as 100 marines, were rowed standing up (perhaps to save space), and only the steersman sat.[32] Substantial fleets of these vessels might be assembled. For example, during the Mane invasion of Sierra Leone, the Mane general assembled 300 boats to assist in his attack across the Tagarin River (now called the Rokelle River). Even if the larger estimates are exaggerated, this still suggests that one or two thousand soldiers might have come to the battlefield by boat.[33]

The watercraft of the coastal regions often were used simply to ferry armies, such as in the mid-sixteenth-century attack that Casamance launched across the Casamance River against a Banyun opponent. Portuguese ships and local craft carried an army across the river which then assembled on the other shore and marched to attack a fortified enemy. The Banyun, however, managed a sortie that routed their attackers. But the day was not over, for two days later, the King of Casamance constructed two forts to block the river, further reinforcing the blockade by a chain, which forced the Banyuns to come to terms.[34] Such blockades were common in the region, for the Jabundos also had blockaded the river in about 1550 when they were at war with Casamance.[35]

The mobility made possible by boats, the difficult terrain, and the small size of polities made the coastal regions particularly prone to raiding and piracy. In his late-sixteenth-century geography of the Rio Grande region, for example, André Alvares de Almada noted that the Chans up one of the rivers came down in small parties in boats "every day" to raid Banyuns, while elsewhere in the same region the redoubtable Bijagos conducted regular raids on the coastline from their islands. The Beafadas of the same area also harboured pirates in their midst.[36] Bijago raids included Portuguese settlements which were fortified, such as Biguba, attacked in 1603, and Guinela, whose chapel, dedicated to Mary, was burned in a 1609 raid.[37] This culture of raiding was a permanent feature of the region, as can be seen in seventeenth-century descriptions.[38]

Europeans brought their own naval skills here as they had in Senegal and, like the French on the Senegal, tried to use their naval abilities to shape politics. Often Europeans at first sought to use their ships to assist African partners, as Hawkins did in 1568, using his artillery to support an attack on a fortified town on the Tagarin River which had resisted siege for a long time.[39] At about the same time, Mane leaders enlisted French ships in their war; they used their artillery to disperse boats of their opponents.[40]

European service was most effective in this sort of allied role, where a European ship or ships could use its artillery to support the ground and marine forces of an African ally. They were not as successful, even right on the coast, using it for their own interests without allies or against the powers of the coast. The English learned this lesson when they sought to use their naval power in Casamance in about 1685 by sending a ship with artillery, which was defeated by well hidden musketeers on the shore who peppered it with fire.[41]

It was more often rivalries between Europeans than a desire (or rather an ability) to dominate Africans that led Europeans to use their watercraft against

Africans. When the French sought to take James Island from England in 1724, French and British warships occasionally fought each other, and a British sloop attacked canoes of the king of Niumi along the Gambia, for his marines were assisting the French.[42]

Following a tradition that probably extended across all the lands of Mali, the towns of the Gambia and Sierra Leone at the start of the sixteenth century were fortified with stockades and multiple protected gates, like the one in Sierra Leone whose walls were breached (perhaps by artillery), set afire, and assaulted by land and sea by Hawkins and his allies in 1568 that was "very strongly impaled and fenced, after their manner", having resisted assault for many years before.[43] Their "manner" seems to have been to use timbers planted in several concentric circles with ditches outside them and complemented with towers for guards and archers to use.[44] The green timber of the stockades often rooted, a technique noted throughout Africa, forming in fact a sort of dense hedge, perfectly designed to hold the ramparts behind it.[45] In the early 1630s southern Sierra Leone was dotted with fortified towns, fenced in with living trees, that provided fortresses for people to flee to "in time of need".[46] These towns and their satellite villages provided the origin of what were called the "war towns" of the nineteenth century.[47]

In the inland part of Sierra Leone fortifications were also critical. The Limbas and Jalunka people were able to defeat the Sumbas in the late sixteenth century in part because their fortifications, which were similar in construction to those of the coast, also included underground hiding places, which allowed picked forces to surprise those who invested them with attacks from the rear.[48]

In the Gambia region, the *cao-sans*, as fortifications were called, consisted of a rampart of earth thrown up behind a sturdy stockade in the last part of the sixteenth century. These were then complemented with guard towers, bastions and parades, from which arrows could be loosed and pitch or other burning substances poured on attackers.[49] The Gambian kingdoms were subject to attack from land as well as water, and seventeenth-century descriptions noted that there were substantial ditches and stake fields designed to hinder cavalry.[50]

These towns may have seemed well protected, but there was adequate siegecraft to take them if time and circumstances permitted, for the king of Kaabu besieged and took Cantor, then razed its fortifications to the ground around 1680, a notable victory.[51] The inhabitants of Niumi sought to take the English fort at James Island in 1768 and brought scaling ladders with them to assist in climbing its walls. The attack was ultimately unsuccessful, and the English were inclined to blame French activities for the use of ladders, though no French were present in the attack and the ladders were actually used by local troops.[52]

In late sixteenth-century Sierra Leone, this siegecraft often included the construction of counterworks, so that both sides were entrenched.[53] This was in turn an extension of the long tradition in Sierra Leone of constructing field fortifications, as camps when the army marched, and in the face of the enemy if time permitted, a technique that may have originated with the Sumbas and ultimately in the savannah areas, but was quickly taken up by other coastal people.[54]

Fortifications played a vital part in the small polities perhaps because of the role of small raiding groups as much as their place in major wars. The Flup ruler of the early sixteenth century, whose territory was in the marshy and river-rich area south of Siin and Saalum constructed a complex stockade around his residence, which was itself garrisoned and protected.[55] The ruler of the island of Bissis mounted artillery on his ramparts in the early seventeenth century, and had posted treetop lookouts, with an eye especially for raiders.[56]

Gunpowder weapons caused a shift in fortification in this area as it did everywhere: walls from which the garrison could fire their weapons, especially those designed with loopholes, joined the ditches, fences, palisades and anti-cavalry devices of the earlier tradition. Francis Moore noted the presence of clay walls when he visited the Gambia in 1731, observing that fortifications were made of sticks "drove all around and filled up with clay".[57] Mungo Park, visiting Madina, the capital of Wuuli, in 1795, made an additional observation which had probably been true since Moore's day at least. The town was surrounded by a high wall of clay and an outward palisade of stakes and thorn bushes; in his time the walls were in ill repair, however.[58]

Eighteenth-century Sierra Leone continued older fortification traditions with modifications for the era of gunpowder weapons. Matthews, writing in 1786, noted that towns were still surrounded by walls made of palisades which had taken root or a mud wall.[59] Both the tradition of counterworks and the innovations of firearms are revealed in Winterbottom's description of the siege of Yangheeakurree that he witnessed in 1796. Yangheeakurree and several lesser satellite towns had been founded in 1785–6 by slaves who had run away from Mandinka masters,[60] and for many years had been protected by Susu, in whose lands they were built. From there the ex-slaves constantly harassed their former masters, resisting all attempts to take the towns by assault. However, in 1796, the Susu became concerned about their own slave population and joined the Mandinka in investing the town. It was an "oblong square" surrounded by a 12-foot-high wall of mud, reinforced by three round bastions, and was easily able to repel several attempts to take it by direct assault. Consequently, the besiegers constructed counterworks, composed of a palisade some 10 feet high that completely encircled the town, cutting off all its food supplies. They then constructed several high towers which allowed the attackers to fire into the town, and set fire to its flammable roofs with red-hot bullets. The garrison responded by destroying all their roofs and loopholing their house walls, and were able to return fire effectively from there. Even an attempt to bridge the wall with a large tree failed. Finally, the Mandinka brought several cannon up from the coast with great effort, and in a few days had battered down the wall and carried the city by assault. They slaughtered the garrison wholesale in revenge.[61]

In interior regions the tradition of building stone or clay walls drew on both an older savannah tradition of fortification and the need to employ these structures for their musketeers. All the Susu towns of the interior regions in the late eighteenth century were walled around at angles and loopholed, often with towers at the gates.[62] The Futa Jallon, at the source of the Niger, also had a longstanding tradition of stone works. When Watt visited the area in 1794, for example, he was shown old and partially dilapidated buildings dating from a somewhat earlier period of complex stone fortifications. At Labe, there was a wall with loopholes and walls constructed at salient angles to maximize the field of fire; at Timbo a square tower, also loopholed, had been built in the wars of the 1760s.[63]

Organization

Although the Gambian kings were heirs to Mali, their military organization seems to have been less centralized. Kings were certainly in supreme command, but smaller units were commanded by lesser nobles. One hint that this sort of organization was used was the frequency with which civil war and the depredations of rulers were said to have fed the slave trade. In this regard the Gambia resembled the Senegal region, even though it did not face the attacks of desert nomads. When he visited the Gambia in 1731, for example, Francis Moore observed that Fooni and Kombo on the south bank were depopulated, their kings "having sold into slavery infinite numbers of their subjects".[64] Many other rulers who followed on both banks seem to have had this rapacious policy, which probably masked internal struggle rather than a callous policy of raiding one's own otherwise loyal subjects. French reports noted that Medano Somo, ruling Nyumi in the 1770s, was an unusually peaceful king, and decided to prevent some of the great men of his country from making a military expedition, as he did not feel that the benefits of such an undertaking would meet its costs. The nobles' power was curbed by him, for he revived a law which then was regarded as a dead letter allowing him to inherit the goods of his nobles upon their death, and presumably he had greater say in their military affairs.[65]

Elsewhere, centralization was less at the regional level, but might still be strong locally. The seventeenth-century Nalu of the Rio Nunez region were regarded by observers as unique in that they fought pitched battles (rather than raids and ambushes) and that their armies were formed in "units after their own fashion", although exactly how these units were recruited or commanded is unclear.[66] But the size and organization of pitched battles might suggest a greater power to mobilize on the part of those who did control the political system.

In early sixteenth-century Sierra Leone, the king was said to decide on wars after meeting with a council of elders, and from this group were appointed the captains that conducted their well ordered armies.[67] The armies of the Sumbas who invaded Sierra Leone in the mid-sixteenth century seem to have been organized to recruit members from among the conquered, for English visitors to the coast as they arrived noted that they enslaved many "Sapies" to work their fields and to serve them, while they themselves lived by war and spoil.[68] In any case the enslaved "Sapies" were all enlisted in the army, which, according to Portuguese witnesses of the early seventeenth century, was what made the Sumbas so powerful.[69]

However, the Sumbas' organizational principles did not survive for very long, and soon they were more or less integrated into the existing network of states and powers. Much of Sierra Leone in the seventeenth and eighteenth centuries seems to have been organized militarily by "towns" in which the rulers of these entities controlled militia bodies raised from their subjects as their soldiers. Forces seem to have been quite small, as was the level of warfare. As Matthews wrote with a certain scorn in 1786, "Every petty quarrel, when there are 10 or a dozen on each side, is called a war." Frequently these small forces were combined in alliances, which might take several years to negotiate, and might result in the largest forces in the coastal regions, around 500 men, recruited exclusively from the young men of each town. Nevertheless, in 1786, when he arrived, Matthews did find most of the country in such a war, composed of a number of allies lined up against each other, including the slave revolt of the Mandinka slaves.[70] Winterbottom, his near contemporary, also spoke of town forces being something in the order of 30–50 men, and most fighting being composed of taking and burning towns by surprise attack.[71]

Sierra Leone and even surrounding regions were also organized at a higher level by the Poro and other societies. The Poro was a religious organization to which the members of all classes of all the towns were initiated. Most observers saw the Poro as a society that helped to maintain the peace, and might intervene if a war had gone on for a long time to re-establish order. They were not above using force to maintain their authority, however, and could probably mobilize as many people to carry out their demands as most towns acting by themselves could, though they represented on the whole more of a democratic than an authoritarian tradition.[72]

A similar sort of unity and military direction also affected the Fulbe. Moore, travelling in their country in the 1730s, noted that they lived dispersed in many independent towns, typically attached to the larger towns of the Mandinka along the Gambia. Although each town was fully independent, and fiercely jealous of that independence, they were capable of great unity in warfare, such that it was impossible for them to be defeated, even though the Mandinka outnumbered them.[73] This sort of unity, not readily explained by the sources, allowed them to assemble the sort of military forces that resulted in the take-over of Futa Jallon and the Islamic revolution after 1727–8.

Conclusion

If cavalry ruled in the savannah, they were completely absent in this region, where the foot soldier and the navies played a more important role. Small polities were the rule, and even those that claimed a larger share of power were rarely capable of anything more than ephemeral success. This was as much a result of the geography of the region as of the specific nature of its warfare, although it may be impossible to sort the two out.

The coastal regions were potentially the most vulnerable to European influence – Europeans had their posts on these coasts, and their ships could penetrate some distance up the rivers. Yet for all this, neither firearms nor ships conferred on them any sort of overarching power. The widespread use of firearms in this region seems to have had almost no effect on politics either – for there was neither more nor less political unity or authority in the 1750s, when the musket had largely displaced the bow on the coast, than there had been in 1550 when Mane armies stormed Sierra Leone.

Chapter Three

War in the Forest: The Gold Coast

West Africa south of about 9 degrees N is covered with a thick tropical rainforest, broken only in the area of modern Benin by drier, more open country. This belt of vegetation completely rules out the employment of cavalry for both epidemiological and practical reasons. Only in the "Gap of Benin" (covered in the next chapter) where the savannah penetrates almost to the coast, do we find the complex co-existence of cavalry, marine and infantry forces dominating war. In the area to the west of the Gap, which Europeans called the Gold Coast during this period, infantry reigned supreme and the nature of the terrain played an important role in the way these forces were organized and fought. Only when the infantry armies broke out of the forest to the north, as the kingdom of Asante did in the early decades of the eighteenth century, did one find encounters between mixed armies.

The coast itself has no natural harbours and a sandbar or offshore islands make the coast hard to approach from the sea. The eastern regions of the area are connected by an extensive inland network of lagoons, lakes and rivers that allowed regular trade in protected waterways between Accra and Benin. Thus in the extreme east of the region, and throughout the Gap of Benin area to its west, the sort of marine complex that dominated the coastal regions of Senegambia was also found, but in the Gold Coast area itself, the coast was less well protected by waterways. The area had ample fishing and salt making along the shore, and goods and even fighting men were often transported by boats, although marine infantry were not so much a factor here as they were eastward.

The Political Background

The Gold Coast region was dominated demographically by people speaking Akan, though there was nothing like political unity of the region throughout the period.[1] Instead, in the early period, the area was especially known for possessing a plethora of relatively small, independent states. Maps from the late sixteenth and early seventeenth century show some three dozen states crowded into the region between the Tano and Volta rivers and lying within the forest zone. Most of these occupied an area some 50 kilometres across, dominated by one town that served as a political capital, and perhaps a few other marketplaces or strategic points, surrounded by a host of small villages.[2]

Europeans who arrived in the area in the 1470s made fairly permanent arrangements with one or other of these little states to establish settlements. At first, it was only the Portuguese who settled, but in the late sixteenth century, English, French and Dutch competitors made arrangements with other state authorities, and by the middle of the seventeenth century a whole host of European nations, including Sweden, Denmark, Brandenburg, Portugal, England and the Netherlands, possessed one or several posts located in the territories of one or other of the coastal states. Because the early trade was in gold, and security of that commodity while it was awaiting shipping was essential, Europeans demanded, from 1482 onwards, the right to fortify their positions.[3] The "trading castles" of the coast were fortified heavily on the seaward side, as dangers of pirates and rival nations posed a definite threat, and more lightly on the landward side, as their rear was protected by the African state whose alliance made their operations possible. In most cases the Europeans paid a rent or tax for the right to maintain their post and construct fortifications.[4]

Europeans always hoped that they could use these forts as bases to monopolize the trade of the coast, starting with the first Portuguese declarations of monopoly in the late fifteenth century, but the divided sovereignty of the African states, their own internal rivalries and the rivalries of other Europeans made this dream impossible. The result, in most of the late seventeenth and eighteenth centuries, was a continuous set of European-inspired intrigues to unseat this or that rival from their posts, or to persuade their African allies to give them exclusive rights to trade, something which virtually every African state sought as far as possible to avoid. Since the European rivalries often involved violence, and since Europeans were frequently closely allied with African states, both parties might become embroiled in disputes and in wars of this sort. But the Europeans themselves were also involved in African politics and sometimes these forced Europeans, not always willingly or happily, to become involved in intrigues of African origin. The result was sometimes complex wars involving both European and African rivalries (along with negotiation, treachery and side-switching), such as the late seventeenth-century Komenda war, undertaken when African polities were still much divided and European competition was at its height.

While the complications of European and African divisions were working out on the coast, the late seventeenth century saw the rise of a new sort of polity in the interior, away from the coast with its forts. Larger and more powerful states, capable of defeating and annexing their neighbours and rivals, were emerging. Denkyira, Akwamu, Axim and Asante came to dominate the interior and fought frequently among themselves from about 1670 onwards. In the early eighteenth century these interior contests took on greater force, with large wars being waged in 1730 and 1742 along with a host of smaller confrontations. In the end, by mid-century Asante had emerged as the winner of these contests and a strong, if not fully unified, kingdom. As the century wore on, Asante power increased and its centralization of authority along with it.

By the century's end, Asante faced only one strong regional rival, that being Fante, a kingdom that had grown by alliance and conquest along the coast, in part in response to the rise of Asante. Although Fante and Asante were already at odds in the mid-eighteenth century, it would not be until the opening years of the nineteenth century that a short but decisive Asante campaign gave it control of Fante as well.

As the African politics changed, European policies did as well. Many of the European powers abandoned the coast in the early eighteenth century, leaving only the English, Dutch and Danes. As Asante rose to power, these groups at first sought to outguess the winners of the complex warfare in the first half of the century, and then to come to terms with Asante as the century wore on. European involvement in African politics declined as these became less important and European rivalries were tamed on the local and international arena.

Warfare was close to endemic in the region for the whole period, though it was waged on widely differing scales and with substantially different weapons and tactics as time went on. Gunpowder weapons, for example, were taken up quite early and were combined with radical changes in military organization at about the same time as regional powers emerged in the late seventeenth century. Here it has been possible to speak of a "gunpowder revolution" in a way that would probably not have been appropriate in the Upper Guinea region.

Weapons and Tactics

The earliest accounts of warfare in the Gold Coast describe the all-infantry armies as being armed with double-edged swords, lances and bows, while protection was afforded by shields.[5] Later and more detailed accounts, however, indicate that these weapons were not ubiquitous, but restricted to certain classes, in fact armies involved several specialized types of soldier differently equipped. Some carried a sword, javelins which were often poisoned, and a shield, while others were equipped only with bows and arrows, and yet others carried only a sword. The weaponry was quite similar throughout the sixteenth and well into the seventeenth centuries.[6] The nobility, the leaders of towns and others of the elite class of the many Akan towns and their specially trained retainers served as the heavy infantry, while the slaves and common soldiers of the militia fought with bows and arrows or with javelins.[7]

Effective use of these weapons required considerable skill and training, especially the throwing of javelins and fighting hand-to-hand with sword and shield, which had no non-military counterpart in hunting as archery might. As a result, professional and well trained soldiers were an important part of the military system of the sixteenth and seventeenth centuries.

Operations

Military operations in the sixteenth and seventeenth centuries were of two sorts, small-scale skirmishes and ambushes and larger set-piece battles, what the Lutheran missionary Wilhelm Johann Müller called "open war", which were fought in quite different ways.[8] The differences were enforced by the demands placed on tacticians by the forested environment of the Gold Coast region.

The west African rainforest was and still is a formidable environment. Because this area had a fairly dense population already in the sixteenth century, with generations of clearing trees and then allowing them to go into long fallow, much of the forest, especially in those areas where population had clustered, was not primary forest, but secondary growth. This often had much more tangled undergrowth than mature rainforest, where tall trees and canopy might block sunlight from the forest floor and make fairly clear space.[9] Instead, the forests of the sixteenth century were mostly likely a fantastic, nearly impenetrable mass of vines and bushes along with tall and medium trees. It was very difficult for individuals to move in such an environment and impossible for armies to do so, unless they followed fairly well worn and defined paths.

These paths could be so narrow that only one or two people could walk abreast. While people could and did move into the bush, it was usually in flight or as a very limited deployment and not as a means of travelling. When Dutch forces sought to drive out the king of Fetu's army that was blocking roads in 1642, his men dispersed into the bush under Dutch fire and could not be effectively pursued,[10] though they certainly also lost their own abilities to function as a military force.

Forested country covered all of the Gold Coast except the narrow coastal strip, which grew considerably wider as one moved east towards the Volta River. Here the ground was much more open, heading to the savannah that marked the Gap of Benin to the east. In light of this terrain, it is only in the eastern part of this region that one encounters much in the way of fortifications. In much of the Gold Coast the towns in the late sixteenth century were open without any defensive works, and the European fortified castle of Elmina was the first such structure to be built.[11] Inland, and in the forests, the forest itself was of sufficient strategic significance to make fortification less attractive. However, on the easternmost end in the area where the unforested coastal belt was thickest around Accra one did meet with fortified towns. There William Towerson saw towns in 1556 that were hedged in with "fences" and with "thickets and bushes" and walled with "long cords" and bound together with tree bark, pointing to an early defensive system that incorporated vegetative as well as dead materials.[12] These were probably the thick hedges that were impossible to shoot through, or even to hew down, that the German doctor Samuel Brun described in the early seventeenth century.[13] In fact, Labadi, the most powerful of the eastern towns in the sixteenth century,[14] "was surrounded by walls and bulwarks" in the last years of the sixteenth century.[15]

Elsewhere, though, the forest served as a sort of fortification, channelling military forces along its paths. In the forest, with its narrow roads and impenetrable bush, a small force could easily delay a much larger one through holding a key point, ambushes were likely, and small units' relative immunity made such raiding operations viable. These operations might be conducted on a wide scale simultaneously with the strategic idea of wearing an enemy down through destroying settlements and capturing and killing people (even before the slave trade added the additional factor of providing people to sell in order to fund munitions imports).

These smaller operations, suited for the environment of the region, were often not really considered war by European observers, but they might be important in larger military affairs. For example, in 1618 Koromanti forces invaded Sabu, not as a large army seeking battle, it appears, but as a group of raiders. They still managed to inflict considerable losses, however, including killing the king's son "not in battle but by treacherous means" according to the visiting German doctor Samuel Brun. As a result of this, Sabu sought to counterattack in kind, using Dutch assistance provided by 30 musketeers and some 300 African soldiers raised from the vicinity of the Dutch post at Moure, but probably using the same tactics as the Koromanti had earlier and indeed as raiders did in general. The force advanced silently along the narrow path until they came to a populated area, where they were able to ambush people and take over some villages, which they subsequently burned. They killed about 300 people in the process, mostly women and children, which they saw as part of a larger strategy of demographic draining – "the blacks say," Brun reported, "it is better to strangle women and children than men, because then they will not reproduce quickly; and the children, if they came of age, would want to seek revenge". When Koromanti mobilized a force to attack them they withdrew slowly along the paths that brought them in, holding off the much superior force and making good use of musket fire and caltrops (an anti-personnel cutting device that lies on the ground or in pits) to inflict heavy casualties on their pursuers.[16]

Whole wars might consist of nothing more than countless repetitions of such attacks, small, quick and destructive with the goal of weakening the enemy in part by sapping demographic resources: "they do not always come to a pitched field," wrote Villault in 1667, "but sometimes endeavor to destroy one another by surprises and inroads, by burning and pillaging . . . their enemy's towns and taking all prisoners they meet."[17] While such actions could weaken and debilitate an enemy, it would probably take a full-scale operation or an "open war", designed to occupy territory and destroy main military forces, to be decisive, and for this larger armies and pitched battles were required.

Major wars were treated formally. The attacking country made a solemn declaration of war, which was subsequently broadcast by heralds and taken to the enemy. A mobilization was conducted and the forces were led to the enemy territory with great fanfare, under the assumption, no doubt, that there was little to be gained in seeking surprise for a force of this size. Such an endeavour might be preceded by a long period of less formal (though perhaps equally destructive) operations, and it might be followed by more of the same.[18] Such operations were relatively rare, and those that led to big battles even less common. Brun was told, following a major confrontation that resulted, according to him, in some 40,000 deaths (and certainly a large number for he saw a great many heads returned from the battlefield), that such a war had not taken place "in a hundred years."[19]

Large armies, like the smaller forces, still needed to use narrow paths to advance, and perhaps might face harassing attacks to slow their advance as they moved onwards, advancing in ones, twos or threes as the roads permitted, without any fixed order of march. When the army arrived at a place where a pitched battle could be offered because there was open space near settlements or that naturally occurred in the forest, they would quickly deploy from their loose marching order to a battle order, in a formation that would be five ranks deep. They closed up well, according to Brun, observing in 1618–19, with shield-carrying heavy infantry armed also with swords and javelins in the front, and archers behind them, who loosed their arrows upwards in order to have them rain down on opponents.[20] Farther back the armies had groups of people armed with swords like choppers, often commoners or slaves, but without the defensive armour that the front ranks held.[21]

Combat was then joined as the ranks advanced, first throwing most or all of their javelins at their enemies (as the archers continued their high arc of supporting volleys) and then closing in for hand-to-hand combat with swords, protected by their shields. A melée rapidly ensued which, like all such hand-to-hand combat, lasted for a short time before one side or the other broke.[22]

War often involved a complex combination of both types of combat operations, though sometimes a long period of hostilities might involve nothing but raids and skirmishes. Even when large armies were mobilized, battle might not be joined quickly. Because of the narrow roads and the nature of the country it was quite impossible, as Müller noted in 1669, to bring an army to the field in any sort of order that a European would recognize. Consequently, armies moved somewhat erratically over the roads in narrow files, two abreast, presumably seeking to occupy important points and to concentrate at some strategic place. Concentration in these circumstances was obviously important, to avoid defeat in detail, so "they have the sense to stay as close together as possible". This situation made "their principal tactic . . . to cut off the enemy's passage: to this end they encamp along the roads and in the bushes by which the enemy must inevitably pass".[23] As Bosman described these tactics in the late seventeenth and early eighteenth centuries, the armies advanced in disorderly bodies, or "crowds" with their commanders in their midst, seeking to engage each other, "man to man or rather heap to heap", presumably in the narrow pathways of the forest. Typically they operated as independent units with perhaps a loose overall co-ordination, for "if one commander sees another in trouble, he is likely to flee". Armies might lie close to each other, skirmishing constantly without ever fighting a major engagement for a whole year.[24]

The Gunpowder Revolution

The art of war in the Gold Coast was transformed by gunpowder weapons much more profoundly than was the case in Upper Guinea, to the point that it is probably appropriate to speak of a "gunpowder revolution". As everywhere, though, the arrival of gunpowder weapons was a gradual process. Perhaps the decisive stage was when the flintlock arrived in quantity and replaced matchlock muskets towards the end of the seventeenth century.

Gunpowder weapons were being used in some quantity very early on the Gold Coast. As early as the sixteenth century, Portuguese musketeers were deployed from Mina to assist their African allies, and when other Europeans sought to enter the trade, to attack or threaten them, as they did with the English who came there in the 1550s.[25] It was only in the last years of the sixteenth century, however, that Africans began buying and learning how to use muskets, as the Dutch visitor Pieter de Marees noted in 1602.[26] Even then, muskets still were largely used by European soldiers under European command for a long time, as it was still common for the Dutch, for example, to lend bodies of a few dozen to over a hundred soldiers to fight in African armies as musketeers, such as the force that Samuel Brun witnessed fighting in 1619. But by this time, there were African musketeers as well, for the king of Sabu sent a detachment with muskets that were "beautifully clean" to support the Dutch about the same time.[27] By the middle of the 1650s, in fact, muskets and corps of musketeers, typically in bodies of several hundred, had become very common in African armies, and thousands of muskets were being sold and employed.[28] In this initial phase of adoption, muskets were probably borne by slaves of the personal guards or perhaps by commoners, though Brun's description of an early-seventeenth-century force from Sabu seems to suggest that members of the political elite bore muskets as well.[29]

As muskets became more common in armies, they added firepower to the missile weapons available to commanders, but as Kea's significant study of the changing military systems of the Gold Coast reveals,[30] they also presented a problem. Earlier use of missile weapons had placed archers behind soldiers carrying javelins and equipped for hand-to-hand fighting, and made effective use of the trajectory of arrows to create a literal rain of arrows as archers loosed an arc over the heads of the advancing heavy infantry. Muskets could not be used in this way and, as a result, in the 1660s musketeers were placed in the far front of the advance, as skirmishers, to clear the field for the heavy infantry when the time came to close in, so that the general course of battle remained the same in Villault de Bellefond's day in the late 1660s as it had been in Brun's in the late 1610s.[31]

In the late 1670s and early 1680s as flintlocks arrived in larger numbers, however, armies began to be reorganized so as to take advantage of the characteristics of the flintlock. Since one of the musket's greatest advantages was its armour-penetrating abilities, not surprisingly the mutually supporting, "well ordered" ranks of shield-bearing heavy infantry were the most likely to suffer. African musketeers strove to overcome the musket's greatest disadvantage, which was its low rate of fire, and at least as far as European observers were concerned, Gold Coast musketeers could fire very fast – "faster than Europeans" according to Barbot.[32] Bosman's description of war at the century's end indicates the co-existence of people using shields to stop arrows and throwing javelins along with considerable musket fire, which suggests that the armies were in transition as more musketeers were being incorporated, but the manner of fighting was still evolving.[33] Javelins were still listed as among the weapons employed by coastal people when Johann Friedrich von der Gröben travelled there in 1682, but his descriptions of those armed forces he actually saw in action mention only musketeers – certainly musket fire was characteristic of warfare at the time.[34] When the local people made an unsuccessful attempt to take Friedenburg in 1695, observers noted that they "fired small shot as thick as hail" into open gun ports, and that same year a Dutch force was surprised when some supposed allies from Komani had their muskets "turned around" but they grabbed them and opened fire when they closed.[35] By the end of the century, whole armies were armed with muskets, especially on the coast, where Fetu's army was noted in 1697 to be composed entirely of musketeers.[36] It was not much later that whole armies even in the interior were so armed. Johannes Rask, writing about army equipment in the area of Accra and Akwamu on the eastern end of the zone as he saw it between 1708 and 1713, did not mention any weapons but swords and guns.[37] Swords, which only nobles carried, were no longer seen as close combat weapons, but were simply used for cutting off the heads of the fallen.

The transition to the musket had transformed some styles of fighting as the musketeer who had been a skirmisher became a main line soldier, though tactics remained true to the musket's first use. It is interesting to note that in the Gold Coast, as everywhere else in Africa, there was no attempt to connect the role of musketeer with pike- or sword-carrying infantry through the use of the bayonet: no trading records show any demand for this weapon. Perhaps this is because the javelin was a thrown weapon that did not automatically translate into the use of a pike.

In any case, soldiers in the musket era fought as if they were skirmishers. They advanced stooping over so that bullets would fly over them, or advanced, discharged their weapons and then crept back to their own units.[38] Engagements were decided entirely by the exchange of musket fire, often at close range. Rømer described soldiers who in their nervousness forgot to load properly, standing not more than "ten paces apart, burning each other [with their gunpowder charges] but no balls come out".

War also became a matter of manoeuvre, as soldiers made much use of cover, and sought to get enemies to fire at them from long distances through taunts and dances, so that they could take advantage when they missed their shot.[39] It is indicative of the degree to which the musket had become the weapon of Gold Coast armies that Asante was said to have won its war with Akyem in 1742 in spite of having fewer troops, in some measure because it had "bribed" or recruited an army from the far north that used bows, and their arrows allowed Asante more missile power in the storms that hindered the use of muskets in the rainy season.[40]

Organization

Rulers of the Akan region typically controlled fairly small polities with a resulting small potential for large armies, and thus might maximize the concentration of highly skilled noble or slave soldiers. War and organization were dependent not only upon the ability of the ruler to raise an effective army from his own subjects, but also upon his capacity to acquire additional military forces from allied neighbours (including Europeans living on the coast), private soldiers of wealthy merchants, and mercenaries. Those countries that could control larger areas, engage in more extensive mobilization and demand support from neighbours would ultimately be the ones that could dominate their neighbours as well as increase their own centralization.

Since at least the late sixteenth century the armies had been organized by towns: the captains of towns had personal bodyguards composed of slaves and of "soldiers", perhaps paid attendants, and when kings summoned they served with their personal troops as well as people of their town's region, presumably serving as a militia.[41] Of these, the professional soldiers were not very numerous; William Towerson mentions a force of some 100 soldiers under three captains coming down to see his ship in 1556, and this was probably only drawn from this personal guard.[42] The militia organization at least from the early seventeenth century served without pay and carried their own weapons when called by their local leader (called *brafo* according to later sources)[43] through beating on a war drum three times to issue a summons to mobilize.[44] They also gathered provisions for the campaign, typically coming with enough for eight to ten days, from their own stores.[45] They were organized according to their local towns and probably served under a captain from their locality. The numbers of troops in such locally organized units were small; Sabu organized some 800 men under ten captains (or some 80 per small town) to assist the Dutch in 1619,[46] while in 1642 400 troops were organized under three captains (133 each).[47] These were probably not full mobilization, for other sources suggest that even small states could, if pressed, mobilize several thousand fighters, though with probably much the same organization.[48]

With relatively small numbers of soldiers under their direct command, leaders who could supplement these forces were more likely to be successful, and there were a number of possible supplementary forces. They could ask the Europeans who settled in fortified locations along the coast after the founding of the Portuguese castle of São Jorge da Mina (later Elmina) in 1482 to provide them with help from their own garrisons of professional soldiers. They might also draw on help from neighbouring states in alliances to bolster their forces against those of their adversaries, either through payment of what Europeans often called "bribes" or through convincing them of a convergence of interests. Finally, they might also hire out forces that were raised for this purpose by successful merchants and mercenary captains who flourished in the region from at least the mid-seventeenth century.

Interstate alliances were the most common and effective means of supplementing a state's military forces. When Fante and Sabu went to war with each other in 1619, the Akani were involved as allies.[49] An even larger alliance was noted in 1622, involving Accra, Komenda and Koromanti against a number of inland states in their own league.[50] In the mid-seventeenth century, there were many such alliances noted: Abrem enlisted Fetu to attack Komenda in a war that grew to include Akani, Mina and Sabu in 1646,[51] and another major war of this sort was waged in 1664–8 involving Akyem, Akani, Fetu and other states.[52]

But the golden age of alliance politics among the Akan states was probably the last years of the seventeenth century and the first half of the eighteenth century, when alliances became complex and shifting and, moreover, when the practice of paying subsidies to various African states to enter wars, supply troops, or remain neutral grew as well. The Dutch factor, Willem Bosman, writing generally about the last decade of the seventeenth century, suggested that an ally could be hired for £2,000.[53] When Akwamu made a war against Accra in 1681, it paid Agona and Akran two casks of gold to assist them, though in the end Akwamu tricked its allies, for which perfidy it eventually paid dearly. It also drew on the support of Akyem through a convergence of interests.[54] Disputes over the considerable sums of money that Akwamu promised to its various allies and then reneged on were still being aired nearly two decades later.[55] The wars between Asante and Denkyira in the first years of the eighteenth century that announced the arrival of Asante as a major power on the coast, and those between Akwamu and Akyem at about the same time, were all complex alliances of several states.[56]

Europeans could provide professional soldiers from Europe, typically equipped with matchlocks and defensive armour and often skilled as well in close-order fighting. The European settlements also had local militias from the small towns that grew up around their posts to supplement their professional cores, so that in many ways they were not unlike other Akan states. Like African allies, they were available for a price unless they could be convinced that their interests were served by the success of their would-be partners. And, like the Africans, they had their own goals. Initially, the Portuguese forces stationed in Mina sought to use their forces to persuade nearby rulers to trade with them exclusively, attacking those areas that traded with French or English vessels, as occurred in 1556, for example.[57] Somewhat later, we have evidence that the Portuguese became involved in local wars which bore on their trade, but often as partners of more complex diplomatic relations that reached farther afield, such as the war between Portugal and its ally in Elmina town and the combined forces of Fetu and Komenda.[58] When the Dutch began to offer serious competition to Portugal on the coast, they presented sizable armed forces to secure allies, serving more or less as mercenaries to African rulers, as they did for the ruler of Sabu in 1618, and working against rulers who had made similar alliances with Portugal.[59] Although the Europeans saw these wars in terms of their trading interests, they involved such large coalitions of African forces, including those as far away as the Akani country, that their diplomacy is as likely to have been drawn from African politics as from European interests.[60] Thus the Dutch involvement in 1622 in a war against a powerful king named Jan Konkon of an unnamed interior country seems to have been more in the interest of the rulers of Accra, Komenda and Koromanti, who were resisting his efforts, than to further Dutch commerce or the Dutch struggle with Portugal.[61]

As more Europeans became involved in the Gold Coast and dotted the coast with their forts and factories, the numbers of their soldiers increased, as did their interest in playing in African politics as a means of defeating their rivals. There is no finer example of this complicated combination of European rivalry merging with African rivalry than the Komenda Wars of the late seventeenth century. European interests continued throughout the eighteenth century, as did their attempts to influence African politics towards their particular ends and to defeat European rivals. African rulers could and did play this game of manipulation from the other side.

Just as European armed forces provided African leaders with possible military units that could expand their armies, there was also the possibility of using the private armies that some of the local merchants had raised from their clients, slaves and supporters, especially during the late seventeenth century. Jan Claessen, a private merchant-strongman, managed a force of over 2,000 men in 1659 when he succeeded in taking the Dutch fort at Fetu.[62]

Ray Kea argues that the revolution in weapons that took place in the late seventeenth and early eighteenth centuries changed not only weapons and tactics, but also the basis for recruitment of armies. The commoner soldier, equipped mostly with bows in the seventeenth century, gave way to the musketeer (formerly perhaps from the slaves and personal guards who still figured quite a bit in Akwamu's army in the late seventeenth century),[63] while the elite heavy infantry of nobles and their slaves and retainers disappeared.[64] Certainly, when muskets became more common in the 1680s, they were carried by the militia soldiers, such as the large force and the detachment seen by von der Gröben in 1688 carrying muskets and accompanied by their wives to the field.[65]

Rask's account of the army of Akwamu in the early eighteenth century describes an army of conscripts and musketeers, brought from their villages by their own leaders in groups generally of 200–400 or more, and bearing their own weapons, carrying whatever rations they could muster, and under standards from their locations.[66] Oldendorp, who interviewed a former military commander who had been enslaved around 1750 and was serving in St Jan (Virgin Islands), noted the connection between kings, "underkings" and lower commands. His informant commanded a unit of 3,000 in the domain of an underking.[67] A survey of the military strength of many of the coastal towns of 1697 found strengths ranging in the low hundreds to the low thousands; all were equipped with muskets at that time.[68] Two of the more powerful subordinates of the king of Akwamu were said to be able to muster 7,000 men each, provided they could make use of the 22 large and small villages of the area, or an average of about 300 each.[69] In 1749 Poppi, ruler of Akyem, counted his people aged 16–60 to make a determination of the total number of men he could put in the field, which in this case was said to be some 40,000 men.[70] Such reckoning was a natural outgrowth of the policy of using, or at least paying attention to, the whole population capable of bearing arms and not just specialized groups.

During the earlier stages of the change, and in the areas to the east, it was still possible for private citizens and for Europeans to continue to play a role in warfare. The rise of merchants who armed their slaves, often with muskets, marked these changes. Some could be quite effective – Edward Banter, a mulatto merchant, was able to use his army to relieve Anomabo fort from a Fante attack in 1699.[71] Jan Kango, formerly an official of Adom, formed his own army and with it made the roads unsafe for travel and trade. He was eventually brought to heel in 1707 by armies from several states.[72] The most famous of these merchant and private commanders was Jan Konny: in 1711 he was subsidizing officials in Wasa to help him in defeating that state, and demanding protection money not to attack Axim;[73] in 1717 Konny wanted to dominate Akyem "by buying a group of robbers who" would pretend to be Asante soldiers and intimidate them.[74] However, such figures became rare in later periods.

In Asante, which emerged as both the most powerful and the most populous state of the eighteenth century, there was the potential for control over the commanders of these locally raised military units through their ability to appoint leaders in some districts and to increase the size and population of the districts. Ivor Wilks has demonstrated how there was a subtle balance between the rights of the king to appoint people to the office of Bantamahene, a major military title whose principal troops were recruited from districts not far from the capital, and the claims of descendants of the first Bantamahene to hold the office to win recognition. That the Bantamehene's troops were recruited locally was revealed when the English traveller Bowditch noted in 1819 what seemed to him depopulation in the district under the senior Asante general. The latter noted that they had indeed suffered heavy casualties in an action ten years earlier from which they had not yet recovered.[75]

Although statistics on the size of armies are always problematic, especially when they come from people who were not directly involved in the operations or mobilization (as European observers were not), it is clear that eighteenth-century armies were larger and were recruited more from general conscription than their seventeenth-century counterparts. Large armies, however, had serious logistical problems, when soldiers had to come bringing their own food supplies and afterwards were required to live off the land. The logistical stresses of using armies of this type counted in several campaigns. The Akyem army broke off fighting in its war against a coalition of Fante, Asin and Akwamu in 1716 because the rainy season was not a good time to fight, as the people who bore arms were needed to work their fields.[76] Similarly, in 1754 the war between Asante and a combined army from Denkyira, Twifo, Wasa and Akyem threatened the whole area with famine, as every able-bodied man was serving in the war and there was no one left at home to attend to the crops.[77] In 1760, Ouwsu Bore of Denkyira proposed the abandonment of their campaign in Asin for the same reason, that the men were needed to plant at home, and without this there would be famine.[78] The army of Anlo was defeated by Popo in 1792 because it had to dispatch a significant portion of its forces back to fetch food, the army having run out, and Popo commanders took advantage of the situation to launch a successful attack.[79]

Kea sees these changes to conscription-based armies as not simply a result of the weapons, as if the widespread use of muskets encouraged the use of peasant armies. It probably did take less training and skill to handle muskets effectively, however, than to deal with the dynamics of sword and javelin fighting. Rather, Kea has argued it was a reflection of a much larger series of social changes that placed more emphasis on peasant production and less on specialized groups of slaves. This was subsequently reflected in military recruitment, and originated in the special circumstances of the larger states that grew up in the interior of the Gold Coast, such as Denkyira, Akyem, Akwamu and above all Asante.[80]

Because demographic resources were crucial in peasant-based armies, moving, mobilizing and recruiting the largest number of people was very important. In this regard, the general economic and social position of the peasantry, and especially its remarkable mobility, played an important role. This mobility was not from military exigencies, nor was it a product of state policy, but rather grew out of deeper institutions in society. Rømer noted in the 1740s that the people of the Gold Coast were very mobile because they built impermanent houses and could always rebuild them quickly in another location. In addition, since they did not own land, they were not bound to a particular spot.[81] Armies could recruit large segments of the population and might move in blocks with all the people. This is surely what was meant when Nimfa, leader of the Akani, was forced to cross the Pra River "with all his people" after his defeat by Asante in 1786.[82]

The military mobility of the rural population in the Gold Coast would ultimately spill over into the neighbouring Allada region to the east during the massive military transformations of the late seventeenth century. The unsettled region between the more powerful of the Gold Coast states and those of the Allada and its neighbours was something of a refugee area where whole groups of militarized people set up bases. In 1682, for example, when Akwamu smashed Alampi, many fled to Keta near the Volta where they quickly became involved, successfully, in a war against Great Popo, as well as other pillaging operations.[83] Sofori "Pickaninie", an Accra general, founded a similar settlement about the same time at Little Popo, and, like the Keta settlers, was known for military prowess and raiding ability.[84]

Success for a mass recruited army relied on drawing on the largest pool of potential soldiers, and population factors were considered strategic. The rulers of Akwamu and their neighbours began a policy of sending small bands of skirmishers, called *sikadings*, to harass border areas of their opponent in the 1720s, and to take and sell many slaves. In addition to the revenue potential of the sale of slaves, the losses might weaken the opponent and cause him to lose military strength. In this way, Owusu Afriyie, king of Akyem, reasoned prior to his war with Asante in 1742 that with "100,000 young men" (*sikadings*) he could weaken Asante by raids on its frontier villages.[85]

The use of skirmishers to weaken opponents had the added advantage that people who were captured could be enslaved and, since the sale of slaves brought in munitions, could directly offset military costs. Indeed, Akonno, the king of Akwamu who made such extensive use of *sikadings*, preferred to use the raiders more to gather slaves than to risk them in direct action, eventually deciding that it was easier to use them internally than to risk them in an international venture. This decision hurt him so badly with his supporters and subjects that he had little support when war with Akyem came in 1730.[86]

Long wars, which kept armies in the field and disrupted countries by stopping off their trade and harassing their populations through skirmishing attacks, could be ruinous. In 1737, for example, the Dutch heard a rumour that Asante was considering ruining Akyem through a long war.[87] This demographic fact was also reflected in the policy of Akyem upon its conquest of Akwamu in 1730. Rather than follow a common strategy of selling off thousands of captives from the defeated region, the Akyem rulers refrained from selling slaves from among the conquered Akwamu. They thought it was worthwhile to retain a large population whose loyalty they thought they could win and who might then assist them in a potential war against Asante. The strategy worked, according to Rømer: within five years they were loyal subjects and soldiers for Akyem.[88] But this strategy was unusual and was followed in this case because the rulers of Akwamu had made themselves unpopular. A more common solution was to deny a one-time opponent the opportunity to recoup his losses and regain military strength by "eating the country" and selling off as many people as possible as slaves.[89] In this way, they could not be a threat to the victorious country by rebelling if held there, or re-forming if left at home. But even here the policy did not always hold, for in 1734 Akyem attacked a section of Akwamu and "all but exterminated" the country, leaving only about 500 families which lived as refugees in the area.[90]

Furthermore, after the defeat, thousands of Akwamu people, along with the armies they supplied, migrated eastward, some settling near Accra and supporting the Dutch post there, others moving into the Volta region to play a substantial role in military affairs there.[91]

Although the conscripted armies were larger than the more professional armies of an earlier age, the general limitations of tactics imposed by the forest environment remained. There, they were still organized in units that proceeded independently, a necessity in the environment. A unit commander who had served in wars in the mid-eighteenth century noted that his unit might be relieved by another in the course of two hours' fighting,[92] suggesting that much of the fighting was on fairly narrow fronts, where not all available soldiers could be engaged simultaneously. The significance of the narrow fronts and problems of mobility are highlighted if one considers that if soldiers really did have to march only two abreast in the forest, and if they marched 1.5 metres apart, it would require a column 750 metres long to move 1,000 soldiers forward. It probably took somewhat less – certainly commanders would try to make it the smallest possible. In fact, a mid-eighteenth-century slave in the West Indies who had served as a commander of 3,000 troops told the Moravian missionary Georg Christian Oldendorp that the army of his king stretched over half a German mile (or about 3 kilometres) on the march.[93] At this rate, a large force of some 20,000 or so troops (numbers which are proposed for some of the larger fighting forces) would have to extend for 15 kilometres if it marched in a single column. Of course, it is more likely that armies advanced over several columns using different routes and rejoining each other should there be a need, but it would still mean that many soldiers had no choice but to wait as actions in restricted areas were fought by their fellows.

Pitched battles on the scale they were waged in the eighteenth century needed open space, and it took a great deal to get it. When Akyem and Asante went to war in 1741, they fought skirmishes for almost a year along the familiar pattern, before committing to a battle. To make a battlefield, both sides sent some 10,000 people to cut trees in order to clear a large open field for a battle where Akyem's army was totally defeated in 1742.[94]

Because the forested roads on which armies moved and manoeuvred formed a complex network, intelligence about these roads was crucial for armies to move with maximum speed, to maintain contact between units, and to plan concentrations and convergence. Such factors probably gave considerable advantages to people fighting on their home ground. When Akwamu went to war with Akyem in 1742, its ruler ignored the advice of his council that he wait for the Akyem army to come to his land, and that he could then fight them on familiar terrain. Instead, he decided rashly on an invasion of his own, into the unknown lands of his opponent. He was at first successful, defeating Akyem forces, but eventually the Akyem army took advantage of the rainy season and turned the tables.[95]

Ntsiful, an early-eighteenth-century ruler of Wasa, was the master of using the forest to his advantage, and of moving the army as a population unit. Thus, he was able to withdraw slowly in the face of a large invading Asante army when his small state was attacked in 1726, fighting several sharp engagements, but always managing to get away with his troops, eventually crossing the Pra river where his pursuers had a hard time finding boats to cross the river.[96] He eventually lodged in Abrembo, to the north of Wasa and, when driven from there by Asante in 1730, he depopulated the country by moving his army to the land north of Fante, where he controlled the roads by occupying key positions, a strategy which European commentators regarded as simply banditry.[97] Asante pursued many other refugees from this war as far afield as Axim, where no less than 10,000 Asante troops encamped and rounded up local people as well as alleged refugees.[98] In fact Ntsiful became something of a legend, for when they were considering war against Asante in 1742, the leaders of Akyem recalled that Ntsiful had fought the Asante to a standstill for 20 years with just 2,000 men through his skill, and they suggested that Akyem should adopt strategies from this experience, and send "100,000" raiders to weaken Asante. King Ba Kwante decided not to follow this advice, and lost the ensuing big battle.[99]

Really large battles such as the one that killed King Ba Kwante were fairly rare in the eighteenth-century Gold Coast, though major wars, sometimes with high casualties, might be waged without ever coming to battle. When large armies were mobilized it might take quite some time before the two armies felt that they could risk a battle, and it might never happen. In a war of 1739 between states allied with the Dutch and those allied with the Danes around Accra, they spent some six months of "ambushes of little importance" before getting serious about the war, but even then no battle was waged.[100]

The tactics typical of the wars of the period are found in Asante's war against Akyem in 1717. The war developed slowly, being declared at least in February. An Asante army advanced into Akyem but only by September was a decisive battle expected. This battle took place between September and October when, on the advice of the formally neutral neighbouring ruler of Akwamu, Asante sent one detachment through Akwamu's territory to take Akyem from an unexpected quarter. However, the ruler of Akwamu warned Akyem of this, which allowed Akyem to meet the detachment, which it pinned down and immobilized, cutting off food supplies. In time, smallpox broke out among the encircled detachment, which was then broken under an attack.[101] Asante employed the same tactics in its war with Akyem in 1764, for when the Akyem army advanced, two Asante forces occupied positions to prevent its retreat and to cut off its proposed junction with its ally Wasa. Asante then effectively cut off food supplies and the Akyem were "half starved" at the time of their final defeat.[102] This was not, of course, exactly siege warfare, but it was a war of position in the paths of the forest in which a well informed army could effectively contain and blockade another army through holding key places until it was weakened through starvation, or disease.

Asante had become adept in fighting in the rainforest, and Asante became the only Gold Coast state to become effective in the very different military environment north of the forest. Asante's armies fought north of the forest in the early eighteenth century. In a lengthy campaign in 1744–5 Asante managed to deal with cavalry armies fighting in a manner not unlike that of the Sudanese cavalry to the west. They used lances and javelins and closed with the sabre. The Asante forces managed to seize and apparently to ride horses themselves, though they can hardly have been an effective cavalry, and reportedly all were killed in one engagement. Their musketry frightened the horses, which allowed the Asante force to withdraw, always surrounded by the cavalry, in good order.[103] Although it was hardly an encouraging beginning, Asante managed eventually to dominate a number of savannah states.[104]

Asante's great achievement, however, was to become the masters of the warfare of the forested south. One of the important factors that allowed Asante to emerge eventually as the major power on the Gold Coast in the last half of the eighteenth century was the construction of the Great Roads, which altered the dynamics of forest warfare in their favour. Although the roads were mostly appreciated by Europeans because of their commercial implications, their military uses were also critical. These roads, which were publicly maintained, and connected capitals and other strategic points to each other, were considerably broader than the smaller paths, allowed the more rapid passage of armies, and deprived leaders like Ntsiful of the opportunity to use the forests to their advantage. Rømer, writing about experience before 1750, bewailed the lack of modern roads that forced traders to move precariously along the banks of streams where the forest was naturally clear. Travellers in the early nineteenth century, by contrast, praised the Asante road network, which they viewed as modern, just as Rømer regarded the previous channels as archaic. There was considerable opposition to the opening of these roads in the forested south, and it was seen as a direct manifestation of Asante power. Its completion represented the completion of the Asante empire.[105]

Conclusion

The nature of the forest of the Gold Coast imposed significant restrictions on the way war could be waged. It banned horses and, for much of the region, also naval forces. Moreover, it created opportunities for certain types of tactics, and particularly for the use of clearings and roads that lay behind Asante's ultimate success in the region.

War in the Gold Coast also had a particularly pronounced demographic dimension, although one that it may well have shared with other regions for which there is less explicit evidence. The idea of moving, stripping or preserving the population as a result of war gave impetus and support to the slave trade as well as the propensity for refugee communities to develop, especially at its eastern end.

Finally, the constant presence of European factors, and the rapid spread of firearms in the region, shaped much of war but, as elsewhere, not as much as one might expect. The small forces that Europeans controlled directly did serve from time to time in the military actions of the smaller coastal states, but for the most part Europeans had little part to play. The Gold Coast has sometimes been cited as an example of the gun–slave cycle at work, but closer examination does not support the cruder model of African wars fought at European behest for purposes of supplying the slave trade.

Chapter Four

Horses, Boats and Infantry: The Gap of Benin

The land adjoining the Gold Coast to the east was open country known as the "Gap of Benin" where the savannah reached down to the coast. Aside from this broad savannah, bordered on both east and west by the tropical rainforests, the most prominent geographical feature of the region was the elaborate coastal waterway on the south. The waterway made it possible to navigate, by small local boats, from Accra on the Gold Coast to the great delta of the Niger river, which had its own complex of waterways that ultimately joined up to the Cross River and the border of what is today Cameroon. The waterway was composed of rivers and creeks that paralleled the coast (joined by several large rivers that ran north and south, of which the Volta was the most important on the west, and the Niger, of course, on the east), as well as large lagoons, the most important of which was the extensive Lagos Lagoon. Virtually none of this waterway was accessible to European sea-going vessels, and even the coast was difficult to reach, for the islands that defined the seaward side of the region had broad beaches and no harbours. Where there were gaps in the islands, the area was still inaccessible to large watercraft because of sandbanks.

On the eastern end of the region, the area around the waterways was either tropical rainforest or mangrove swamp, but the Niger's delta and related waterways made it a maze of fairly shallow and small creeks that spread their way through the forests, providing the major means of transport in the area. This combination of forest or dense vegetation and river made it a different environment from the savannah or swamp that surrounded the waterways in the west, joining eventually with forest near Accra.

The area thus defined had the potential for all three of the major African forms of fighting – cavalry in the savannah north and throughout the central part of the region, marine infantry in the watery coastal and delta environment, and regular infantry everywhere. Naval power and cavalry power were thus important in their own spheres, and everywhere infantry had a role to play, whether as common footsoldiers or as marines.

In addition to the limits and possibilities imposed by the vegetation and physical environment, there were limits imposed by the disease environment. Although much of the land in the Gap of Benin was good cavalry country, the local disease ecology did not make it good horse breeding or raising country. As a result, the major military powers of the south could not maintain horses, even though they lived in cavalry country. It was difficult for them to resist cavalry armies, but because horses could not live for long in the south, those northern areas where horses could be maintained could not sustain their power in the south once the dry season had passed.

The Political Background

The kingdom of Dahomey, which came to dominate the southern part of the Gap in the middle of the eighteenth century, faced a double dilemma posed by these environments. On the one hand, it could never control the coast because it lacked an adequate fleet, and on the other it was constantly harassed from the north because it could not maintain a cavalry. It is not surprising that Dahomey's rulers lived so much by war, for they were almost incapable of winning any war decisively, and were constantly vulnerable.

In the sixteenth century, most of the coast was dominated by two major kingdoms. In the west, the kingdom of Labidan in the region around Accra was noted as the most powerful state. In the east the Empire of Benin dominated the Niger Delta and the coastal waterways that reached westward almost to Accra. Only the coastal towns around Calabar on the Niger, and probably the many Igbo communities of the northern and eastern parts of the delta, avoided Benin's might. Benin's navies and marines advanced west during the early sixteenth century; in 1539 emissaries from both Labidan and Allada on the coast were found imprisoned in the Benin court. Indeed, Benin's power seems to have been growing, for its navy was still very active along the coastal lagoons, and only the city state of Ijebu seems to have maintained its independence in the area. Two centuries later, traditions of Accra looked back on the age of Benin domination as a sort of golden age, in contrast to the world of divided sovereignty that followed.[1]

In the interior, the kingdom of Oyo probably overshadowed much of the cavalry country, though the course of events in this region is only vaguely known at present. Based on traditions collected in the late nineteenth century, it seems that in the early sixteenth century Oyo dominated most of the north, but found its power contested by the kingdom of Nupe along the Niger. Indeed, at some point, probably in the middle of the century, Nupe managed to defeat Oyo, sack its capital and destroy it as a regional power. It was only in the early seventeenth century that Oyo recovered and began a long stretch of growth, becoming a major empire that could reach southward by the end of the century.[2]

Towards the end of the sixteenth century, Benin's power declined and most of her western territory was lost. A new set of smaller regional powers emerged in place of Benin, with Accra gradually becoming dominant on the extreme west, but fitting more into the politics of the Gold Coast in the period that followed. Warri became more important in the east at one end of the Niger delta complex, where it managed to hold its own against Benin, and the Igbo territory north of Calabar was decidedly divided, into as many as fifty small entities, a situation which remained for the rest of the precolonial period.

The Gap region of the coast increasingly fell under the power of the kingdom of Allada, which exercised an apparently weak authority over its neighbours on the coast and some distance into the interior. After an apogee in the mid-seventeenth century, on the other hand, Allada too underwent a loss of territory. Popo and Whydah emerged as important local powers west of Allada by the end of the seventeenth century, and in the interior the once dependent Fon state of Dahomey started its rise to dominance, where it would soon collide with Oyo to the north and the coastal powers to the south.

Europeans did not take an immediate interest in the Gap region in the sixteenth century, although they did establish diplomatic relations with Labidan and Benin. Portuguese mercenaries served in the army of Benin in the early sixteenth century, and are represented in the art of the time loaded with weapons. As late as 1600 Benin might still call on Europeans for occasional support, but their presence was still sporadic. Most of their relations in the sixteenth and early seventeenth century took the form of purely trading establishments, with occasional establishment of factors. However, after the 1670s, European factors were more firmly established, especially in Whydah and Allada and then, in the early eighteenth century, even in Benin. European factors concentrated in Whydah, where they were allowed to fortify their establishments and where they became active in the factional politics of the kingdom. Although these forts were unable to withstand a sustained attack, their guns might be important in providing support for refugees. European commercial rivalries and alternate attempts to monopolize commerce both suffered from and contributed to the activities of the many coastal refugee states and their navies.

The rise of the important imperial powers on the Gold Coast in the late seventeenth century had a substantial impact on the western parts of the Gap. Akwamu, the most important of the eastern Gold Coast states, managed to crush Accra in battles between 1677 and 1681, and its further expansion eastward brought more of the region bordering on the Volta under its influence. But Akwamu's victories, while quite decisive on the Gold Coast, resulted in a flood of armed refugee groups from Accra and then from the smaller states, along the Volta moving eastward. Some of these occupied the lower Volta and established local dynasties, while others moved into the coastal waterway, maintaining themselves on the sometimes barren islands and coastline. When Akyem defeated Akwamu in 1730 the process was repeated, and Akwamu refugees moved eastward as well.

In short order, the military refugees, finding themselves in an inhospitable environment and lacking the resources to maintain themselves, turned to raiding and robbery as support. Mercenaries from the region occupied by refugees became important all along the coast, serving in various armed encounters as the political situation changed during the critical period of 1680–1730. These mercenaries and refugee dynasties played an important role in the struggle for control of the coast that followed.

Dahomey's ambitions dominated the eighteenth century, which began with a concerted drive to control the coast. In 1724 Dahomey armies crushed Allada, and three years later they smashed Whydah. But neither victory proved decisive, just as Akwamu's victory over Accra had not been, farther west at an earlier time. The ruling family and part of the army of Whydah withdrew to the west to the coastal islands and carried on a low key war against Dahomey from then onward, adding to the already complicated mix of refugee armies on the islands and coastal waterways. A part of Allada's elite and army at the same time withdrew eastward and established itself along another set of islands at Porto Novo, a process that was repeated as Dahomey sought to control the kingdom of Weme east of Allada, whose refugees, along with some from Allada, established Badagri. Dahomey tried in vain to bring these coastal areas under its control, but lacked sufficient naval resources to do so. Although Dahomey established a mildly loyal rump dynasty in Allada, which provided Dahomey armies with naval support, it was insufficient to turn the situation to Dahomey's advantage.

Dahomey's extension eastward along the coast was at least partially helped by the final loss of Benin authority in the region. Following 1689, Benin began a long and very harmful civil war that ruined its ability to conduct long-range military operations and even to hold on to some parts of its empire. At least one consequence of this was an increase in piracy, particularly Ijo piracy in the western part of the delta, which was not really suppressed when the civil war in Benin was brought to an end in 1732. Although the following years saw a re-emergence of Benin in its immediate region, and by the 1770s its occasional participation in military operations in the Lagos Lagoon, it was never again able to assert itself in the areas to its west.[3]

Just as Dahomey's armies were moving to the coast, Oyo began to extend its power southward. Although raids from Oyo into the region had been going on since at least 1682, Oyo military activity increased in frequency after a great campaign that humbled Dahomey in 1728 and continued through the 1740s. Although Oyo could not maintain its cavalry permanently in the south (and thus was unable simply to annex the area as it had other regions in the north), it could raid the area extensively and at great cost to Dahomey. Consequently, in 1747, Dahomey agreed to humiliating terms and paid Oyo tribute to prevent continued visitations of the northern cavalry. Oyo, which had relations in the 1770s with some of the coastal states, especially Porto Novo, manipulated Dahomey's own interest in the south to its advantage, but neither state ever established real control over the coast.

While Dahomey was thwarted in the south, it still sought to extend control northward inland into Mahi country. This broken and mountainous region was divided into many small polities, and Dahomey became involved in dynastic politics that sought to unite them. In the 1730s Dahomean armies began seeking to impose a king in the area from one of the elite families that was connected to Dahomey's own royal family, and no doubt to extend its own influence. Like the long series of campaigns waged against the small states of the coast, the Mahi wars proved to be indecisive. They were also problematic, since Oyo was also interested in the region. The eighteenth century ended with an extensive and reportedly successful campaign by Oyo into Mahi, though even this campaign does not seem to have brought long-range consequences. The power of both countries collided with the expansion of Asante in the Gold Coast interior. In 1764, an Asante army making a probing expedition was smashed by one from Oyo that helped to define the boundary between the two most powerful states in the region.[4]

Weapons and Tactics

The earliest descriptions of warfare indicate that all infantry in the region carried shields, swords and lances of one kind or another (typically called *asagayas*) and used arrows.[5] Illustrations and descriptions of these weapons in the early eighteenth century show a triple-barbed pointed javelin, which could be thrown accurately from about 30 paces. Shields were very large, four feet long and two wide, so that they covered the whole body. These shields were made of elephant or oxhide, and were proof against arrows and most javelins. For closer fighting, men carried a three-foot-long heavy sword or cutlass.[6] Finally, people of the coastal areas at least used a short throwing club, like the clubs in Upper Guinea, capable of breaking bones and hurled with great accuracy in a manner resembling the throwing of a javelin. Bosman believed the people of the Gold Coast (probably Accra and Akwamu, the states most involved in this area) feared these clubs more than a musket.[7] These weapons, supplemented by muskets in the middle of the seventeenth century, remained a constant mainstay from the earliest descriptions until well into the eighteenth century.

The initial organization of Allada and its neighbours in the late seventeenth century probably reflected the earlier periods as well, in which the structure of armies and their tactical organization was designed to lead to a hand-to-hand encounter. An account of the 1690s describes Allada's armies as being organized in tightly disciplined companies for parades or marches, but when they were deployed in the battlefield they spread out like "groups of sheep".[8] Indeed, their parade order was remarkable, if one believes the plates that accompanied the account of Desmarchais, which shows the coronation parade of the king of Whydah in 1725. In the picture, the army of Whydah is shown in dense formations that would have made a European proud, with musketeers and pikemen in separate formations.[9]

But the parade order was probably only to facilitate rapid marching, for the soldiers clearly did deploy into loose companies, "great platoons without ranks and without order" once in the presence of the enemy. If they had superior numbers they sought to envelop their opponent's formation, but when armies of equal strength met each other they did little beyond probing attacks, each withdrawing without fear of being pursued; only, in fact, when a complete defeat was imminent did they fight bravely and desperately.[10] Another early-eighteenth-century French visitor thought small mercenary forces from the Gold Coast refugees could defeat Whydah, even though the king could allegedly raise huge armies, because the dispersed deployment meant that they fought without order, and were thus weak and vulnerable. Each unit fought separately, and by the early eighteenth century they were beginning actions with a phase of musketry, although it was conducted at considerable range, so that shots were often ineffective, though they could penetrate the shields, probably their most important function. Musketry was often considered intense if a few people fell.[11] This early phase of musket fire probably came from skirmishers posted forward, since musketeers did not carry shields and were thus not expected to engage in the later phases of battle. In many encounters, if generals judged that the issue could not be decisively decided and opted to withdraw, they might not go farther than a musketry skirmish.

There were times when armies did engage each other closely, so that an archery phase began after the musketry phase, and the "sky is obscured by arrows" as they advanced, probably, like their counterparts in the Gold Coast, shooting them in an overhead trajectory. Then the forces commenced a closing attack, as the infantry hurled their javelins, while covering themselves as best they could with their shields, and at last they closed competely for hand-to-hand fighting with sword and cutlass. The loose formations of which the European observers complained were probably designed to give room for the soldiers to fight hand-to-hand, while at the same time reducing the chances of the javelins and other missile weapons hitting their targets, since attacking loose formations required aiming. Once battle was joined, "no one then thought of giving or receiving quarter" until one side or the other broke. Then, throwing aside their arms, the defeated fled as best they could, vigor-ously pursued by the victors, who sought to capture, garrotte or enslave as many as possible.[12]

Tactics of the armies of the region went through a slow evolution as weapons changed, moving as elsewhere from an ultimate reliance on hand-to-hand fighting to looser organization and much more dependence on firepower from muskets. Gunpowder weapons were employed quite early in the region. As elsewhere, Portuguese mercenaries provided the earliest of these. They were already serving in Benin in about 1515, probably with guns,[13] and in 1516 the king of Benin seized a Portuguese bombard for his own use.[14] When Andreas Josua Ulsheimer came to the Lagos Lagoon region in 1603, his captain was recruited by the king of Benin to use their artillery to assist in bombarding a rebel town in the area. The Dutch force with two large guns joined some 10,000 Benin soldiers in the assault, which succeeded when the main gate of the walled town was forced after half a day's bombardment.[15]

In the sixteenth century, though, these gunpowder weapons were virtually always used by Europeans and for specialized purposes, especially in sieges. African armies began importing and using gunpowder weapons in their own forces only by the mid-seventeenth century. A few Dutch muskets were being deployed by soldiers in Warri's army or navy alongside arrows and javelins by 1656.[16] In 1662, visiting Capuchin missionaries noted that the king of Allada had muskets stored in his palace.[17] The Sieur d'Elbée, visiting Allada in 1670, witnessed a parade of troops and noted that as well as spears, shields and swords, the men also carried "muskets in good order".[18] By the time an "unhappy war" broke out between Offa and its neighbours in 1681, large supplies of gunpowder were considered crucial for continuation.[19] However, these weapons were much slower in displacing the more traditional weapons, for in all these instances gunpowder weapons continued to be carried and used side by side with clubs, shields, swords, lances and archery, both in the Gap and the Delta, where a visitor to Old Calabar in 1713 noted no firearms among its troops.[20]

It was some time around the second quarter of the eighteenth century that gunpowder weapons came to dominate the field. Whydah had more muskets than other coastal powers, but they were still not the dominant missile weapon for them, being employed, as in the Gold Coast, as a skirmishing weapon in the early stages of combat. The emerging kingdom of Dahomey, which invaded the coast in 1724 when it attacked Allada, started using firearms more often and dispensing with other weapons. As early as 1727, when King Agaja of Dahomey wrote to King George I of England, he noted that, "I am gret admirer of fire armes, and have allmost intirle left of the use of bows and arrows, though much nearer the sea we use them, and other old fashioned weapons," such as the throwing club and javelin. He expressed a strong desire to replace his "old fashioned weapons" as soon as possible if he could learn to manufacture powder or firearms.[21] The army that William Snelgrave reviewed that same year still carried shields and swords, although he noted that they were largely armed with firearms.[22]

Gunpowder weapons proved to be of some value to Dahomey soon after. The cavalry armies of Oyo that invaded Dahomey in the period between 1728 and 1747 were entirely horsed, using bows and arrows as their missile weapons, lances and "cutting swords". When they met Dahomey's troops the gunfire frightened the horses, preventing them from making a home charge. As a result, Dahomean infantry was able to stand in the field against them, though defeating them proved more difficult.[23]

In the following years, however, gunpowder weapons did become general. When the navy of Warri received the Portuguese vessel that brought Capuchin Domenico Bernardi da Cesena in 1722, many carried muskets and pistols, and fired salutes with their guns.[24] By the 1780s the musket had replaced all other missile weapons, and the sword had become for the most part an officer's weapon. The soldiers of a great alliance of small states lying along the Volta that fought alongside Danish forces in the campaign against Agona were equipped solely with muskets, carrying only a variety of daggers as a personal weapon.[25]

The evolution of tactics in all musketry wars is revealed clearly in Isert's detailed account of an action between an allied force of some 4,000 troops and a probably smaller force from Agona on 11 April 1784. The allied force advanced in a dispersed order, by platoons of 25–100 men, across a field against an enemy who had posted themselves on the edge of a forest. Pickets were deployed to find and fix the enemy and then platoon after platoon advanced at a run, stopping some 50 paces from their opponents to form a single firing line, steppping back to reload after each round. The larger engagement divided into a number of local affairs, but as the Agonas had many of their forces concealed in the woods they were able to emerge unexpectedly and threaten the more advanced of the allied troops. To meet these threats, reserve platoons, held back from the first assault, were committed as needed, and the fighting continued until nightfall when both sides eventually withdrew from the field.[26]

Marine Warfare

In addition to the usual infantry weapons, soldiers of the Gap and Niger Delta region made extensive use of watercraft. Already in the sixteenth century, travellers noted the size of canoes made in the Delta, carved, as most African watercraft were, from a single log that was hollowed out.[27] Those in the New Calabar region were 50–70 feet long and 6 feet at the beam, capable of carrying 60–80 people, and were paddled rather than rowed. They were protected by shields mounted on the sides, and marines in them used javelins as their principal weapons.[28] When the Capuchin priest, Juan de Santiago, visited New Calabar in 1647 he saw them with figureheads representing Catholic saints salvaged from Portuguese wrecks.[29] The watercraft of late-eighteenth-century Warri's navy could carry, it was said, up to a hundred men who could paddle the craft very fast, and were aided by simple sails (they did not know tacking, irrelevant in river navigation in any case). They, like the boats of Calabar a century earlier, were protected from enemy fire by shields built onto the boat.[30] These large craft represented the capabilities of Warri, the strongest and most centralized naval power in the region; the Ijos, living in a decentralized society and given to piracy, had smaller craft, which could carry 50–60 men nevertheless.[31]

The watercraft of the coastal regions facing the Gap varied widely in size and capacity, though they were perhaps in most respects like those of the delta. While the watercraft were primarily used as troop carriers, the soldiers themselves might have considerable firepower. Thus, in the attack on Shagbrno's forces at Little Popo in 1753, the Dahomeans advanced against their foes, who withdrew through swamps to the offshore island. As Dahomean troops followed overland, the retreating forces suddenly returned, and using their watercraft sailed back along the island. The Dahomeans, caught in the open and unable to return to their own boats, were virtually all killed by musket fire from the passing boats.[32]

The Allada navy advanced considerably in firepower by mounting light artillery on its watercraft, a feat credited to Antonio Vaz de Coelho, an African who had been carried to Brazil as a slave, and then returned and offered his technical help to Allada. In a 1778 operation, Allada possessed two armed boats, each of which had four brass swivel guns and 24 large calibre blunderbusses mounted on it, which they used to good effect to cover the army's retreat in a debacle against Epe.[33] The navy again proved its worth when Allada was invaded by Weme in 1785 and, although Weme's infantry completely defeated Allada's ground forces, the naval forces saved the day.[34] Mounting artillery on canoes was not restricted to Allada, for when English captain John Adams visited Bonny in the 1790s its watercraft were equipped with a bow cannon "of large calibre" with which they had twice defeated New Calabar, forcing all its trade to pass through Bonny.[35]

Considerable forces might be moved on watercraft, though generally such forces were quite small. According to French sources, when Lagos and its allies attacked Badagri in 1788, they moved some 40,000 troops in 2,000 craft (or 20 soldiers per boat).[36] While these numbers seem exaggerated, movement on a scale even resembling this probably required considerable water, such as was only found in the Lagos Lagoon. Certainly the kingdom of Warri in the Delta region was more a naval power than anything else, for a visitor of the mid-seventeenth century believed that it had an army of 60,000 (probably an exaggeration), "the majority in water with canoes".[37] Indeed, visitors of the 1780s described Warri as the most formidable power on the coast because of its navy, maintaining that the kingdom scarcely fought on land, but rather forced its enemies into submission by cutting off water routes of food, for many regions in the area around Warri were dependent upon trade to deliver food supplies to them in exchange for salt, fish and overseas goods.[38]

Fortifications

It is curious that the people of the Gap region built no fortifications until the early eighteenth century, since all their neighbours did. To the east, the towns of the Lagos Lagoon, Benin and even the smaller towns of the Niger delta had been fortified with walls and ditches since the sixteenth century. To the west, there were fortified towns in the Accra area in the sixteenth century. The European fortifications constructed in the late seventeenth century, probably the first built in the area, were considered helpful though not inviolable. In fact, they were so easily taken by assault that Labat contended that the people of Whydah let the Europeans settle amongst them so that the inhabitants could pillage the European traders from time to time.[39] The forts certainly did not stop Dahomey's army in its triumphant march into Whydah in 1727: all the forts were burned and their directors taken prisoner.[40] The tactics of taking a fort were revealed in the actions of the British commander at Whydah in 1728, when Dahomey sent an army there to round up dissidents who had taken refuge in his and the nearby French fort. The British commander burned all the villages around the fort when there was a sea breeze, so that Dahomeans could not do it when there was a land breeze that would carry flames to the fort. Lacking cannon, the Dahomeans sought to burn the French fort in the same way, after their unsuccessful infantry assault with only small arms, foiled when British artillery from the nearby fort fired into their ranks. Nevertheless they did fire the French fort and blow up its magazine, which had some 1,500 refugees within.[41] The fort was subsequently rebuilt, however.

The tactical situation might be altered by the presence of a fort with its firepower, even if it had not been invested. In one of the numerous Popo–Dahomey confrontations near the forts in Whydah on the morning of 12 July 1763, the English fort shelled the advancing Popo force of some 8,000 with grapeshot made from musket balls as they moved along the beach against a Dahomean detachment of 1,000 men. The Popos were sufficiently disorganized by this action that they were broken, and Dahomey exploited the situation to its advantage by launching a counterattack which stalled its attackers long enough for reinforcements to arrive. By 2 o'clock the Dahomeans had achieved a complete victory in which 30 out of 32 Popo officers were killed.[42]

However, European forts could be taken by direct assault, as Dutch Keta was in 1737. After investing the fort closely, Dahomean infantry scaled the walls with ladders, while they tunnelled under one of its bastions, causing it to collapse the third time artillery was fired from it.[43] Similar tactics were employed to take the much stronger Portuguese fort in Whydah in 1743. This fort had a steep wall and moat and mounted 30 guns. It succumbed when sappers undermined a bastion and upon its collapse, the Dahomean infantry swarmed in, while the Portuguese commander João Basilio fired the magazine and blew himself up.[44]

On the other hand, African authorities did view the possibility of European fortifications as a potentially valuable asset. When Portugal was considering establishing itself at Jakin in 1730, the exiled king of Allada explicitly asked them to build a fort, so that he could be protected against Dahomey by it.[45]

In fact, the Dutch helped with fortifications, though Dahomey ended up taking the fort in a surprise attack in 1732, from which the principal inhabitants escaped by the time-honoured coastal means of flight by boat to a fortified island.[46]

In the turbulent world of the Volta delta, the possession of a fort or fortified island was also of interest. Thus the Danish factor Sparre constructed a fort in large measure to protect and support a varied group of refugees on the Volta island of Ada when Akwamu pressured them after its own defeat by Akyem on the Gold Coast in 1730. The fort was no sooner built than Akwamu sent a marine force in 100 boats to take the island, but failed. They were subsequently bought off by a ransom of 17 slaves and went further to the east. From that point onward Ada was a refuge for a variety of people in the region, albeit a somewhat temporary one.[47]

The constant threat of Ijo pirates to the lands under the Warri forced them to consider fortifications of their own type. Palisades and barricades restricted boat movement and allowed for both the observation of and attack on ships or canoes that entered the area. In addition there was a system of alarm bells that noted the arrival of a Portuguese ship, for example, in 1722.[48] Farther inland, Olaudah Equiano, enslaved from the Igbo country around 1755, recalled that village compounds in his home of Essaka were surrounded by a moat and palisade.[49]

In the face of the Oyo threat, Dahomey sought to fortify the country, apparently with the help of a renegade French officer named Galot, who taught them the rudiments of field fortifications with artillery.[50] A Dutch observer noted on the eve of the 1728 invasion that the king of Dahomey "has made deep ditches around his entire country, as well as walls and batteries, mounted with the cannons he captured at Fida [Whydah]".[51] In fact, these fortifications, which probably included a great deal of wood and trees, and which were therefore what Snelgrave referred to as the bushes, were critical in Dahomey's defence. The ditches, bounded by artillery, were forced by Oyo troops after a long fight, but the army was effectively stopped in the engagement. In another account, or probably another engagement, Dahomean troops dug trenches and posted their army in two corps, one facing the trenches and the other on the flank. As Oyo troopers advanced into the trenches an extended battle developed, which lasted for some four days. Dahomean troops from the flanking detachment launched attacks and withdrew to trenches afterwards. These same tactics were employed by Kpengala's army defending the capital of Abomey in 1742, where the principal defence was a dry ditch without breastworks and where the Dahomey infantry did well until reinforcements from Oyo finally overwhelmed them.[52] Both these accounts reveal how the infantry armies of Dahomey dealt with the challenge of cavalry using fortifications; they also reveal that the army, once engaged, could not defend the rest of the country, and only the shortage of water and fodder forced Oyo's ultimate withdrawal.[53] Dahomey did not stop with its fortifications: in 1772 the royal residences were surrounded by a nearly square wall of mudbrick some 20 feet high and close to one mile on each side with blockhouses on each wall. The town of Abomey itself, however, continued to be encircled only by the dry ditch, crossed by bridges each with a garrison, but still without a breastwork as earlier.[54]

Allada also constructed fortifications after the mid-eighteenth century. After a war with Weme in 1785 in which Allada narrowly escaped defeat, it constructed a moat and a "strong clay wall" along the common boundary.[55] The city of Allada was also fortified by the 1790s, possessing a strong wall and ditch system with loopholes cut into it, as well as fortified and loopholed houses within the town.[56]

In the broken Mahi country to Dahomey's north, the local much divided polities used inaccessible mountains as natural fortifications, so that operations there by Dahomey's army were typically composed of sieges of these fortified mountains, where food might be stored for a long time. These mountains were refuges for a great many of the civilian population, as well as strategic strong points. Dahomey's campaign of 1731 into Mahi was so long and protracted that the army revolted in the midst of it, because Agaja punished commanders for failing to take the strongholds by assault. Even when a successful assault was made, in the rainy season, the Mahi were able to withdraw successfully with relatively few losses.[57] When the Mahi were attacked in 1752, they withdrew to the mountain of Boagry, which was so steeply bordered and difficult of access that, while it was easy to defend, it could not be escaped from should the defence fail. The Dahomean army cleared the countryside and made camp before the mountain, which had been further fortified by the digging of earthworks in its vulnerable areas. However, the Mahi defenders had sufficient room in the mountain to plant crops and were prepared to wait out the Dahomean attack, while constantly harassing the Dahomeans with skirmishes. Finally in frustration after a year's waiting, the Dahomean general, the Agau, tried a direct assault, and after several days of bitter fighting with heavy casualties, the Dahomeans carried the Mahi works and destroyed the garrison.[58] The cost of this operation was not forgotten for, when the Dahomean army again besieged Boagry in 1764, the commanding officer refused to make a heavy assault. When he was dismissed for cowardice, he deserted to the Mahis, and his presence perhaps helped Mahi repel the attack that his reinforced successor launched against the fortified mountain.[59] The problem of fortified mountains bothered Dahomean forces on a smaller campaign against Agona in 1778, where their opponents made use of caves to fortify themselves, although Dahomey was able to smoke them out effectively.[60]

The refugee dynasty of Whydah, driven from their home by Dahomey in 1727, fortified two islands off the coast, and mounted artillery to command vulnerable crossing places. There, since Dahomey lacked a navy capable of ferrying troops across elsewhere, the former king was safe, though the sandy soil was unsuitable for planting and his subjects were miserable.[61] The local environment favoured those who could keep their mobility. In the long run, however, the islands proved to be excellent fortresses, and the mobility provided to the refugees by their boats allowed them to harass Dahomey constantly, while giving them the freedom to return to safety should larger campaigns fail.[62]

One way to deal with such an island was to blockade its food supply, as Dahomey did to the island of Popo where the exiled king of Whydah had his base in 1733, since the population far exceeded local resources and the rulers depended upon the extensive intercoastal water traffic to keep themselves up. Although the king was prepared to sue for peace, no terms were agreed upon and the siege did not have a decisive result.[63] When an allied force of Oyo, Dahomey and Lagos sought to blockade Badagri in 1784 the Lagos force sent 32 large watercraft to participate in the sea blockade, while harassing those on shore. The defenders ended up losing many prisoners and were weakened by the naval forces.[64]

In 1774, the Dahomeans managed to defeat Whydah's army on the mainland, so the Whydahs withdrew to the fortified island of Foudou-Cong, another refuge for Whydah troops. To follow their enemies, the Dahomean troops cut trees and planted them in the water to make a causeway, which they used to cross to the island and defeat the garrison. Although the Whydahs had some 700 canoes to move their troops out they found they could not pass the causeway, and had to remain in their boats for some months, living off fish.[65] The tactic of bridging to the islands, while requiring considerable effort, was tried again in action against Jakin in 1776, where Dahomean forces built three bridges to the island placed so that they could be mutually supporting.[66]

Organization

The military forces of the various states in the region were recruited largely from the peasantry, but also from more professional groups of mercenaries and bandits, serving frequently under their own commanders. An important point of centralization for any state was the degree to which its leadership was able to control and manipulate the locally recruited forces and their commanders. In early-seventeenth-century Benin, commanders were always surrounded by their troops, though these seem to have held their commands from the king, and represented the largest and perhaps the most centrally disciplined army in the region at the time.[67] The supreme commander of the Benin forces, styled the "fieldmarshal" in mid-seventeenth-century Dutch documents, was held to be second only to the king.[68]

Commanders in the forces of Whydah, a smaller and much less centralized state than Benin, were styled "fidalgos and captains" in the 1680s.[69] In late-seventeenth-century Popo the army's lowest unit was composed of platoons of 20 men, who were under "cabociers".[70] In early-eighteenth-century Whydah, military forces ultimately fell under the command of local authorities, who recruited and led them. The local leaders kept their troops distinct on the battlefield, even though, in the opinion of some outside observers, these leaders were not always very competent. In addition, some of these village leaders had special functions, such as the Souga, who commanded the king's fusiliers.[71] Each of these governors was required to arm and equip a fixed number of soldiers, though the soldiers themselves were required to provide their rations.

Within their commands, the leaders in turn divided their troops into "platoons" for tactical purposes, though the basis for choosing members of the platoons is not known; it may well have been based on the local village commanders.[72] The units were probably quite stable, however, for when Whydah's army was routed by Dahomey in 1727 its defeated soldiers straggled back "by platoons".[73] The village-based units probably did not actually mobilize the entire population capable of bearing arms, although the potential for such large forces may explain the difference between the size of the forces that Whydah was supposed to be able to muster and the actual field forces it deployed.

These local forces, controlled in their supply and recruitment by local people, made ensuring loyalty to higher command and government problematic. One way of creating loyal forces was to recruit them from one's own family, which with clientage and polygamy might amount to several hundred or even more potential soldiers. When a civil war broke out in Whydah in 1708, claimants to the throne had mobilized family members on a large scale into significant military forces.[74] Whydah was in fact troubled by civil wars when these local nobles or captains fought with each other, deploying the troops under their command, so that, instead of fighting duels as was done in Europe, they fought whole wars complete with pillaging and enslaving of the opponent's people.[75] One such war took place in April 1726 between the English Captain (so called by Europeans because the English fort and trading post lay in his jurisdiction) on one side and the combined French and Portuguese captains on the other.[76] While these forces were adequate for civil war, they were not enough to mount an effective defence of the country. The French Captain, Asu, commanded some 3,000 troops when he faced the army of Dahomey in 1727, a number too small, in his opinion, to hold out without adequate support from the other military leaders. Moreover, he noted, his command included many women and children, suggesting that the armies raised by such officials were likely to be drawn from a levy *en masse*, perhaps stiffened by better trained soldiers.[77]

Also, as in the Gold Coast, the population of the Slave Coast area was mobile and capable of moving as a block from one place to another. Thus, when Whydah was conquered by Dahomey in 1727, a significant number of people both military and civilian withdrew to Little Popo, where they resisted Dahomean occupation and attempts to extirpate them for many years.[78] The independent commands moved along with the population into exile from Whydah. When Huffon of Whydah fled to the island of Little Popo, Asu continued as commander of a large army on his own island, making an unsuccessful attempt to re-occupy the mainland in 1729.[79] Eventually, when Asu died in 1733 and Huffon a few weeks later, there was a complex succession struggle in both camps, in which Dahomey became involved and nearly managed to finish this refugee army.[80]

In the area around the Volta, there was a complex combination of local and private forces. Local people were joined during the course of the late seventeenth and eighteenth centuries by large contingents of refugees from the Gold Coast to the west and the Gap region to the east. Few of the distinct groups had many soldiers, and warfare was often a complicated and unstable system of alliances, held insecurely together by the taking of solemn oaths. A large war in the region in 1769, for example, involved negotiations over who was and would be loyal to whom. A key moment came when Aveno, which had sworn at some earlier time to support both sides, decided to come in on the side of Ada against Anlo.[81]

The smaller state of Calabar in the Delta had a variant on the system of private commands, known in later literature as the "canoe house". These houses were headed by private individuals who had a say in government through collective decision-making mechanisms, and are perhaps attested in a late-seventeenth-century document signed by "Amaral, ship captain".[82] The Delta region presented problems to all who wished to build centralized power; even Benin's sway there was limited by local entrepreneur nobles whose loyalty to Benin was conditioned by their possession of canoe fleets. One such entrepreneur, "Caboceer Baba", used his fleet to help the Dutch become established in their base near Benin in the early eighteenth century, until Ijo pirates extinguished his command.[83] In Warri, on the other hand, a much more centralized government prevailed, and the soldiers, a "simple militia" as Moreau de St-Méry called them in the 1780s, were mixed in among the regular population, but were ready to march when called. They were supported by taxes in a public treasury, and thus completely loyal to the state.[84]

Dahomey, a more powerful and potentially centralized state, grappled with many of the same issues as it rose to power in the early eighteenth century. One method was to create military forces dependent on the king alone, and to separate, as much as possible, the loyalty of soldiers from commanders and transfer it to the king or the state. To ensure the loyalty of the officers, the king made their appointments temporary and reserved the right to relieve them at will. In this way the Agau charged with attacking Mahi in 1764 was relieved when he was too inactive and the Mayhou was sent to relieve him.[85] In the 1770s, Norris, visiting the palace of Dahomey, noted specifically the temporary nature of military commands.[86]

In addition to taking steps toward creating a dependent officer corps, Dahomean rulers also sought to create special permanent military units sponsored by the state and loyal to it. There was a fairly small regular detachment, a royal guard composed of "heroes" with special uniforms, and already by 1727 fully equipped with firearms.[87] When a detachment of the royal army passed Whydah after engaging in a successful expedition against Tuffo, it was said to have 3,000 troops divided into regular companies and carrying colours, as well as some 10,000 "rabble" following it, carrying supplies and performing various support tasks. These were regular soldiers, perhaps more numerous than in most armies of the time, and they were replenished by taking in boys, who were given to the soldiers "at publick charge" to raise and train for a military life.[88] These boys were obtained, according to mid-eighteenth-century information, by a levy on all the villages.[89] It is possible that this is the system described by Norris, whereby children of certain wives the king distributed to various young men belonged to the state. They were subsequently raised apart from their families and then integrated into the army later, when they had forgotten their family ties.[90]

The rulers of Dahomey were anxious to maintain a professional and thus politically dependent army, for when his regulars suffered heavy losses against the Oyo invasion in 1728, King Agaja replenished some of their ranks with women, drawn from his wives and perhaps the origin of the famous "Amazon" corps of later Dahomean history. This may have been the earliest attempt to mobilize women into Dahomey's army as combat troops; they were clearly employed as a sham to make the numbers seem greater, and marched in the rear of the formations. In time more women and eunuchs under arms were constituted in this force. Norris counted some 40 women on guard with muskets at the royal palace in Calmina, and some 90 more attached to a returning army that he reviewed.[91] In 1781, the king was able to march off with a force composed of 800 armed women.[92]

In addition to women, Dahomey's regular army included mercenaries and other professional soldiers of a variety of origins. As in the Gold Coast in the late seventeenth century, armies might be augmented by recruiting mercenaries from the various militarized people, or hiring the forces of other states. Whydah, locked in a war in 1688, brought forces from both Accra and the Gold Coast in to its side.[93] Likewise, Allada "bribed" forces from Akwamu and Sofori to attack Offer in 1692, and subsequently they invaded and ruined Whydah as well on Allada's behalf. Whydah for its part hired people from Keta to assist it.[94] A unit encamped in Sabe about 1730 to watch the activities of Huffon, the former king of Whydah, now safe on Popo island, replenished its strength by recruiting bandits and other loose people – perhaps from the various rebel or defeated armies of the Volta region.[95] In the 1780s Dahomey was replenishing its considerable cumulative losses by recruiting from its conquered people, after a serious loss in which some 400 members of the royal guard fell. A French observer noted that a considerable portion of the Dahomey army was composed of Mahis who had been drafted into service, even though the Dahomeans did not count them as worth much.[96]

However, these measures never fully overcame the problems of recruitment and hence, even in Dahomey, soldiers were loyal to their commanders, or at least might follow them against the policy of the king, so that when the troops were pressed by Agaja to continue their war in "Yahoo", probably Mahi, in 1731–2, whole units deserted, including one of 4,000 commanded by one of the king's sons, who took his men to Weme.[97] Army commanders bearing specific titles often commanded detachments of the army and operated quite independently: the 3,000 soldiers that attacked Jakin in 1733 were split, one portion under the Zohenu and the other under the Fosupo, but this suggests that the officers were not immediately attached to their units.[98] Nevertheless, army officers clearly had access to soldiers who would support them personally. When the Mayhou, another commander, revolted in the succession of Tegbesu around 1740, he was able to raise a force estimated at 20,000 in a short time, though loyal forces under the Agau defeated and slaughtered them.[99]

Some indication of the structure of these local armies is revealed in Norris's account of the invasion of Dahomey by the former king of Whydah in 1743. To meet this challenge, the Caukaow raised his army, the viceroy Eubiga assembled all that could bear arms in the town, and the *caboceiros* of Sabe increased their own forces, though they were still badly outnumbered by the invaders. Clearly these officers were raising or maintaining military forces locally in the area of their command, and the forces were not permanently under arms.[100] In 1745, the Tanga, a local Dahomean officer at Whydah, possessed a strong personal guard, as well as the devoted loyalty of the remaining soldiers that he raised for a rebellion against Dahomey and an attack on the English fort. The loyalty of his troops was ensured, it was said, because he used his many wives to give wives to other young men who then served him well.[101] Shagbmo, another Dahomean officer, concerned that he would be accused of treason, in 1746 fled to Popo, taking with him a part of his army, where he continued to be a thorn in Dahomey's side, a role continued even after his death in 1767 by his son.[102]

The officers, endowed with considerable revenue from their positions, raised and paid troops from their own resources, the king supplying only ammunition, as we learn from a report of a campaign of 1728.[103] Ferreira Pires observed in 1797, "the king's wars are sustained at the cost of his cabeceiras". The king supplied, as before, munitions and equipment, and shared the spoils with the commanders, purchasing their slaves for fixed prices and paying a bonus for enemy dead.[104] Before undertaking a war in 1789, the king of Dahomey had to purchase considerable quantities of guns and especially gunpowder, much of it on trust from European merchants.[105]

The military forces of the islands and the Volta basin lacked the centralization of the Dahomey army, and form a contrast to it. They had many relatively small units under commanders who were considered general officers. A force from this area that attacked Whydah in 1763, for example, composed of 8,000 troops, had no less than 32 "general officers" each with his own umbrella (an insignia of office), or about 250 men in each command.[106] When Danish officials assembled an army to attack the Agonas in 1784, they noted that commanders bearing umbrellas commanded units of 25–100 men. As this force moved into battle "each village unit marched separately in platoons", presumably recruited and fighting together by their residences.[107] This army assembled slowly, for every day new units arrived, including that of Lathe, a rich merchant from Popo who had his own personal force.[108]

Beyond the problems of recruiting soldiers, and forming units that leaders could rely on, armies had to be maintained in the field, and problems of logistics probably limited army sizes considerably. The supply problems of maintaining large permanent forces probably explain the low numbers of the Dahomean army given in a late-eighteenth-century source – surely the largest in the region, suggesting that it numbered only about 3,000 and that the garrison at Glewhe was only some 300, for these were the small numbers permanently under arms.[109] Supply, even for small forces, proved a problem once the first rations, which all soldiers were expected to be carrying when they reported, were exhausted. In the war between Accra, Whydah and some of the Volta River refugees on the one side and Popo in 1694, the siege of the latter town was supported by provisions from the whole country, which had begun suffering great privations after just a month.[110] Many of these soldiers, however, when not on campaign, were demobilized and worked in agriculture in their own villages.[111] Indeed, this is exactly how the Dahomean army was initially overcome by an attack from Popo in 1763, for their commander had to recall soldiers from the fields, it being planting time, before he could lead a successful counterattack.[112]

Problems of supply were especially critical to the armies of Oyo operating in Dahomey. While the Dahomean army could avoid defeat by withdrawing into fortifications or other bad cavalry country, they could not do any more than harass the Oyo troopers. Cut off from their regular food supplies, the army suffered quite a bit, and were required, as William Snelgrave thought, to "eat their slaves". Oyo for its part, however, could only remain in the country for the forage season, after which its army had to withdraw, unable to make a permanent occupation.[113]

Operations

We can glean some details of operations from an account of the battle between Dahomey's army and the combined forces of Whydah and Popo when the former king of Whydah, hoping that Dahomey was sufficiently distracted by Oyo's invasion of 1729, sought to re-occupy his town and country. Between them, Whydah and its ally were said to have gathered 15,000 troops, while the Dahomean force that came down from the north to engage it was depleted by the detachment of one force that was still raiding to the east and its own losses from the war with Oyo. On 16 July 1729 battle was joined, as the Whydah-Popo army divided into three units, one under Asu (a Whydah commander) and a second under the king of Whydah, while the Popo soldiers formed a third command. The council of the allies was divided, for the Dahomean force, made to appear larger by the addition of some female soldiers in the rear of their march, seemed to the king of Whydah to be too large. Nevertheless, his co-commanders disagreed, and battle was joined. Asu and the Popo divisions moved in with a withering attack on the Dahomean right, and were so successful that they forced it back. However, the Whydah troops on the other flank were less successful and broke themselves, in spite of the king's efforts to stem the tide by lancing some of his own soldiers. With that break, the Dahomean right wing rolled up the allied left and was able to take Asu's men in the rear, and then to drive the Popos from the field as well. In the rout, the king of Whydah only saved himself by taking refuge in the English fort, and then removing to the safety of his coastal island.[114]

In an action at Serrachee in 1775, the Serrachee forces managed to break the lines of the Dahomey army and penetrated to a reserve unit posted with the baggage and commanded by the Sawgan. Having already sent his forces into the breach unsuccessfully, the Sawgan fought his opponents with musket and then with sword until captured.[115]

Warfare on the rivers, islands and lagoons was complicated. Not only did this environment limit movements in some ways, but the use of boats expanded and changed the way operations were conducted, even if infantry tactics might remain the same whether the soldiers were on land or serving as marines. When Popo revolted against Whydah in the late seventeenth century, Whydah forces, reinforced by some French marines sent to reinforce French commercial interests in Whydah, built floats to attack the town. However, the floats came under such heavy fire from the fortified houses of Popo that they had to break off the attack, and resolved never to attempt it again.[116] When Dahomey invaded Whydah in 1727, its troops had to halt at the border marked by the river, and the Whydah troops, seeing that the Dahomeans had no capacity to cross with boats or even by swimming, felt themselves safe. But eventually the Dahomean army found alternative crossings and, flanking the Whydah army, crushed it.[117]

Dahomey's war on Epe in 1778 demonstrates the complexities of operations in the coastal environment, where marine warfare from boats was often the norm. In addition, the restricted environment of swampy regions often made warfare here not unlike the forest warfare of the Gold Coast region to the west, where strategic use of clearings and roadways allowed carefully planned and placed forces to keep much larger armies at bay. Dahomey sought to overcome its traditional lack of water mobility by enlisting the Allada navy in its efforts. Four divisions of Dahomey troops advanced overland into Epe territory and were mostly victorious, but one 800-man-strong Epe detachment withdrew into a swampy area and delayed the Dahomeans for a long time by holding a pass into it with great tenacity and courage. Meanwhile, the Allada force landed its marines, but the Epe king who commanded the forces facing them managed to break their ranks and captured their transports, taking them to nearby Weme. The Epe then re-embarked in the boats and attacked the remaining Allada army, routing it. From there, they moved against the Dahomean rear as it crossed the swamp where the Epe detachment had delayed it. Although the Epe were successful, the Dahomey force were still able to plunder the country and withdraw.[118]

The war against Badagri in 1783 took similar turns. Using support from Allada, Dahomean forces took Badagri's beach, and then crossed the river at its mouth, with Allada watercraft ferrying their infantry across. At this point, however, the Badagri army withdrew into the swamps and used the restricted mobility of this area to harass and ambush the Dahomeans as they advanced, eventually cutting them off. Fortunately for Dahomey, the commander of the force was able to cut his way through the surrounding force, regain the boats, and withdraw from the river.[119]

At the other end of the region, the 1784 campaign by an alliance of people from the Ada and Accra region and the Danish against Aguna and its allies involved another sort of amphibious operation. The flotilla of the allies went upriver in a sizable number of canoes, many armed with a small bow cannon, and led by a raft containing two larger pieces. In all 115 watercraft crossed the river under fire to meet their allies, but the Agona people, skilfully entrenched, were not hurt by the fire of the artillery, and the direct water assault was called off. Eventually the force of some 2,500 landed upstream and proceeded inland, when confronted by extensive earthworks that lay behind a marsh at the town of Atocoo. These were attacked the hard way, by a frontal attack as infantry waded in the marsh up to their armpits in order to attack the works, while two other units worked through even more difficult terrain to take the works on the flanks. But neither group attempted a direct assault; rather they drove the defenders out by 45 minutes of sustained musket fire at close range.[120] In another action involving the same principals in 1792, artillery fire was used to break and confuse the defenders behind their earthworks by setting fire to the bush and creating a panic which caused the defenders to break and run, leaving their leaders to commit suicide.[121]

Conclusion

The plight of the kingdom of Dahomey, straddling the world of amphibious operations along the coast and over to the Volta in the south, and facing the cavalry armies of Oyo in the north illustrates the unique character of this region. The rulers of Dahomey, even more than those of its predecessor, Allada, managed as best they could in a difficult environment where their success rested on mastering both the waterways and the cavalry savannahs, at a time where they themselves were unable to breed or maintain horses, and relied on allies for naval forces. They never quite managed to master either, and this puts rather a different light on Dahomey than the one shed by its depiction by Abolitionist writers of the late eighteenth century, of a constantly aggressive and usually successful kingdom. While there is little question of its aggression, its success was often limited.

As already noted, Dahomey's relative lack of success underscores once again the ambiguous impact of firearms. Dahomey wanted to take up firearms quite early, but never wholly re-armed with them. It failed most conspicuously against the mounted soldiers of Oyo, who were virtually without the weapons until the nineteenth century. As is so often the case in military history, Dahomey's successes were as much the product of determination, discipline and generalship as they were of the magic of technology.

Chapter Five

War on the Savannah: West Central Africa

The landscape of west central Africa, like that of the Sudan, was a broad savannah. The tropical rainforest of the coast north of the Zaïre River and stretching inland into the heart of the continent was, unlike the rainforest of west Africa, sparsely inhabited. The heart of the region lay south of the forest then, a terrain of frequent mountain ranges especially once one moved inland from the coastal plains, broken by plains and flat plateaux.

From a strictly terrain point of view, west central Africa should have been fine cavalry country, and thus have a military history quite like that of the Sudan. But horses were never able to survive in the climate of the region. Furthermore, although the Kwanza and Zaïre rivers bore considerable boat traffic, west central Africa also did not have the marine culture of the west African coast or even the Niger river. Consequently, west central Africa was the land of infantry, where even reconnaissance was done by fleet-footed scouts.

The Political Background

The kingdom of Kongo dominated sixteenth-century west central Africa. The other large kingdoms of the area, Ndongo and Loango, both claimed, at least in late-sixteenth-century and early-seventeenth-century traditions, to have been founded by or descended from Kongo, even though that was probably not true. Only the kingdom of Benguela, located south of the Kwanza, and perhaps some of the states located farther inland, about whom we know much less, traced their origins elsewhere and lived outside the shadow of Kongo.

Not only did Kongo dominate the region in prestige at the start of the sixteenth century, but it was growing more powerful throughout the century. Kongo expanded both to the south into the mountainous region that divided it from Ndongo, and towards the east along the Zaïre and towards the Kwango river during the course of the century. Here it met challenges which shaped the military history of the period. As Kongo expanded southwards it met the growing power of Ndongo, which had begun its own conquests, reaching westward from its original base in the highlands between the Kwanza and Lukala rivers. Mid-century Ndongo rulers feared Kongo's ambitions even as they pressed their own power southward across the Kwanza and eastward towards the Kwango.

South of the Kwanza power was divided, but another important state, the kingdom of Benguela, dominated the great central highlands and presented a rival to Ndongo expansion from which there were several wars in the mid-sixteenth century. Several states extended along the Kwango River and met the challenges coming from Kongo and Ndongo with varying degrees of success. In the northeast, the kingdom of Nziko managed to hold Kongo off and stop Kongo expansion, while the "Seven Kingdoms" of Kongo dia Nlaza, an old state south of Nziko, fell to Kongo attacks and was incorporated into Kongo between 1550 and 1580. South of that along the Kwango the great kingdom of Matamba paid tribute to Kongo as early as 1517, but managed to avoid integration into either Kongo or Ndongo throughout the century and the first quarter of the next.

Europeans arrived in west central Africa in 1483 with the Portuguese explorer Diogo Cão, who established relations with Kongo in an emotional and important meeting of civilizations. Kongo's king, Nzinga a Nkuwu, accepted Christianity (taking as a baptismal name João, from the king of Portugal at the time), and in short order institutionalized the Christian religion and adopted European literacy, dress styles, and a new and extensive commerce on the Atlantic.[1] Portuguese mercenary soldiers served in Kongo's armies as early as 1491, and were included in its campaigns to the south in 1512. Thanks to a special relationship with Portugal, symbolized by exchanges of letters in which each monarch addressed the other as "brother", Kongo's claims to extensive territory were recognized by Portugal, who assisted Kongo in making them good.

Portugal also entered into relations with Ndongo, beginning in 1520, initially through the initiative and guidance of Kongo. Though nothing lasting came of the first tentative diplomacy, in time renegade Portuguese were active in Ndongo's court and in its army, causing strains in the relationship between Kongo and Portugal. These strains were increased when

Portugal renewed more independent relations with Ndongo in 1560, and then increased when the "Jagas" invaded Kongo about 1568. While the origin of the "Jagas" is debated, they seem to have originated in or just beyond Kongo's eastern provinces and their invasion temporarily drove King Alvaro I from his throne. From his refuge on an island in the Zaïre River, Alvaro appealed to Portugal for aid, which was dispatched in the form of a strong force from the Portuguese colony of São Tomé in 1571.[2] Although the Portuguese assistance allowed Alvaro to regain his throne, it also permitted Portugal to establish even more direct relations with Ndongo. At about the time that Portuguese forces were sent to Kongo, the Portuguese crown, recognizing that Kongo was not then in a position to oppose them, issued a charter to Paulo Dias de Novais to establish a colony on the Angola coast around the mouth of the Kwanza river.

Although he was to build a colony in Africa under Portuguese authority, Dias de Novais nevertheless entered into formal relations with both Kongo and Ndongo, and offered his small army to the king of Ndongo. For some four years, from his arrival in 1575 until 1579, Dias de Novais served Ndongo, assisting in the punishment of rebels near his base on the coast at the island of Luanda. In 1576 the Portuguese force left Kongo, and King Alvaro tried to recover his lost prestige by re-asserting his authority and assisting Dias de Novais in Ndongo, perhaps hoping that by working with the Portuguese he would be able to share in the influence that Portugal might gain in Ndongo.

Such a situation could not last, and in 1579 the renegade Portuguese in Ndongo who had arrived before Dias de Novais and were in danger of being displaced by him persuaded the ruler to expel Dias de Novais from Ndongo. The expulsion of Dias de Novais met with an immediate response from Kongo, which dispatched a large army southward to rescue the Portuguese and punish Ndongo, but this army was unable to continue a campaign in Ndongo and had to withdraw. In the meanwhile, Dias de Novais had managed to recover and held off Ndongo's attempt to drive him from the coast or the handful of fortified bases he had built along the Kwanza. In fact, in the following years Dias de Novais, using Portuguese boats on the Kwanza and recruiting the assistance of dissident former subjects of Ndongo, managed to build a creditable military force that began making direct attacks on Ndongo itself in the late 1580s. However, shortly after the Christmas of 1589 Dias de Novais's forces closest to Ndongo were crushed at the battle of the Lukala and had to retreat with heavy losses to their earlier domains. An uneasy peace between the two was established and remained for some years.

In the meanwhile, there had been important developments in the kingdom of Benguela and on the great highland region south of the Kwanza. Although the process is unknown to us at present, Benguela and surrounding regions were destroyed by a new and powerful military force that called themselves Imbangala, but were known to the Portuguese as "Jagas" even though they had no relationship to the group that had invaded Kongo and nearly overthrew Alvaro I a quarter of a century earlier. The Imbangala probably originated in the central highlands, in all likelihood from armed forces of Benguela or other, less well known states in the highlands. They took the form of marauding bands, headed by military officers, that lived by permanently pillaging the countryside. They grew and replenished their losses through incorporating people, especially adolescent boys, whom they captured in their raids, and at least initially were said to practise infanticide and cannibalism.

By 1600 the Portuguese were trading with them for slaves from their many captives, and some Portuguese (and at least one renegade Englishman) were serving in their ranks in the same sort of mercenary capacity that had typified Portuguese involvement in the region earlier. As the lands between the highlands and the Kwanza river were becoming depopulated and desolated, some Portuguese officials began inviting Imbangala to come north of the Kwanza to help them in their own wars, probably as early as 1615.[3] In any case, the governor, Luis Mendes de Vasconcelos, with the assistance of several Imbangala bands, launched a new and very successful war against Ndongo in 1618–21. Ndongo was badly defeated, had to concede considerable land, and sued for peace. Even though the new queen, Njinga Mbandi of Ndongo (1624–63), put up substantial resistance, her right to rule was challenged from within Ndongo, and using an alliance with her rivals, Portuguese forces with Imbangala allies defeated her (and her own Imbangala allies) in a series of campaigns in 1626–9 that all but drove her from Ndongo. Njinga managed to rebuild her army in the eastern regions of Ndongo and in Matamba, which she conquered in 1631. Using these newly collected forces she returned to harass the Portuguese colony in the following years.

The arrival of a Dutch expeditionary force in Luanda in 1641 set up a showdown between Njinga, her Ndongo rivals and their Portuguese allies, and the Netherlands. As a result of a series of campaigns the Dutch were driven from Angola in 1648 and, after more inconclusive fighting, Njinga and the Portuguese agreed to a peace and *status quo* in 1655. Within twenty years of this initial understanding, the extensive wars over the throne of Ndongo and the colony of Angola came to an end. Angola expanded little more, and the political geography of Angola was more or less fixed for the next century and a half.

While the war between Portugal and its allies and Njinga was going on, the Portuguese governors also continued expanding into the "Dembos", or the mountainous region between the colony and Kongo. In the 1660s the two clashed over rights in the region, causing King António I to lead an army into the Dembos region in 1665. In the battle of Mbwila, in late October 1665, one of the largest in central African history, Kongo's forces were badly defeated. However, the battle did not change the political balance either in the Dembos or between Kongo and Portugal. Portugal did try to follow up its success in the Dembos by invading Kongo, aided by one of the pretenders to Kongo's throne, in what would become a chronic and inconclusive civil war between potential successors of António I. Even though it was divided against itself, Kongo was still the most important military power in central Africa. The army of Kongo's province of Soyo managed to crush the Portuguese force and its allied army at the battle of Kitombo in 1670, an engagement which effectively ended Portuguese ambitions in Kongo until the middle of the nineteenth century.

The civil wars in Kongo matched members of various branches of the royal family who fortified themselves in provinces of the country and contested the kingship and ownership of Kongo's centrally located capital city of São Salvador. When a strong contender occupied the city and was properly crowned, there was peace, but no contender was able to unite all the factions under one authority, and so when strong kings died or when their heirs contested the throne, the civil war was re-opened. Thus Pedro IV restored the country in 1709, but it was split again in the 1760s and then again in the 1780s in active and lengthy episodes of civil war.

Portugal founded a new colony at Benguela bordering Angola's great central highlands region in 1617. For a long time, Portugal had little interest in the interior behind this post, which had been badly disturbed by the Imbangala movement. By the mid-seventeenth century, most Imbangala groups had come to terms with the existing powers, and highland kingdoms of the following period were a mixture of new states founded by Imbangala bands, and older kingdoms which had survived or re-organized in the cauldron of the Imbangala period. The extensive kingdom of Bembe seems to have been a weakly centralized but powerful government over much of the highlands, sharing power on its eastern side with another similar state called Muzumbo a Kalunga.

In the eighteenth century the Lunda Empire, whose original home was in the Shaba region of modern Congo-Kinshasa, began a long expansion to the west, and by the 1750s Lunda armies, or refugees driven by Lunda advances, were fighting all along the Kwango river especially against Matamba and Kasanje, an Imbangala state built on the Kwango. By the end of the eighteenth century Lunda forces had consolidated a huge empire east of Kongo and Ndongo and were in regular diplomatic and commercial relations with all the coastal states, including Angola.

In addition, two new and powerful kingdoms, Viye and Mbailundu, arose in the central highlands region and consolidated control over major sections of that area, displacing the older kingdom of Bembe by the middle of the eighteenth century. In the 1770s they became involved in wars with Portugal which saw considerable fighting, and, although it was indecisive, Portugal did manage to get its nominal authority accepted, by installing one rival line or another on the thrones of both kingdoms, reinforced by a poorly enforced treaty of vassalage. The century ended with another period of stability that lasted until well into the nineteenth century.

Much of the fighting in the area around Portuguese Angola in the eighteenth century involved attempts by the Portuguese government to monopolize trade out of the region by excluding foreign merchants from the coast, or by forcing neighbouring African countries to trade only with Portugal. To this end, the Angola government launched many military campaigns into the Dembos region, capped by the construction of a fortress at the junction of major trade routes in 1759, and further by a series of advances from a similar fort at Caconda in the central highlands. While none of these measures, nor an abortive attempt to conquer and control the trade of Cabinda in the Kingdom of Ngoyo north of Kongo in 1783, allowed the crown to monopolize trade, as they hoped, they did lead to many campaigns, punitive expeditions, and attempts to win African co-operation by forcing treaties of vassalage upon them.[4] Portugal, however, was too weak to leave permanent and effective garrisons anywhere outside of the old nucleus of their colony, whose borders had been fixed in the 1680s.

Weapons and Tactics

Early central African armies were characterized by their combinations of what might be called light and heavy troops. Light troops, by far the most numerous (and in some armies the entire force), relied on individual skill and ability to manoeuvre to succeed in battle, while heavy troops (always the minority in every army) relied on defensive weapons and formations to carry the day. The Kongolese army was a good example of a combination of these two: fairly small numbers of shield-bearing heavy infantry made up its core, surrounded by thousands of more lightly armed troops. When the Portuguese entered central African wars on their own in the late sixteenth century they developed their own special heavy infantry core with the use of tight formations, firearms, armour and swords. However, not all armies were organized as were the Kongolese or Portuguese armies: in most of the areas south of Kongo and outside of Portuguese-led forces, the entire armed force consisted of light infantry.

The earliest reports of the Kongolese troops who received the Portuguese embassy of 1491 do not mention its famous heavy infantry, and describe only lances and bows.[5] Early sources are sketchy however, and the later-sixteenth-century sources that do contain military details describe shield-bearers (*adargueiros* in Portuguese) who were, according to an account of 1577, the best troops in the region.[6]

The Kongolese continued with their shields even when their military utility declined in the face of muskets. Musketry could easily penetrate these shields, though they performed the useful function, at least according to Cadornega, of hiding the actual position of the troops, while perhaps still preventing arrow wounds, since archers continued to be an important component of central African armies until the later eighteenth century.[7] Indeed, in the Battle of Kitombo in Soyo in 1670, Portuguese soldiers carried shields that they had captured in an earlier engagement with the Soyo army, and hoped to show their own prowess in hand-to-hand fighting with swords, using the captured shields as well. In spite of this, however, they were overwhelmed by Soyo's troops.[8]

Those soldiers in Kongo and in the neighbouring regions that did not carry defensive arms instead developed great skill in fencing and in dodging lance thrusts, arrows, or javelins. Jesuits who first witnessed the armies of Ndongo and its immediate neighbours in the 1570s wrote, "all their defense consists of *sanguar* which is to leap from one side to another with a thousand twists and such agility that they can dodge arrows and spears".[9] The physical agility of central African soldiers was notable, astonishing visitors, and required arduous physical training that was constantly renewed, especially in special military reviews and dances where virtuosity was displayed. The Imbangala, who were wholly devoted to fighting, were particularly adept at this mode of warfare, but it could be found everywhere.[10] When the Kongolese ambassador to the Low Countries, Miguel de Castro, passed through Dutch Brazil in 1642, he amazed his hosts with a display of skill and agility with a broadsword,[11] and even more dramatically, Queen Njinga so impressed the missionary priest Cavazzi who was visiting her court in 1660 with her agility, despite being near 80 years old, that he complimented her for it. "Excuse me, Father," she told the priest, "for I am old, but when I was young I yielded nothing in agility or ability to wound to any Jaga [Imbangala], and I was not afraid to face twenty-five armed men", a boast that was typical of the military culture.[12]

The two types of armament were noted in contemporary records as being a means of distinguishing armies. Kongo's shield-bearing infantry was considered distinctive enough that a series of pictures from the late seventeenth century set aside Kongolese soldiers from those of Ndongo or the Imbangala by their shields.[13] In fact, a spectral combat alleged to have been waged over Kongo's capital of São Salvador before the battle of Mbwila in 1665 matched a shield-bearing Kongolese against an unarmoured Imbangala.[14]

Operations

Fighting with great ability and particularly giving room for individual manoeuvre meant that armies fought in an open order with considerable space between the men. The significance of this means of organizing troops became apparent to Luis Mendes de Vasconcelos, who came to Angola as governor in 1617 with experience of the wars of Flanders behind him, and had composed a treatise on the art of war. His decision to force his soldiers to fight in tight formations as would have been done in Europe resulted in heavier casualties from arrows and javelins, and on the advice of old soldiers, he adopted the African system of fighting.[15]

Light troops in sixteenth-century wars were predominantly archers who also carried weapons for hand-to-hand combat. Usually the archers would loose their arrows as a preliminary to combat, but even among light troops the archery phase of battle was shortlived, as troops closed for hand-to-hand fighting, with sword, lance and battleaxe. The bravest sixteenth-century soldiers went into battle with only one or two arrows, and after these were loosed they planned to close.[16] Some, but not all, archers used poisoned arrows. In eastern Kongo, noted for its poisons, a Jesuit report described the effect of *cabanzo*, a very fine poison which caused considerable casualties in the fighting between a royal force and those of rebels in Mbata province in 1623.[17]

Armies, once mobilized and moved toward enemies, marshalled their various types of soldiers in order to accommodate their levels of skill and training, and the effectiveness of their weapons. In the earliest periods, military formations were organized in large masses on the battlefield, and battles tended to be set-piece affairs decided fairly quickly on carefully chosen ground. In these, masses of soldiers engaged in a brief period of archery, followed by a rapid closing and hand-to-hand fighting, decided by armour and skill.

When Mpanzu a Kitama, the brother of Afonso I of Kongo, attacked Mbanza Kongo in 1509, his army was organized into battalions, with his own in the lead, "raining arrows" as he sought to weaken Afonso's forces with arrow strikes. Afonso's men endured the arrow strikes "there being already a great number of arrows over us and they wanted moreover to charge us with azaguayas [lances] and swords" for the phase of hand-to-hand combat, when Mpanzu a Kitama's men suddenly and unexpectedly broke and ran, witnesses, Afonso would have us believe, of a vision of armed horsemen following Saint James.

In Ndongo, large armies preparing for a set battle organized their units into similar mass units called *mozengos* or *embalos*, and a battle order often arranged them into three, a centre and two wings. Frequently the first attacks from this formation were by a special detachment chosen for its courage and skill, called the *gunzes*. The Ndongo army that attacked the Portuguese at Talandongo in 1583 used such a three-part formation, as did the Portuguese-led force that opposed it.[18] In addition, armies might be subdivided into independent commands called *lucanzos* which could be dispatched for special tasks. The Portuguese caught one such *lucanzo* commanded by Kakulu ka Kabasa crossing a river in 1586 and managed to defeat it unit by unit.[19]

When the Portuguese began fighting in Africa under their own command, probably even when serving as mercenaries under Kongo, but certainly after Paulo Dias de Novais had to fight Ndongo after 1579, they developed their own special formations, modelled to some extent on that of Kongo. The Portuguese troops, with their armour, musketry, long swords and tight formation, formed a sort of fortress on the battlefield that held on to the baggage and served as a reserve. African allies then made formations on the wings and attacked or retreated as the fate of battle determined. The presence of the Portuguese fortress helped to anchor their allies, and provided a secure reserve that could stand on its own, as it did in the battle of Mbwila, but often was lost when the allies finally broke and abandoned it.

Battles in the sixteenth and seventeenth centuries were often decided quickly when one side or the other, unable to bear the pressures and stress of combat, broke ranks and fled. The Ndongo armies that fought against the Portuguese in the late sixteenth century fled in panic when beaten, and the fleeing soldiers sometimes cut down their own comrades who impeded their flight. For this reason, very strong units were placed in the rearguard to stem this flight or, if necessary, to cover its retreat. Often these armies did not re-form at another place, but returned to their homes.[20] This was a typical response; Kongo armies were also reputed in the early eighteenth century to be incapable of re-forming once their main forces had broken.[21]

Central Africans were quick to adopt the use of firearms, though slow to replace their traditional weapons with them entirely. Initially, these weapons were used in central Africa, as elsewhere, by Portuguese mercenaries.

According to instructions given to the leader of Portuguese mercenaries in 1512, they were to be equipped with muskets and crossbows, and included horsemen, though experience would soon show that horses would not survive in central Africa.[22] But the mercenaries were not entirely satisfactory, for Afonso complained of their cowardice and incompetence to the king of Portugal in a letter he wrote describing his campaign to the south around 1513.[23] The Portuguese were still valued as fighters, and soon Portuguese serving freelance and without royal permission were found among the ranks of Kongo's enemies, first in Mpanzalungu near the Zaïre, and then later in Ndongo, for the crown could not easily enforce its agreement with Kongo to have its subjects to serve exclusively there.[24]

But the Kongolese, who showed great enthusiasm from the very beginning for all things European, were quick to work on using European weapons themselves. Afonso of Kongo was interested in these weapons for his own use very early: in around 1510, he was asking for "bombards and muskets" to assist in burning a house of idols that was likely to bring revolt.[25] Indeed, in 1512 he received elaborate crossbows as gifts from the king of Portugal.[26]

The same rapidly developing interest was shown by Ndongo, Kongo's powerful southern neighbour, once it was presented with the prospect of working with Portuguese mercenaries. When Paulo Dias de Novais arrived in Angola in 1575, he immediately hired his 700 soldiers out in mercenary service to both Kongo and Ndongo at different times, assisting both countries in subduing rebels during the four-year period when he enjoyed good relations with both.[27] It was not long, however, before Ndongo had to face Portugal as a enemy, and in this situation it did not waste much time in developing its own musketeer forces. The army that Ndongo deployed to attack Portuguese forces in 1585 included 40 musketeers organized by Ngola Kilongela, an African who had seen service in the Portuguese army.[28]

In spite of these initial developments, firearms did not replace archers very quickly in any of the armies in west central Africa. Certainly they proceeded more slowly than many west Africans did, even when the superior flintlocks of the eighteenth century arrived. The weapons carried by Kongolese troops that appeared at a St James Day call-up and military review of 1701 at Kibangu, capital of Pedro IV, included some muskets, but also swords, clubs, lances and bows. At this point the shield and personal manoeuvre were still considered the most important tactics.[29] In 1701 the forces that were ready for war in Nkusu, Kongo, were all archers, while the majority of those appearing in a similar parade in Soyo in 1702 were archers.[30] In a mid-eighteenth-century report on Kasanje, the state along the Kwango river founded by Imbangala bands in the mid-seventeenth century, ambassador Correia Leitão noted that the troops continued to carry bows and use hardened wooden lances as well as firearms which were obtained "in abundance" from Portuguese sources. Kasanje's musketeers were regarded as being equal to the Portuguese in competence.[31] Leaders of armies based east of the Kwango River did not consider the relative lack of firearms a major military problem. Lunda armies that had arrived on the banks of the Kwango from farther east in the 1750s were largely equipped with lances and swords as well as shields that could resist arrows. According to Manuel Correia Leitão, who left a long report about Lunda military capacities in 1756, they regarded firearms as cowards' weapons and refused to use them.[32]

Even the Portuguese-led armies did not become majority musketeers until their neighbours did, although the core of Portuguese regular soldiers carried firearms from the seventeenth century onwards. Portuguese armies sent to the central highlands in the large war against the Jaga Kianbela in 1718–22 included bodies with bows, and in a climactic battle on 9 June, in which the Portuguese-led force stood against waves of attacks, the sky was obscured by arrows and javelins deployed on both sides.[33] The force that Portugal sent into Kisama about 1734, composed of 100 musketeers and 1,000 archers, is perhaps typical of such early-eighteenth-century armies.[34]

In fact, it would seem that it was not until the later years of the eighteenth century that muskets at last replaced bows and arrows for all soldiers. When the regent of King Pedro V faced down forces of his rival for Kongo's throne, José I, at São Salvador in 1781, a witness noted that all 30,000 soldiers in the army of José were armed with "musket and ball".[35] Those forces that faced Portuguese armies in Nsulu (along Kongo's south coast) in 1790–91 were composed mostly of musketeers, though archers were still not completely absent.[36] The detailed campaign diary of a Portuguese expedition through the Dembos in 1793–4 seems to suggest that their opponents always used muskets, or at least that they were constantly under "fire" presumably from guns.[37]

Artillery were a different sort of firearm, and their use seems more or less uniform throughout. Only small numbers of guns were ever employed, more by the Portuguese than by any other power, but used both as a siege and, loaded with grapeshot, as an anti-personnel weapon. The Portuguese introduced artillery into central African battlefields in the seventeenth century. Artillery played a significant role in supporting the Portuguese formation in the key seventeenth-century battles of Cavanga, Mbwila and Kitombo.

African powers were less inclined to use artillery, and it seems that only Kongo took it up as a regular part of its arsenal. Soyo began using artillery in the seventeenth century, perhaps starting with the guns captured at Kitombo in 1670. In any case, seven guns were paraded for a French emissary when he visited Soyo in 1702.[38] The Kongolese continued using artillery throughout the eighteenth century, for in 1790 Portuguese forces faced Kongo units that sometimes employed artillery.[39]

The Portuguese believed artillery to be very important in their own campaigns. The detailed diary of a punitive expedition of 1793–4 that snaked up the coast of Kongo and then cut inland to the fort of Encoge, returning by a different route to Luanda, regularly employed its small artillery force to break up enemy attacks, shell fortified villages, and advance on other strongly held positions. Virtually all their attacks were supported by artillery, and they rarely failed to achieve their immediate objectives, since the appearance of the guns was enough to cause harassing forces, who do not seem to have possessed any big guns, to withdraw.[40]

Fortifications

Central Africans made extensive use of fortification in their wars from the earliest records in existence, and they figured prominently in many wars throughout the period before 1800. Fortifications in early Kongo included the use of walls and anti-personnel traps, for when Afonso fortified Mbanza Kongo against his rival brother in 1509, he had holes equipped with "an iron" dug around the city to channel his opponents' attack to his army that was assembled in the central public square, but he did not attempt to defend the palisaded walls that surrounded the town, perhaps because he had too few soldiers to man the walls. In the end, his brother was killed when he fell into one of these holes in the rout following his defeat.[41]

Ndongo armies made field fortifications as well. In the 1585 campaign against Portugal, Ndongo constructed four or five forts "of wood and straw after their fashion" each a day's journey apart to cover their retreat.[42] These forts were palisades with covers of leaves that allowed the garrison's strength and movements to be hidden while covering them as they shot, and they were not primarily intended as a barrier to prevent infantry advance.[43] In Kisama, south of the Kwanza, forces that opposed the Portuguese expedition against them in 1594 withdrew to forested and broken country which became natural fortresses of this sort, both to engage the Portuguese unseen and to avoid their cavalry.[44] The tactic of withdrawing to forested areas in the face of invasion was still characteristic of Kisama in the eighteenth century, when a Portuguese invasion of about 1710 noted it.[45]

Field fortifications were not just static defences to protected vital areas, but were also valuable for armies on the move. The Imbangala of the early seventeenth century entrenched themselves behind palisades at every stop, complete with gates for each of the commanders and a separately entrenched section for the overall commander.[46] These Imbangala fortresses were perhaps stronger than those customarily built in the region, since their typical tactic in dealing with a new region was to build a fort in one section of it, and then have the residents exhaust themselves in attempts to take it. After some days of these attacks, the Imbangala commander sent out an ambush force of some 1,000 men behind the place where the local people were assembling and then defeated them by catching them between the ambush force and a sally from the garrison.[47]

The civil war period in Kongo led to the development of natural fortifications that allowed substantial civilian populations to live in moderate security, by taking advantage of one of the region's prominent geological features, the steep-sided, flat-topped mountain. The most famous of the eighteenth-century fortresses was Mount Kibangu at the head of the Mbidizi River. Steep natural slopes prevented easy approach to the mountain except through a few limited routes which could be easily blocked. Thick forests or steep slopes were so typical of these natural forts that the Kikongo terms for them, *nfinda* (forest) and *tadi* (rock) became synonymous with fortified location.[48] Lesser capitals were also located in similar locations. One of the Dukes of Mbamba, Manuel de Nóbrega, was forced to withdraw from an exposed lowland capital to a forested flat mountain in the "Alps of Mbamba" following attacks by his rival from Luvota in 1702.[49] This town was well protected with pit traps covered with grass and ditches and was able to repel an attack in 1707.[50] Even smaller settlements became fortified, such as those of Wandu in 1705 defended by ditches and trees, or constructed in forested mountains.[51]

It was also common in the Dembos area between Kongo and Ndongo for armies to be redeployed into rocky fortresses if they were unsuccessful on level land. Portuguese campaigns in the early seventeenth century in this region were typically composed of open battles followed by sieges.[52] These rocky redoubts were also refuges for raiders, as indeed, the Portuguese sought to dislodge Angoleme a Kaita from his *empure* or fort where he maintained his supplies, in 1644, after having defeated him in an open battle.[53] Fortifications continued to be important in the Dembos area in the eighteenth century. Portuguese troops marvelled at the complex fortifications of redoubts, hidden roads and mutually supporting bulwarks as well as naturally occurring but carefully used features such as hills and especially dense forests which protected the town of Mbanza Kina in 1794. The Portuguese commander, after a successful attack, ordered the destruction of fortifications and cleared the forests as a means of razing them.[54] In general, the Portuguese, who have left us details on these sorts of operations, attacked forts with artillery, especially mortars, which were particularly effective, though sometimes they also undermined them or set explosives on them.[55]

In the central highlands of Angola, the normal tactics involved extensive use of fortifications. Portuguese forces attacking the Jaga Caconda in about 1685 noted that he was entrenched in a fortress or *ekipaka* behind "his customary lines of sharpened stakes".[56] Central highlanders could look back on a long history of fortifications when they faced eighteenth-century Portuguese campaigns. The Mbailundu war of 1773–6, for example, involved extensive operations around fortifications and their *ekipacas* were "very well delineated, including bulwarks, ditches and trenches, with covered roads which protect them from all types of fire", which they could use to hide troop movements and keep supplies.[57]

Watercraft

Although central Africa was infantry's paradise, the naval aspect of war so widespread in west Africa was less important in central Africa. In the course of the seventeenth century, Portugal seems to have secured naval control of the coast and rivers of west central Africa, though Europeans were not equally successful in west Africa. The rivers and coast of sixteenth-century central Africa were defended by large watercraft not unlike those of west Africa. They were carved from a single log and, according to early-sixteenth-century accounts, could carry a ton of merchandise or 150 people. The king of Kongo of the same period was supposed to be able to assemble 800 of these, probably along the Zaïre.[58] One of these boats co-operated with a Portuguese vessel to capture a very strongly armed French ship off Soyo in 1525, partially by attacking and capturing a shore party that had landed on a longboat.[59] The incident probably explains why a guide for French shippers in the central African region of about 1530 cautioned all who traded there not to pass any village but to wait for a boat to come to them from the shore and bring royal permission from Kongo.[60]

One rarely reads of Kongolese naval forces or exploits after the second half of the sixteenth century, though the tradition does seem to have been continued on the coast north of Kongo. Seventeenth-century Ngoyo was famous for its large fleet, whose sailors or rowers rode on large watercraft and in 1670 were sent to support Soyo in its war against a Portuguese invasion. They carried a number of missile weapons including firearms and, like the infantry of Kongo, were protected by shields.[61]

Ndongo also employed fleets of rivercraft as its navy. One large army assembled in 1586 crossed the Lukala River on eight "great canoes", each of which held 80–90 people. However, Portuguese naval superiority seems to have eliminated the capacity for any of Portugal's African rivals to do much more than raid along the rivers. The dominant powers of Kisama, the district south of the Kwanza, certainly used watercraft in their frequent raids on Portuguese shipping in the Kwanza, though never to mount any large-scale operations.

Portuguese mercenary service included use of their own naval vessels, whose size and armament made them particularly useful in central Africa. In 1491, shortly after King João I received baptism, he set off to attack rebels who lived on islands in the Zaïre and was joined by Portuguese bringing their ships (and artillery) up the river.[62] But it was on the Kwanza River that the Portuguese shipping proved to be valuable, and not just to assist African powers. It was probably their naval superiority that allowed the Portuguese to hold on in Angola after the falling out with Ndongo in 1579, for they could support and relieve their waterside forts very effectively. In 1580 the Kwanza fleet of two galeotas, a caravel and two smaller boats was able to relieve besieged Portuguese and raid the river banks, for food and to find local rulers ready to help Dias de Novais against Ndongo.[63]

Organization

Central African armies were a complex mixture of conscript and professional soldiers. The differences between the two reflected in part a professionalization of skill or discipline, particularly by heavy infantry forces, and in part the vagaries of state power. Professionals answered directly to the higher levels of state, while conscripts tended to respond to more local control, as they were recruited from local districts where they lived. The structure of recruitment and the degree of cohesion in an army were often a result of the degree of centralization in the country as a whole, since local armies were likely to be loyal to their commanders. The kingdom of Kongo managed the high degree of political centralization that it enjoyed in the sixteenth century through political control of its military organization, which was tied directly to political structure, and armies were raised from and attached to units of government. The earliest Portuguese reports of 1491 tell us that each nobleman in the royal entourage controlled an army, and noted with clear exaggeration that their commands included as many as 10,000 soldiers.[64] When King Afonso I (1509–42) faced a rebel army raised by his brother, his principal followers were mobilized from the province of

Nsundi,[65] while his brother had several other great lords with him in the fight, as well as people from within and without the city "which is great".[66] Some years later, in an elaborate plot to overthrow Afonso's grandson Diogo (1545–61), the conspirators hoped that they could bring in the "army of Nsundi" and the "army of Nocolla" to assist them.[67]

But these provincial armies were not the private property of the noblemen in question, for the nobility in Kongo served in their posts at the will of the king, and could be removed as easily as they were installed. Afonso himself had been summarily relieved of his province and its attendant command when his father became concerned about his conversion to Christianity.[68] His later successor Diogo removed nobles from their offices, sources of income and military commands at will.[69] Thus, as long as Kongo rulers retained the right to appoint and dismiss their provincial officials, they also retained full control over their army organization and its chain of command. Not surprisingly, seventeenth-century traditions of the origin of the country saw a military analogy in the organization of the country, for the first king in the legendary past was said to appoint his officials as "captains" not for life, but for as long as the king wished.[70]

The military organization at the provincial and local level was anchored on the rights of state authorities to issue a general call-up of the population to arms.[71] Many who responded to the call were ultimately sent home; most others were employed; in the supply train rather than as soldiers, at least in the sixteenth and seventeenth centuries. But there were among the citizens of each province a core of soldiers who were required to serve and could not even send substitutes when called.[72] The heavy infantry in Kongo, an elite force with considerable skill, were generally considered to be nobles, and lived on subsidies paid from the state out of its revenues in the province, thus making them a professional core. At the local level these nobles, rulers of villages at most, were known as "fidalgos mobatas" or village nobles, and probably represented the core of heavy infantry to which the ordinary "mobatas", their subjects, were attached. During a revolt of 1621, Afonso Mvemba a Mpanzu, a dissident member of the royal family, managed to build an army by winning the allegiance of these nobles, and then was able to defeat a loyalist army raised locally in the province of Mpangu. Afonso's army included many archers for the "mobatas, that is the country people did a great massacre with cabonzo [arrow poison]" on their opponent's force.[73]

Such forces might not be very large in relation to the total population. When unexpectedly threatened by a Portuguese force from Angola in 1623, the Duke of Mbamba called up his army to meet them, and was able to face his attackers with a contingent of 200 heavy infantry, as well as 2,000–3,000 archers, probably drawn from the "mobatas", a less well trained but perhaps pre-designated section of the population, from a province whose total numbers were in the 50,000 range (or perhaps 15,000 adult males).[74]

Rebellions in Kongo typically found their military strength in the ability of the rebels to win the loyalty of the military in their provinces. The nature of the Kongolese state made rebels uninterested in seceding with a province, since most rebels had fairly shallow roots in their provinces. Because one province could not easily stand alone against the others, rebellions were fairly rare, typically by desperate people, and usually restricted to civil wars at the time of succession over who would be king. Established monarchs were extremely difficult to unseat from within.[75] This was exactly the plan outlined by the plotters in the 1550 conspiracy, by D. Francisco, an unsuccessful rebel in around 1562, and in the rebellion of 1621 in which Alvaro III, a young and unpopular king, faced his humiliated brother, who was able to muster armies in the provinces in hopes of overthrowing him.[76]

To Kongo's south, the lands of its neighbours in the mountainous highlands that separated Kongo from its southern rival Ndongo and in Ndongo and its neighbours, armies seem to have followed similar patterns. In the sixteenth century, armies were typically in the command of local lords, known as *sobas*, and served them. There were a great many *sobas* in the area under Ndongo, certainly more than 100, and so each one contributed fairly few troops. Unlike in Kongo, however, the king of Ndongo was not fully free to replace or move *sobas*, and thus the loyalty of these armies was much more in doubt. He did possess a range of officials who organized and ordered armies when they were gathered, but the gathering of the mass of the troops fell to the individual *sobas*, who seem to have also maintained command over their small units.[77] Sometimes these local units could be quite numerous; Namba Kalongo, after having been forced to submit to Portugal, brought some 3,000 soldiers to the colonial army.[78]

As a part of constructing more centralized power, the rulers of Ndongo developed more professional and loyal units. The king of Ndongo himself had a number of units that answered only to him. In 1585 these units were known as the "flower of Angola", and some were commanded by members of the royal family who normally resided in the capital with the king.[79]

As the Portuguese moved from being mercenaries serving as heavy infantry in the armies of Kongo or Ndongo, into moulding their own military forces, they relied heavily on the existing military culture of Ndongo to supplement their own soldiers. The Portuguese forces that grew up in these circumstances were a complicated collection of mercenaries and regular troops, raised in many respects in the same way that Ndongo's were. After their expulsion from Ndongo in 1579, Portuguese officials sought to emulate Ndongo and recruit soldiers from among the *sobas* who were prepared to switch their loyalty from Ndongo to Portugal. Like Ndongo, however, they also looked for more professional and loyal soldiers that would answer to them. One such group, probably already in existence in Ndongo and brought into the Portuguese army, were apparently permanent professional forces called *kimbaris*. The Portuguese listed 8,000–10,000 "Chorimbaris", all archers and not heavy infantry as the professionals were in Kongo, as the backbone of their force in 1585.[80] These forces, however, were supplemented by slaves of Portuguese residents, including those who were resident in Kongo and came to join the Portuguese host. Thus, when João Rodrigues Coutinho came to Angola in 1602 with important reinforcements from Portugal, he was joined in his first major campaign against Kisama by "mulatoes and negroes" of Kongo.[81] The Portuguese army of those days was filled by Kongo nobles who came down to Angola to serve, along with about 100 of their followers, in the Portuguese army and were given the title of *tandala* or commander over the forces of the *sobas* who supplied most of the manpower.[82]

The methods used in Angola were also followed in Benguela, as the Portuguese sought to extend their power along the Angolan coast, and eventually into the central highlands, in the early seventeenth century. Here the Portuguese began with a close alliance with a local ruler who saw them as a means to defeat his rivals and raise his power. However, the Portuguese, fearing his power, and the fact that most of the soldiers ultimately looked to him as a leader even in the Portuguese camp, challenged him. To this challenge he boastfully replied that the "Portuguese are women on land, only on the sea are they men". In the ensuing campaign in which the Portuguese sought "to show him whether the Portuguese are women or men", they managed to destroy his town, after a night march and a long encounter matching muskets and arrows.[83]

After 1600 the Portuguese expanded this initial collection of allied *sobas*, professional units, mercenaries from Kongo, and slaves, with the Imbangala. The Imbangala originated, as far as documentation allows us to tell, south of the Kwanza in the Kingdom of Benguela, probably the northern edge of the Angolan central highlands. Possibly they began as military units in that or nearby kingdoms, and from an early time divided into several units or bands. The Imbangala units, unlike those of the kingdoms and *sobas*, were purely professional soldiers, who lived through war and not through other means, but, unlike the other professionals, they answered to no command outside of their own units. They lived in armed camps, and travelled constantly, pillaging areas as they came to them, moving on when they had finished. Their entire population was either combatants or support people; they had no real civilians. They recruited new members and replaced those who had fallen by capturing slaves, primarily adolescent boys, and then training them to fight. As these boys proved themselves loyal and fit, they were integrated into the unit.[84]

Competent as fighters, and self-sustaining in their own violent manner, the Imbangala forces completely changed warfare in Angola for some fifty years. Such forces could not exist independently for long, and during the middle years of the seventeenth century all the settled powers of Angola: Portugal, Ndongo and Matamba, solved the problem either by incorporating Imbangala units into their armies as regular units, by destroying them, or by allowing them to form their own states, of which the most famous was the kingdom of Kasanje, founded in about 1635. Many Imbangala eventually founded smaller states in the central highlands of Angola, original home of the Imbangala bands. One such state, for example, was Gando, whose ancient rulers were overwhelmed in Portuguese campaigns of 1685, but which was revived by a coalition of Imbangala and traditional rulers who created a military alliance. The new allies swore to expel the Portuguese from the area, and marched on the fort at Caconda in 1718. Led by the Jaga (Imbangala) Kiambela, they agreed on tributes, weapons and military forces, though no doubt each unit maintained its independence in peacetime.[85]

When Kongo's central power collapsed in the civil wars between rival kings that followed the Battle of Mbwila in 1665, its previous military organization continued to function as before, though for different and sometimes rival commanders. Various pretender kings, and sometimes local appointments of these kings, established their authority over the provinces and with them their military forces. By gaining control over the provinces, pretenders were able to raise armies and to control local appointments, even if they lacked the ability to dominate the kingdom as a whole. Thus, the military continued to be responsible to the state, which was governed in the same way as it had been before, save that it was typically smaller in scale and its borders less secure.[86]

In the competitive environment of the civil wars in Kongo, however, commanders may have been more demanding in their military call-ups, to increase the size of their armies. In the 1690s, the general call-up required everyone who could not desert, as many did, to appear bearing weapons and fifteen days' rations. Serving under their local lords, and flying unit flags, they marched out to do battle as ordered. A call-up in Soyo in the late 1680s could bring in as many as 20,000–25,000 potential soldiers, though perhaps not all would serve as combatants.[87] When Capuchin Marcellino d'Atri passed through the southern part of Kongo during war in 1702, he found that virtually the entire able-bodied male population had been mobilized to fight (or had fled from the call-up).[88] Those in political power who controlled the appointment of the local lords could still count on an obedient army, but court intrigues might undermine that, as several rebellions in Soyo reveal. In 1674 and again in 1686, an appointed relative of the Prince of Soyo led rebellions with military forces drawn from the province of Kiowa that were more loyal to him than to the ruler.[89] As in Kongo, the ability of the ruler to control his appointments was variable, since the appointed officials might rebel, but the rulers usually continued to maintain their right to appoint offices and commanders at will.

Under pressure of the civil wars Kongo also developed private armies not connected directly to political organization, but loyal directly to an adventurer of noble pretensions. Small armies of this sort were present in the 1690s. One such army, commanded by Pedro Mpanzu a Mvemba, originally came from forces in the province of Mbumbi, where he built a base and refused to be relieved of command when his original superior, the Duke of Mbamba, was overthrown by a rival faction.[90] A similar but larger army was constructed by Pedro Constantinho da Silva about the same time, perhaps initially from forces in the province of Wembo. This army was so mobile and loyal that he moved his troops from Wembo to Kibangu, far from their original homes, and then from there to São Salvador, where he was defeated only after a long fight by King Pedro IV in 1709.[91] In the late eighteenth century, such armies were more commonplace in Kongo, often shading into the gangs of bandits, as did the troops of "Mbwa Lau" (Mad Dog), a notorious army commander whose force engaged in highway robbery in the 1780s along with several other such renegade military units.[92]

This sort of mobility was based on the capacity of the Kongolese population to move as a block and follow leaders. The fact that the Kongolese constructed their houses of temporary materials, often rebuilt them in a year or two, and did not recognize the legal concept of private property in land, helped to make the population mobile, and thus armies and the entire population that supported them could and did move in support of their leaders.[93] While this potential was probably always latent in the Kongolese population, the period of intermittent civil wars after the late seventeenth century reinforced it.

The establishment of a solid political configuration in the area south of Kongo after about 1670 ended the period of chaos caused by the Portuguese wars and the arrival of the Imbangala. Armies in this later period continued to be recruited as before, as units of various origins gradually became professional, and treaties and arrangements gave one state or another the right to call up forces from local rulers.

An eighteenth-century certificate to a lesser noble in the Portuguese circle, the Dembo Kakulu ka Henda, reveals the sort of service that such subordinates provided. Kakulu's troops served in a campaign in Benguela in 1718, a considerable distance from their homes. They provided two companies of troops, probably archers.[94] Silva Corrêa's description of a "typical" mobilization for the Portuguese army around 1785 was also probably used in some measure by many of its enemies as well. The preparations for raising a force of 5,000 or more could take over a year, as the commander sent to Portuguese subjects, African vassals, and the various African allies requesting that they supply forces, which they might do if the campaign suited their needs or desires. Often, however, even the closest subjects bound by strong treaties of vassalage might send virtually no one, and the government was often powerless to prevent it. Potential soldiers frequently vanished into the bush when the call-up was made and mere token forces appeared. Even the Portuguese residents of the *presidios* and towns of Angola often refused service, for the military campaigns were expensive and dangerous and frequently also endangered their commercial interests. The most reliable soldiers were the "paid infantry", who served directly under the governors' command, and the "*empacaceiros*" (antelope hunters) who were also professional soldiers but serving under their own commanders, who answered in turn to African rulers (*sobas*) who had sworn vassalage to Portugal.[95]

Logistics

However they were raised, armies needed to be supported in the field, and logistical problems posed serious limits on the size and operational range of armies throughout Angola. Armies were required to report with foodstuffs when mobilized, but most campaigns required more time in the field than the supplies that soldiers could bring would cover. To some extent additional food could be obtained through foraging, although in most of central Africa rural population was thin and could not support an army for very long. In addition, the absence of more than token cavalry forces, and even these only in the Portuguese army, meant that the population could flee with its foodstuffs. This required armies to carry their own food supplies, often carried and provided by the soldier's wives or conscripts, hence the term for them: *mulherio e gente inutil* (womenfolk and useless people).[96] The baggage train of an army in Angola was called the *kikumba*, and was typically disposed in the middle of marching formations when on the move, and carefully placed to be secure in battle. When the Portuguese fought the battle of Cavanga against Queen Njinga in 1646 they placed the *kikumba* in the midst of their forces so as to give the soldiers an incentive to fight harder, since their own wives were there. Indeed, they might well have, for the decisive moment in the battle came when the conscript soldiers of the *guerra preta* (black army, African soldiers serving the Portuguese) rallied and defeated Njinga's soldiers who were looting their baggage.[97]

Portuguese troops invading Kongo in 1670 lacked local food supplies and were provided with many sacks of *nzimbu* shells, used as local money, since this campaign was carried out in conjunction with a Kongolese army and directed against Kongo's rebel province of Soyo. There was also hope that the forces could be supplied by sea, as they were advancing up the coast, but in this they were disappointed.[98] In the same way, the commander of the Portuguese force that invaded the central highlands in 1755–6 issued an order forbidding the seizure of local foodstuffs, contrary to the usual custom, so as not to extend the war to those whose neutrality he sought to maintain.[99]

Warfare in the central highlands usually involved as much a search for food supplies as military encounters. The investing of fortified locations took on logistical significance as the defenders of these places seem to have been effective in concentrating food there and denying it to those who would besiege them, as the Portuguese discovered when they began campaigns there in the middle decades of the seventeenth century.[100] In the 1718 defence of Caconda, the Portuguese commander was able to replenish his supplies with a surprise raid on the fortified capital of a nearby African ruler.[101]

According to Elias Alexandre da Silva Corrêa's treatise on war in Angola in the late eighteenth century, foraging armies were a bane on all areas where they moved as the country was stripped of food and famine followed the wake of such a force. Stored food supplies were especially vulnerable, and no amount of diplomacy could prevent even modest armies from causing major damage to both friendly and enemy country. This prospect made war as unwelcome to the permanent Portuguese residents of Angola as it was to those who might be attacked.[102] In all of this, Angola presented the curious spectacle of a country apparently built solely to maintain the slave trade, and yet one in which the acquisition of slaves by war was rarely welcome.

Operations

The conduct of operations in central Africa changed considerably through the period, particularly as weapons changed and tactics evolved along with them. We can trace the evolution of operations in Portuguese Angola with particular precision, thanks to the detailed documentation that the Portuguese left as participants in them. In the sixteenth and seventeenth centuries, the set battle involving large forces and concentrated in one decisive encounter seems to have been far more important than such affairs would be in the eighteenth century.

In a major battle of 1585, the army of Ndongo launched its attack against the Portuguese army under André Ferreira Pereira, whose 8,000 African archers and 130 Portuguese musketeers were disposed in the usual three-mass formation including, no doubt, the Portuguese deployed as a mass. Portuguese sources attributed outrageously high numbers to the African force (600,000 to 1,200,000 – actually 6,000–12,000 would be more likely), but were probably accurate in saying that its numbers were spread out over a league and a half to two leagues of front (or perhaps eight kilometres), and included some 40 musketeers. Portuguese troops advanced to the battlefield, blinded by a morning snow (not impossible in the tropics at these elevations) that cut their vision. Ndongo forces attacked the Portuguese stronghold in waves. The first wave, commanded by Sangi a Ndala, probably the *gunzes*, called the "flower of Angola", composed of members of the royal family and the court, attacked the Portuguese centre, and when this failed it was followed by another wave from the second line. Following that, the two wings, commanded by Kari kia Luanji (right) and Kabuku kia Mbilo (left) attacked the Portuguese flanks, and when these had failed to break them, a final attack by the reserve forces also was engaged, still unsuccessfully.[103]

When Matamba's army faced the Portuguese at the Battle of the Lukala on 29 December 1589, it used a variant of this pattern of attack. It was disposed with the customary masses in the centre as well as a wide flanking half-moon formation which managed to envelop the Portuguese-led force between itself and the main army. The latter, disregarding its own losses, relentlessly pressed its attack, this time successfully, on the Portuguese centre, deployed as was customary for Portuguese heavy infantry, as a mass.[104]

As musketeers became important they were dispatched into the vanguard of attacking armies. Queen Njinga's forces at the battle of Angoleme a Kaita in 1644 attacked a Portuguese force disposed in a half-moon formation with its flanks protected by hills in a frontal assault. It was led by the *empacaceiros*, the descendants of the *gunzes* of earlier times, but equipped with musketry, though still advancing along with "clouds of arrows".[105] In Kongo, the musketeers joined the shield-bearing heavy infantry in attacking formations. The Count of Soyo, attacking Portuguese forces just north of the Mbidizi river in 1670, had his musketeers intermixed with the shield-bearing infantry as they advanced. In the end, the Portuguese artillery loaded with grapeshot inflicted such casualties that the unit had to withdraw.[106]

The same basic tactics were employed by King António I when Kongo fought with its fullest force against the Portuguese at the Battle of Mbwila on 29 October 1665. Kongo brought its army, said to have 100,000 soldiers (but surely considerably less), 800 shield-bearers and 190 musketeers into the Dembos region to support the ruler of Mbwila from a challenge by his aunt, Dona Isabel. She, along with her own small army of some 400 troops was in turn supported by the Portuguese, who deployed some 6,000–7,000 "bows" as well as 466 musketeers and *empacaceiros*. When the two armies were in sight of each other, the Portuguese deployed defensively with a strong front guard and lesser bodies deployed on the two flanks, while holding a strong force in the rearguard as a reserve. The Kongolese troops of the vanguard under the command of the Marquis of Mpemba, composed of all the musketeers and half the shield-bearers as well as some 4,000 infantry, pressed hard on the Portuguese troops, who were deployed in a diamond-shaped formation from which the infantry made sorties. After a hard fought engagement in which the Portuguese believed their two field pieces were critical, the Kongolese vanguard were forced to retreat, at which point the remainder of the Kongolese forces, including its reserve of 400 shield-bearers commanded by the king himself, renewed the attack. This attack completely enveloped the Portuguese and drove off all the flanking troops. The infantry engaged the Kongolese army and the battle ended when King António, wounded by two musket balls, retired from the battle and was killed by a sortie. The Duke of Bengo, commander of the rearguard and baggage, managed to withdraw with the Kongolese survivors, although without the baggage.[107]

War in the central highlands of Angola, on the other hand, involved long campaigns, rather than large engagements, although often some sizable engagements and sieges might be mingled in. In a campaign of 1716, Gando ya Kitata organized the pillage of Portuguese merchants, and after an initial sharp engagement fled and joined forces with another minor ruler, Kanyakutu, who made a stand against Portuguese forces at a river. When the Portuguese commander succeeded in outflanking them while making a diversionary attack on their main force, he was able to capture many of them when the *kibuka* (fort) fell.[108]

As tactics evolved in the eighteenth century, the pattern remained essentially unchanged for the Portuguese forces, though their African opponents gradually evolved different ways of fighting to those practised in the seventeenth century. A core of paid soldiers, Portuguese infantry, protected the baggage in battle and provided a solid core from which it made occasional sorties, though as in the earlier centuries a good deal of the actual fighting continued to be done by African allies. The *empacaceiros*, professional soldiers recruited from Africans, and the Imbangala regiments joined the core of the army, though their tactical deployments were more in line with those of their opponents.[109] Given their employment, it is not surprising that Portuguese paid soldiers and even *empacaceiros* did not suffer heavy casualties in many engagements, indeed sometimes none at all. Only if they were left completely unsupported would they be firmly and fully engaged, and then they might suffer terrible losses.

The manner of fighting battles changed quite substantially for the African armies of west central Africa in the late eighteenth century, perhaps because gunpowder weapons became more predominant, and consequently Portuguese tactics evolved in response. The campaigns that the Portuguese waged in southern Kongo and the Dembos region in 1790–93 reveal the new art of war in detail. Both the Portuguese army, composed as usual of a core of Portuguese troops and a larger army raised from a variety of African subordinates, and its Kongolese opponents were organized in small companies, or platoons, which operated mostly independently. As armies approached each other, a series of lengthy skirmishes commenced between platoons that were highly mobile and fired from cover, firing "without order", which probably means aimed firing at will rather than volley firing. These troops would withdraw when the fighting became too intense. When main forces did become engaged, a large action started, in which the Kongo armies might form dense columns with a narrow front and 15–20 ranks deep, which attacked first with musketry and supporting artillery and then with *arme blanche* of swords. These columns often co-operated with each other to form semi-circles and sought to envelop their opponents. True to their history, the Kongolese infantry still carried shields that proved useful in hand-to-hand fighting. In the operations of 1790, the Portuguese commander reported fighting nine "battles" and six "shocks", probably reflecting the difference between the intense skirmishing and the heavier action of the columns.[110]

When fighting among themselves in the civil war, Kongo armies seem to have employed much the same tactics. Raimondo da Dicomano gave a general description of war in the 1790s. He noted that forces were raised by a general levy, and although all troops carried firearms, they carried only small supplies of ammunition. War was composed of a lengthy firefight that ended when one side broke. Often these wars were attacks on settlements conducted by half the attacking force while another portion sought to fire the houses or could be used as a reserve to capture prisoners.[111]

Larger battles were possible, however, if the stakes were important enough. Portuguese punitive raids did not have such stakes, but interestingly, the one time when the great 1793–4 campaign failed to take a town or disperse its forces was when the Portuguese sought to capture the famous shrine at Quibaxe in Nambu a Ngongo. In spite of serious attacks and artillery fire beginning on 24 May 1794, the defenders eventually drove the Portuguese back and they in turn abandoned the action.[112] Similarly, the massive battle of São Salvador waged in 30 September 1781 between rival kings José and the regent of Pedro V, lasted most of the day and left the battlefield littered with the dead.[113] But this was not a punitive expedition to burn villages and move on; the fate of the kingdom was at stake.

The interaction of intense action and rapid retreat certainly characterized late-eighteenth-century war. The campaign diary of the 1793–4 Dembos campaign reveals that the Portuguese force, which with its allies numbered as many as 8,000–10,000, was under fire from small attacks and skirmishes almost constantly for days on end. At times, it would dispatch columns of several hundred, supported by artillery, to undertake special tasks, such as destroying villages. Typically these attacks would be strongly resisted by musket fire, but eventually the opponents would flee, often after experiencing artillery fire. Even strongly defended positions, such as Mbanza Kina with a complex of interlocking bulwarks and mutually supporting redoubts, were defended only for a few hours before being abandoned.

Apparently, the people of the region were not prepared to defend homes for very long (they often managed to keep food from the marauding column) probably because, like all housing in much of Africa, it was easily constructed and rebuilt and not worth dying for. In the end they did wear the Portuguese down, so that a considerably reduced and tired force returned to Luanda, suffering more from pinprick attacks and shortages of supplies than from any single great battle.[114]

Conclusion

West central Africa illustrates two interesting points. First, it showed how war was conducted in open country without cavalry, and secondly it revealed the potentials of Europeans in Africa.

The climate of west central Africa permanently limited the capacities of cavalry, and in spite of extensive attempts to do so, the Portuguese were never able to use cavalry as a significant arm. Outside of occasional use of the Kwanza and Zaïre rivers by both Portuguese and some of the African powers, the naval factor was less important than infantry. Indeed, infantry ruled the battlefield in west central Africa as in no other part of the continent.

The Portuguese built the largest European colony in Africa in their hold-ings in Angola, but the success of the colony was limited. No major African power was conquered, and Portuguese arms only succeeded to the degree that they adopted a considerable amount of African military culture, as well as using thousands of African soldiers trained and usually led by their own commanders in that culture. In many respects, the story of Europeans in Angola is an important counterexample to the success of Europeans (including Portuguese) in the Americas.

Chapter Six

War, Slavery and Revolt: African Slaves and Soldiers in the Atlantic World

The Europeans and the Slave Trade

To millions of people all over the world, the enslavement of Africans is best illustrated by the capture sequence in the television version of Alex Haley's novel *Roots*. In the film, the protagonist, Kunta Kinte, an inhabitant of Juffure in Niumi on the Gambia River, is alone in the woods when he is suddenly beset by a group of "slatees" led by an American factor. Using a large hunting net, they bring Kinte down and, in spite of his attempts to run and fight, capture him.[1] Speaking from a strictly statistical viewpoint, such a story is unlikely. However, since the slave trade involved thousands of active participants over 400 years and millions of square kilometres, it is impossible to say that such an event did not ever happen, or even that it could not happen at Juffure in 1769. After all, the fact that the English director at James Fort on the Gambia was instructed in 1765 to intervene if traders should seize free people illegally[2] certainly implies that at least sometimes English traders did capture people directly and illegally. But given the general military situation it is obvious that such activities had to be marginal to the larger slave trade. Certainly, the Gambia was not routinely the scene of unchecked slave raiding of this sort, given the tight control that the rulers exercised over the activities of European traders there. Slatees, in fact, were Muslim traders who bought slaves in the farther interior, not the thugs who helped factors wrestle people to the ground on the banks of the Gambia.[3]

The Kunta Kinte episode probably better reflects ideas that have grown up in American folklore about the slave trade than a documented reality; such ideas may well have influenced Haley or his elderly relatives and shaped the imaginative parts of *Roots*. Michael Gomez, analysing folktales told by African Americans to the Works' Progress Administration in the mid-1930s, noted that a consensus tale consolidated in the late nineteenth century of their ancestors' enslavement had emphasized that Europeans had captured them directly, usually by trickery, though a substratum of stories also implicated the African elite in assisting in this project.[4]

In fact, as we have already seen, most recently arrived Africans in the Americas, when interviewed by people like Alonso de Sandoval or Georg Christian Oldendorp, spoke of their enslavement in more or less the same terms as can be documented from the records of European trading companies and other eyewitnesses. Most were enslaved in Africa as a result of wars between African armies, or by raiders and bandits that arose from these wars, or from the breakdown of social order that often accompanies war, especially civil war. Only in Angola, and then mostly in the seventeenth century, were Europeans primarily the leaders of the armies that enslaved Africans. Some, though not the majority, fell victim to a judicial process, and very few were enslaved by the processes described in American folklore. It is obvious that, whatever may be found in the folklore, and however much it may be believed by the descendent community, the vast majority of Africans who were herded on the slave ships had been directly or indirectly the victims of wars between African armies.

Historians have long ago recognized the reality depicted in the documents, even if the public has not followed them as quickly. Where there has been more debate, however, is in the issue of the causes of these wars. As noted above, since the debate about Abolition, commentators have divided over the issue of the motivation for African wars. Philip Curtin has characterized this debate as a distinction between the economic and political model of enslavement.[5] One group ascribes wars to the influence of European traders and a corrupt segment of the African elite. This coalition fought its wars along what Curtin described as economic lines, in which the entire object was to capture people for sale. Sometimes, in the language of modern commentators, such as Boubacar Barry,[6] the slave trade becomes personified as a sort of evil spirit that changes societies into militarized slave hunting organizations as it moves inland from the trading entrepôts along the trade routes.

The other vision is what Curtin calls the political model, in which the slave trade is simply an afterthought to wars that would have been waged in any case. In the political model, the motivations for African wars must be sought in African politics and diplomacy, and not in the working of trade or the influence of Europeans. The Anti-Abolitionists who first developed this idea sometimes argued that, as African leaders were naturally warlike, their wars needed no special diplomatic explanation. Others, following the lead of commentators on Dahomey in particular, argued that losers might have been slaughtered on the battlefield had it not been for the demands of the merchants. Thus, Dahomey's annual Customs, with its human sacrifices, was the alternative to the slave trade. Archibald Dalzel, who had the advantage of being able to quote Dahomean rulers on the topic, suggested that they were so interested in human sacrifice that recruitment of victims for the Customs was far more important than the trading opportunities. Werner Peukert has gone farthest to champion this idea in recent times, suggesting that Dahomey's wars were motivated by "cultural factors".[7]

There is substantial evidence for both models, and in fact the truth lies in a complex combination of both. The Senegambian region has been frequently described as fitting the economic model, in which rulers, acting in apparent whim, seize people at the suggestion of Europeans for sale. As early as 1500, Portuguese visitors believed rulers on the Gambia were prepared to make war solely to supply them. "When the caravels of Christians come," noted Valentim Fernandes in 1506, "the lord assaults the first village he can whether of friends or enemies and seizes men and women enough."[8] Alvares de Almada also noted a case in 1575 in which he believed the ruler of Saalum made a war solely to pay a debt he owed him,[9] in 1638 the wars of Senegal were described as wars to rob people and not of conquest, and in 1670 the count d'Estrées believed that if the king of Kajoor had no slaves to sell, he would enslave and sell free people.[10] André Bruë, the French factor in Senegal in 1719, writing privately to the company and certainly without thinking about Abolitionist issues, believed, probably with cause, that the ruler of Kajoor was considering an attack on the Seerer kingdom in order to obtain the wherewithal (48 slaves) needed to meet a debt to the company, though the presence of a Moorish army in the Fulbe country frightened him enough that he delayed it.[11] Such a matrix lay behind French intrigues to bring the Moors into the Senegal valley in 1737–8 and play into the alliance politics with gifts of guns and munitions.[12] Geoffroy de Villeneuve, who visited Senegal in 1785–88 and wrote extensively about it for Abolitionist causes, identified three different small wars in that time which he claimed were caused entirely by merchants persuading, sometimes through alcoholic drink, the rulers of Saalum, Siin and Kajoor to undertake expeditions they were otherwise unwilling to set out upon. In a famous incident in 1775, the French factors believed (and later English testimony confirmed) that the English had more or less paid the Moors and the king of Kajoor to invade and pillage Waalo, by advancing them "blue cloth and muskets"; indeed, in the fighting some 8,000 people were captured in less than six months. As a result, a slave could be bought for a "single cloth in the streets of Senegal".[13]

However, all these statements need to be placed in the context of the local politics, which, when known, tend to reduce the purely whimsical nature of the wars. More often Europeans were content to benefit from wars they claimed no part in starting; the French factor on the Senegal noted in 1754 that they had "no interest being mixed up in their business" concerning a war in Bundu, but another war in Bambara country in which they were equally uninvolved was producing an "abundant slave trade" from which their merchants were benefiting.[14] In the case of the 1775 war, for example, the predatory alliance would have been impossible without existing rivalries between Kajoor and Waalo, a recent usurpation within Waalo by a party hostile to the Moors, and the longstanding Moorish interest in maintaining control in Waalo.[15] Likewise, de Villeneuve himself noted in the context of the three wars he observed that were motivated by debt or alcohol that there was a major war between Saalum and Kajoor in 1786 (caused, he says by the "ambition of the Damel" [king of Kajoor]), and the pillages might equally be rooted in that rivalry.[16]

Even the lesser operations, raids on the civilian population, incursions of Moors, and attacks by the Bambara, were governed by the rhythm of these wars, even if not directly a part of them. When a body of 200–250 Moors made an incursion into Waalo in 1722, for example, the motive for this raid was said to be the failure of the current ruler to pay a customary tribute.[17] Certainly many of the "Little Pillages" were linked to larger conflicts, as were the mutual pillages of villages between Kajoor and Waalo during their war of 1748.[18] For example, Mungo Park's observations on the small pillage type of war in Bambara region (part of Kaarta and Segu, on Map 4) reveals some of the same logic: typically the origins of these pillages were longstanding resentments about past insults and rivalries, particularly in areas where mutual raiding had been going on for a long time – any pretext or perceived weakness was enough to send a body off on one of these attacks, and indeed, Park believed that sometimes a single individual might take off on an almost suicidal mission of revenge.[19] In such a context, it would be easy enough for merchants offering some muskets on easy terms to provide an immediate pretext.

The closest that one gets to a purely economic model of enslavement is with small groups of raiders and bandits who were not attached to the state and its policies. For example, Alvares de Almada mentions small groups of boat-borne raiders in the riverine areas of Casamance that he called "*gampisas*", who conducted raids and captured people to sell.[20]

Unlike Senegambia, which began exporting slaves from the start of its contact with Europe, the Gold Coast exported very few slaves until the last half of the seventeenth century and even then slaves did not dominate exports until into the eighteenth century. But Europeans were involved in Gold

Coast wars from the very beginning, hoping to increase their own trade, or sometimes drawn into wars by the rivalries of the African states. Yet in this early period, even with European involvement in African wars, Europeans bought or obtained very few slaves. In the early seventeenth century, the Dutch found themselves supporting an unpopular king of Sabu because he was friendly towards them. In 1618, for example, 30 Dutch musketeers and some 300 African soldiers resided at Moure, a Dutch-controlled area. But at the same time, Sabu was prepared to help the Dutch against the Portuguese, sending the Dutch some 800 troops to assist in war against their Portuguese rivals.[21] The Dutch were able to drive the Portuguese off the Gold Coast altogether between 1637 and 1642 with the help of these African allies, who had their own scores to settle in the area.[22]

As other European powers clustered on the coast in the last part of the seventeenth century, the rivalries increased between them, joining longstanding political rivalries among African states. Here, Europeans also offered "bribes" or "dashey" to African rulers, usually sums of money or trade goods, as the Dutch factor did in 1683 to get Ahanta and Chama to attack Adom, against whom they were said to have a bitter hatred; this was in order to roust their English rivals from the region rather than as a ploy to get slaves.[23] In fact, a Dutch retrospective memoir of 1679 noted that warfare had been so continuous since 1658 that it had made the gold trade almost impossible because of blocked roads, but the Company had been compensated by purchases of slaves. At this point, however, the Dutch still regarded the wars, even with their benefit of slaves, as something to be ended, and were proposing to continue the longstanding European tradition, going back to the days of the Portuguese presence, of mediating disputes to restart blocked trade.[24] When the king of Komenda ordered people from Quiffer arrested in 1692, and then took their seized goods to "bribe" his neighbours to join him in the ensuing war, the Dutch were prepared to lend him money in order to prevent the war.[25] Komenda in turn became the scene of the Komenda war which began in 1694 and was still winding down at the end of the century. The war began when Komenda attacked a private, but wealthy and powerful, merchant named John Kabes. The English joined the fight on Kabes's side, and the Dutch on Komenda's. Both sides in turn paid presents to a wide number of African powers to join the fight, stay neutral, or even to appear to join one side and switch to the other. Eventually the initial coalition of forces was so changed by defections, counter-bribes and military action that it could hardly have been recognized.[26] Slaves in quantity were obtained during the wars by both the English and Dutch, but the war itself was more than simply a European-inspired war to capture slaves, and in fact Kabes's original fault was mining for gold on a hill that the Komenda king said was sacred.

It was during this same period that the Gold Coast went from being an exporter of gold to being an exporter of slaves (indeed, in the sixteenth century, Gold Coast merchants had actually sold gold to import slaves). This change, which was soon noted, not necessarily with pleasure, by Europeans, was blamed on the import of firearms and the fomenting of rivalries that this caused. The Dutch factor, writing in 1730, was explicit: "that part of Africa which as of old is known as the 'Gold Coast' . . . has now virtually changed into a pure Slave Coast; the great quantity of guns and powder which the Europeans have from time to time brought here has given cause to terrible wars" and the resulting captives were enslaved and sold, "which in turn animated again and again those people to renew their hostilities".[27] Indeed, this same sentiment was expressed by Africans to the Danish factor Ludvig Rømer about 1745. "You are the cause of our troubles," he was told; "your merchandize causes us to fight each other and sell people", once there were many thousands of families here, "now one can scarcely count 100 individuals".[28] This germ of an idea eventually would make the Gold Coast the symbol for the gun–slave cycle in Abolitionist literature, and subsequently in some modern historiography.

In fact, the period was one of great turmoil and change: as we have seen, army size and organization changed, gunpowder weapons were more widely used, and more important, the interior powers such as Akyem, Denkyira, Akwamu and especially Asante emerged as great powers and came to dominate the coast. Ray Kea has suggested that there were local and deep-seated social changes behind their emergence, and the ability and desire to import guns, to be paid for with slaves or their decision to retain gold goes deeper than simply a response to European gun sales.[29] At the same time, these forces had little immediate need of the sort of support that Europeans had provided earlier, and in fact, Europeans were much less active in the actual political process than before, although hardly any less interested.

Identifying these various motives for wars, or reducing the direct European impact in causing wars, does not mean, however, that the prospect of capturing slaves was absent from all war planning. In outlining causes of wars as he understood them, Dutch factor Willem Bosman listed plunder, alliance entanglements and the recovery of debts, for which the taking of slaves was a sure means.[30] To this might be added various wars caused by marriage entanglements, stolen women, repudiated wives and the like, such as the war between Asante and Denkyira in 1701, caused by an issue of this nature, that resulted in the wholesale plunder of Denkyira and the desertion of its territory for a time.[31] There were, in fact, important political and military considerations that made the type of warfare that became widespread in the eighteenth century feasible and attractive to military decision makers.

Rømer, the Danish factor in the 1740s, described the custom of "eating the country", in which the population of a defeated area was as nearly stripped as could be done in one campaign. Such a practice was important militarily, and indeed had underlaid at least some of the Akan military thinking for some time. In 1618, long before there was much of an export slave trade, Brun was told that capturing and even killing women and children was valuable because it would reduce the population of a potential enemy.[32] But one must imagine that in Brun's day it was not really feasible to practise genocide, if for no other reason than that it would so increase resistance as to render war more expensive and violent. The possibility of reducing military capacities by selling off slaves, however, did become feasible when the wars of the late seventeenth century demonstrated a European willingness to buy slaves in such numbers that depopulation, especially of males of military age, became feasible. Indeed, it was just this logic which, according to Rømer, lay behind Akyem's decision not to "eat" Akwamu in 1730 – because planners in Akyem believed that they could actually persuade the people to give their loyalty to Akyem and therefore to be retained.[33] However, even here the respite must have been short, for elsewhere Rømer himself says that Akwamu's population was so "exterminated" that only 500 families remained.[34] Indeed, the destruction of the country might not have to be achieved in an open, declared war: the hosts of *sikading*, or raiders, might depopulate frontier areas and weaken enemies.[35]

Needless to say, the fact that these operations could also finance the purchase of munitions and, if necessary, bribes to other rulers to join or stay neutral in wars, meant that war and the slave trade were joined in very practical ways. While this sort of logic probably applied everywhere, it was particularly visible in the Gold Coast.

The rise of Dahomey and its wars against its neighbours are often cited as an example of another sort of result of the slave trade, that is, the rise of a slave-trade-oriented military aristocracy. Dahomey enjoyed a widespread but probably exaggerated reputation as a militarized "Black Sparta" in the nineteenth century, and much of its historiographic reputation stems from propaganda of the late nineteenth century, when its military prowess was touted, as was the addiction of its rulers to the slave trade.[36]

In the seventeenth century, the Slave Coast region was characterized by wars reminiscent of those of the Gold Coast, and many of the same observations apply there. Indeed, I. A. Akinjogbin's most interesting contention in his classic study of Dahomey's rise was that the great interior kingdom's rise was in part to settle the unrest caused by the arrival of Europeans and the disruptions caused by their trade and meddling.[37] As in the Gold Coast, however, the meddling was at least in part conditioned by the ambitions of the Africans, as Allada's former authority in the area fell apart and contenders from its former provinces fought each other, while in each new state family factions fought over the rule. Such struggles certainly gave Europeans an opportunity to play a role, well illustrated by Whydah's civil war of 1708, in which rivals for the throne enlisted French and English support, while the Europeans in turn each hoped that their candidate would grant them exclusive access to the market in slaves.[38] But commercial interests drove these European contentions, rather than a desire to stimulate the slave trade.

Dahomey's drive to the coast in the early eighteenth century has been the subject of considerable debate, primarily over whether it was driven by a desire to obtain trading routes to European shipping, or whether it was responding to the ideological and constitutional crisis among the related states of the area created by Allada's decline.[39] Certainly Dahomey was invited to invade by various dissident parties in the civil wars of the coast. But once Dahomey's presence on the coast was established after 1724, many of the country's wars could be reduced to a search for security against the rival displaced dynasties of the countries that Dahomey had partially conquered, rather than the activities of a militarized bandit aristocracy that lived on the proceeds of the slave trade. These dynasties managed to establish themselves on the littoral on islands or other inaccessible spots and raided Dahomey constantly. Even Dahomey's war against the Mahi, its other great eighteenth-century preoccupation, might be explained as it was in contemporary documents, as a support for the establishment of a unified dynasty under a family related to that of Dahomey. Indeed, Dahomey's explanation for the pro-gramme was that it would reduce transit taxes by unifying the region under a single king.[40]

Dahomean rulers themselves summed the situation up very well. In about 1785, when Parliamentary debate about the slave trade was hot in England, and Dahomey had become the symbol in Abolitionist literature of a slave-raiding state, Lionel Abson, the English factor, read newspaper accounts of these debates to Kpengla, king of Dahomey. Kpengla was not pleased with the characterization of his country, and said "We Dahomeans are surrounded by enemies who make incursions, we must defend ourselves. Your countrymen, therefore, who allege that we go to war for the purpose of supplying your ships with slaves, are grossly mistaken." He then went on to say, "In the name of my ancestors and myself I aver, that no Dahomean man ever embarked in war merely for the sake of procuring wherewithal to purchase your commodities." Instead, he linked Dahomey with war (of defence) and the slaughter of human victims in annual ceremonies (called Customs) to honour his ancestors. He attested to having killed thousands, and even alleged that in the time of his ancestors, before Europeans came, prisoners were killed "to a man".[41] The authenticity of the speech has been questioned. It was published by slave-trade defender Archibald Dalzel, who frequently illustrated his chronicle of Dahomey's wars by showing how often thousands of captives had been killed in the Customs.[42] But it is not inconsistent with other evidence of a largely political and diplomatic programme underlying Dahomey's military activity.

However, as in the case of the Gold Coast, the taking of slaves still had to figure in wars whose ultimate motivation might have been something other than taking slaves. William Snelgrave, for example, noted that in 1729 Agaja, the king of Dahomey, was surprised to find an attack from Whydah had disturbed his plans – for at the moment he had "another army inland to take slaves, for as I have formerly observed, he drives no regular trade in slaves, but only sells such as he takes in his wars".[43] Although this source does not give the location or other activities of this second army, obviously Dahomey needed to collect slaves to continue its trade, and this trade was clearly necessary for the supplies of munitions, among other things. In fact, Agaja was concerned at that moment about a shortage of troops, clearly the product of a complex demographic and financial circumstance. The wars had already stripped much of the country of potential soldiers, and he was forced to expedients – recruiting of bandits and mercenaries, enlisting his wives to meet the shortfall, and finally promising refugees free passage home and then enslaving them when they returned.[44]

The same sort of demographic considerations that influenced war in the Gold Coast also lay in these campaigns: once when English factor Robert Norris refused to buy some slaves as they were too old, the king ordered them killed. When Norris suggested that they could be spared to work boiling salt he replied that doing this would "set a bad example," and "keeping people in the country who might hold seditious language: that his was a peculiar government, and that these strangers might prejudice his people against it, and infect them with sentiments incompatible with it".[45] Such sentiments reflect the danger of retaining prisoners of war, as well as allowing them to return home or remain in the lands that had been attacked and conquered. Genocide was not an option, in spite of Kpengla's proud boast about his ancestors, but export was, and opened up possibilities that were otherwise unavailable strategically, just as it had in the Gold Coast.

The connection between war, European influence and the slave trade are most problematic in west central Africa. The role of the Portuguese in sponsoring the development of the slave trade in Kongo, and subsequently their development of the colony of Angola, which was dedicated to the export of slaves, have dominated historical discussion of the region. West central Africa may well have exported more people per capita than any other region, and Angola was the only place in Africa where Europeans had a genuine foothold in a sizable territory with the military resources to undertake wars solely under their own direction.

The export of slaves played an important role in the earliest European contacts with Kongo and its neighbours in the late fifteenth and early sixteenth centuries. The earliest Portuguese assistance to Kongo was paid for in slaves: in his instructions to Gonçalo Rodrigues in 1509, King João III specified how his expenses should be met from "whatever grants the King [of Kongo] should give you from the prisoners and captives the said Manycomgo makes in the war".[46] This military assistance was integrated into Kongo's efforts to expand its territory, but also to bring back slaves to support the growth of Mbanza Kongo.[47] Thus, in his campaign against the Mbundu to the south in 1513, King Afonso I of Kongo retained some of the slaves and returned them to the capital, while granting others to the Portuguese.[48]

The Portuguese colony of Angola was founded by a parallel process through Portuguese assistance to Kongo's southern neighbour of Ndongo, which began in 1520. It was probably to protest against this Portuguese assistance to Ndongo that Afonso complained to the Portuguese king in 1526, saying that Portuguese merchants had made his vassals too rich and they no longer obeyed him (he considered Ndongo a vassal), and that his own nobles and relatives had been seized.[49] Portugal's decision to colonize Angola came from this growing relationship, which also included an informal assistance given by Portuguese from the island colony of São Tomé and in response to Ndongo's own embassies to Lisbon. Paulo Dias de Novais's expeditions, first in 1560, and then in 1575, represented first, more assistance, and then, when conditions in Kongo favoured it, colonization.

It was only after Ndongo expelled and attacked them that the Portuguese actually attained (with considerable help from Kongo) some sort of rights over Angolan land and built their colony in the early 1580s.[50] Even during this turbulent decade, though, the Portuguese regarded the number of slaves bought at markets where "kings, lords and all Ethiopia sent to sell slaves, a very ancient usage", as they "are served with pieces [slaves] instead of money" as much more important than their own war captives. The people whom Portuguese merchants bought at markets were enslaved, according to Portuguese sources, when "some vassal commits treason against his lord, and rises up with his whole estate, or commits crimes with the wives of the lord".[51] For the Portuguese there was a balance to be had between direct enslavement of Africans and purchasing those who had already been enslaved by their African neighbours.

The history of the Angola colony is an interesting working between what can be described as security wars, designed to defend the colony (such as the wars of the 1580s), extend Portuguese control (the campaigns against Ndongo from 1619 to 1681), gain influence over its neighbours, or monopolize trade from the coast (especially the wars of the eighteenth century), and wars that might be safely designated as slave raids. The Portuguese crown supported wars to defend the colony, but not simply those to attain slaves. Nevertheless, governors especially favoured wars of all sorts, whatever their instructions, primarily because they could get more financially from the colony by direct seizure of people than through taxing exports of people enslaved outside the colony and bought by Portuguese merchants or their agents.[52] To this end, many governors undertook wars that had little strategic interest and appear to be simply wars to gather slaves, especially during the period 1619–81. The settlers in the colony, on the other hand, were not always as anxious to fight in these wars, as it hurt their own commercial interests, and put their lives and property in danger. Local interests vigorously protested the wars of Luis Mendes de Vasconcelos in 1619–22 on exactly these lines,[53] and would subsequently denounce governors João Fernandes Vieiria and André Vidal de Negreiros for similar actions between 1658 and 1664.[54] Indeed, António de Oliveira de Cadornega, the chronicler of the wars to 1680, protested that many mistook all the wars as simply "wars for negroes" and failed to see other causes – a statement that confirms the idea that some wars were, and that some were not, solely for capturing slaves.[55] Even in the eighteenth century, when Portuguese-directed wars were less numerous, the governors had a hard time convincing the residents that they should fight, and they continued to regard wars as more harmful than helpful to their commercial interests.[56] In any case, the royal government often did not profit also, since the costs of wars might not be defrayed by the sale of slaves if the operation did not net a large number, as many did not.[57]

The Imbangala, a militaristic sect that developed in the central highlands of Angola in the late sixteenth century and subsequently were involved both in the wars of Portuguese conquest and the War of the Ndongo Succession (1619–81) on both sides, may well have also been motivated by the search for slaves, although their rationale for movements was often simply to spoil land and to drink wine from the palm trees by their own destructive method. Certainly our first witness of their activities, Andrew Battell, bought slaves from them in large numbers and noted their singular proclivity for rapine.[58] Indeed, Governor Luis Mendes de Vasconcelos wrote to complain that the residents of Angola were using the Imbangala as "hunting dogs to get slaves"[59] (though in the end he was not averse to using them himself). At the same time, the Imbangala recruited people, more or less as slaves, to serve in their own armies, and not just to export.[60]

The Portuguese believed that the new powers that emerged east of the Kwango river in the mid-eighteenth century were essentially motivated by a desire to enslave people to participate in the overseas slave trade. According to Manoel Correa Leitão, the Angolan ambassador to Kasanje on the Kwango in 1755–6, the rulers of Malundo, across the river, and their neighbours "live for war, and this only to imprison people to sell". They continued these wars, even though their casualties were heavy. The total losses were even higher, for they only sold the "tenth part of those they kill". This did not prevent them "giving quarter to Pieces of India [slaves]".[61]

The Kongo civil wars which sporadically consumed the country from 1665 until the early nineteenth century are, like the wars of the Senegal valley, readily understood as struggles by various royal lineages for power, with the capture of slaves as a secondary consideration. When Alexander Falconbridge, the steady Abolitionist writer, noted in about 1785 that, when no ship visited Ambriz for a period of five years, the "absence only restored peace and confidence" and when a ship did come that confidence was destroyed and a war was organized to supply it,[62] he knew little of the history of the area. He was certainly not conscious of the re-emergence of the rivalry between the line of kings loyal to Pedro V at Luvota just inland from Ambriz, and those from the upper Mbidizi valley championing José I, which resulted in a major battle in September 1781 that enslaved thousands of people.[63] It would be quite a stretch to imagine that Pedro's partisans decided to launch their attempt to re-occupy São Salvador solely to fill the holds of English and French slave ships which were expectantly waiting on the coast, or that this was foremost in the minds of José's partisans as they countered this movement successfully.

However, one result of the civil war was a general breakdown in order, which allowed bandits of a semi-political sort to operate. One such bandit was Pedro Mpanzu a Mpemba, once a political appointee, who took refuge on a flat-topped mountain when replaced by a rival in the early 1690s. There he took to raiding caravans, selling his captive slaves to merchants in Luanda.[64]

In addition to this unsanctioned, illegal activity, Kongo warfare and political tension often involved smaller scale raiding, such as the attack of 1701 in which forces of King Pedro IV attacked a village, seizing 58 people as slaves, because the village was said to have switched its loyalty to one of his rivals.[65] When Raimondo da Dicomano visited Kongo in the early 1790s, he described these low key operations as "village wars", a series of ambushes and blockades that netted few slaves individually, but perhaps had a larger impact over the years.[66]

Raiding of this sort was typical of Portuguese operations in the eighteenth century, in which refusal to accept vassal status, harbouring tax evaders, trading outside established zones and the like were punished by attacks in which people were stripped from the country and villages burned. This was described in the instructions of one column operating in the central highlands, as the usual custom.[67] Moreoever, in and around the colony of Angola, local rulers who were nominally subject to Portuguese rule often engaged in low key wars, succession disputes and raids on each other, such as appear in the few local archives that survive, for example around Kakulu ka Henda in the 1770s.[68]

In short, African leaders did not have to act as the "slatees" of *Roots*, simply the bribed assistants of Europeans, in order to respond to demands of the slave traders. If African economies were too large and complex to be seriously affected by the changes in foreign trade, the strategic significance of imported munitions in many areas still made African rulers anxious to get on good terms with traders and to maintain all forms of trade with them. It is not the gun–slave cycle in its original form, but it is an influence of some significance nevertheless.

African Wars and American Revolts: African Soldiers in America

The fact that most Africans exported from Africa as slaves were captured in wars has considerable implications for the history of the Americas. Europeans almost never kept by-name shipping lists of the slaves, and so for us they are nameless people, counted up by age, sex, and perhaps by nation, but rarely as individuals. It is only recently that historians of the Americas have come to realize that Africans often came with skills that could be put to use in American societies: they could grow rice, for example, or raise cattle and ride horses.[69] We are more aware that they possessed their own aesthetic conceptions in dance, music, design and language that have impressed themselves on most of the cultures into which they were integrated. But we have not always realized that many among them were soldiers, if not by profession, then at least by experience.

In spite of our documentation of African wars, we are remarkably unsure about how many of the people embarked on slave ships were actually soldiers taken from a losing army. Soldiers often managed to escape defeat on the battlefield, by withdrawing or simply by fleeing, and in such cases the real victims were often villagers who were then at the mercy of the victorious army. These non-combatants, though the victims of war, were not soldiers. On the other side, most civilians took considerable precautions to put themselves out of harm's way when wars began, by removing themselves at least temporarily to woods and hills where they would be difficult to find or round up. To the degree that armies enveloped each other, or that bodies of soldiers thus surrounded might find themselves forced to surrender, soldiers were captured and exported. Certainly both situations occurred, but the exact percentage of soldiers must remain an open question. Whatever the percentage was, however, it was certainly high enough to make the African veteran a factor in American life.

In many cases, when a slave ship arrived in an American harbour, the merchants and planters who rushed to the harbour to buy the cargoes were quite unaware of how their new labourers-to-be had become enslaved. Although they often had stereotypes about slaves from different parts of Africa, and sometimes these conventional conceptions affected their purchasing decisions, few took any trouble whatsoever to learn anything about the Africans' homelands. Thomas Thistlewood, a Jamaican overseer and later plantation owner who kept a detailed diary of his life in the island in the mid-eighteenth century, was deeply and intimately involved in the daily lives of his slaves, recording their inter-relationships and even listening in the evening to the folk stories of "Nancy" (the spider Anansi) that they had learned in Africa. But in all the thousands of pages that he wrote, Thistlewood never seems to have learned about their lives in Africa.[70] Only a handful of American slave owners seem to have actually known what Oldendorp knew about the Africans' background – that many thousands of them were prisoners of war.

But they did become painfully aware of this military background when the slaves decided to revolt. There is considerable evidence that Africans with military experience played an important role in revolts, if not by providing all of the rebels, at least by providing enough to stiffen and increase the viability of revolts. At least to some degree, therefore, American slave revolts were extensions of African wars.

The idea that military skills from Africa may have manifested themselves in slave revolts needs a few elaborations, however. As with many other types of cultural transfers from Africa, we need not and probably should not assume a simple transfer of tactics, unit organization, weapons and the like from an African model to the Americas. This is not to say that some of these elements might not transfer as cultural items, for example, the use of a particular type of drum music, and possibly even certain basic assumptions about infantry tactics that might rest on home training. But military systems are nothing if not flexible, and African soldiers in America must necessarily have made use of multiple African military cultures as well as the limitations and opportunities created by the American social setting, geography, ecology and the like.

The possibilities of transfer of military training and its use in America are well illustrated from the very first slave revolts recorded in the Americas. When fairly large numbers of slaves were brought to Hispaniola, the first Caribbean island settled by the Spanish in the early sixteenth century, they soon led to concentrations of plantations on the southern side of the island. The Caribbean was served in these early days largely by the slave trade from Senegambia, which in turn was fed in some measure by the civil war in the Jolof empire, and by Jolof campaigns against Siin and Saalum in the Gambian region. The combination of infantry and cavalry tactics that had evolved in that region certainly stood the enslaved prisoners of those wars in good stead in their new circumstances in America when they staged their first revolt, albeit without all the opportunities for weapons that they may have wished for.

The Spanish chronicler Gonzalo Fernández Oviedo noted that the core of this rebellion, which started on the sugar plantation of Diego Columbus on the second day of Christmas, 1522, was made up of slaves of "the Jolof language", who, having killed their own overseers, advanced towards the small colonial town of Azua, attacking the plantations along the way and augmenting their numbers from the slaves held on them. They paused for the night before the large plantation of Licienciado Zuazo with its slave labour force of 120 people. Overnight the Spanish gathered a force of cavalry and at first light advanced against the rebels.

The Jolofs, upon seeing the advancing Spanish cavalry gathered together, "with a great shout, formed a squadron, awaiting the cavalry". The Spanish force charged the squadron and tore through it, causing some casualties, but the rebels, for all this, kept their order and threw many "stones, clubs, and javelins" at the horsemen. The Spanish wheeled about to attack the rebels from the rear and found them having re-formed to await the second charge. It was only after the second charge had passed through them that the squadron broke ranks and fled to the hills and forests, leaving six of their number dead on the field and wounding one of the Spaniards seriously.[71]

The tactics of the rebels certainly suggests experience of infantry forces confronting cavalry. Their decision to maintain a tight formation at all costs reflects typical ways in which infantry handle cavalry, and their actual ability to do it reflects a probable experience in this type of engagement. In this regard, their performance on the whole was better than that of the Tainos, original inhabitants of the island who, lacking any experience with cavalry, could not stand up at all to Spanish horsemen.

Of course, one could not consider this a typical Senegambian infantry– cavalry encounter. The rebels did not possess their full complement of weapons, and had to use stones and clubs instead of archery, javelins and swords. They possessed no shields, but taking this into consideration, they did the best they could.

But it would not be long before slaves of Hispaniola would have horses and weapons. A number of slaves ran away to the Bauroco section of the island, originally held by Enriquillo, a rebel Taino ruler, but by the 1530s they were operating on the island on their own. Under two leaders, Diego de Ocampo and Sebastian Lemba, each of whom had his own captains under him, they launched raids on outlying plantations, skilfully riding horses, wearing armour made from hides, and showing great dexterity with lance and club. It took several extensive and costly campaigns in 1545–7 with hundreds of soldiers to defeat them and round up their followers.[72] Islander landowners had employed Jolofs and other Senegambians with equestrian skills in their ranches raising cattle[73] – indeed they were resistant to royal orders that they desist from employing slaves to manage their cattle. The Spanish attributed their employment in cattle rearing to their skill "both in the saddle and with the lance", and while the first might be born of cattle raising and developed in America, the second was surely born of the African experience.[74] The leaders, Jolofs as well, passed into island legend and were even immortalized in poem.[75]

Another instance where African military experience probably played a role in American revolts comes from Jamaica in the late seventeenth and early eighteenth centuries. Here a series of powerful revolts led by "Coromantees", as Akan-speaking people from the Gold Coast region were known in English-speaking America, threatened the island on a number of occasions. Indeed Coromantee revolts would trouble Jamaica, and occasionally the other islands and the mainland (where they revolted in New York in 1712), throughout the eighteenth century. In 1675, upon hearing of an alleged conspiracy in Barbados, Governor Adkins advised that the Coromantees were a great threat to the island, as they were warlike and robust.[76] In 1685 a powerful Coromantee revolt of some 150 slaves rocked Guanaboa. Rising on the Widow Grey's estate, the rebels managed to get a good number of firearms, but were forced to retire when an attack on Prince's estate nearby resulted in the loss of the "conjuror" on whom they depended for spiritual support. Nevertheless, they kept some order and withdrew to some rocks when confronted by cavalry, where after a firefight they were dispersed, the 30 best armed making other attacks before retiring.[77]

These poorly documented revolts, however, were only harbingers of larger and more powerful revolts that would follow. The revolt on St Jan in the Danish West Indies reveals something of how the African background might work in the American setting. This revolt, which broke out on 23 November 1733, began with the seizure by the rebels of the Danish fort with its military supplies. They also sought to ambush the militia as it assembled, but this failed and the planters and a number of loyal slaves regrouped in a single plantation, leaving the rest of the island in the hands of the insurgents, which they then re-organized under their own authority.[78] Ray Kea, who has analyzed some of the records of the revolt, is able to show that a good number of the leaders of the revolt had been people in positions of command and authority in Akwamu before its defeat by Akyem in 1730.[79] It seems reasonable that such officers would be likely to mobilize some of their former soldiers who had also been exported from the Danish positions on the Gold Coast to the Virgin Islands for the revolt, and indeed they wasted no time in doing so. In the substantial fighting that continued until late May 1734, the rebels successfully defeated several attempts to capture them and to retake the island, primarily by using the type of tactics that worked so well on the Gold Coast, laying ambushes and using the dense forests and its roads to force opponents to fight at a disadvantage. Like Ntsiful, the wily ruler of Wasa a few years before, the St Jan's insurgents were able to maximize their effectiveness against their more numerous opponents by taking this careful approach. Their gravest danger, already noted while the revolt was still under way, was their inability to replace ammunition and powder. In fact, they took the extraordinary step of offering to sell slaves in exchange for powder to Danish and English merchants and planters.[80] This was probably the cause of their final loss, when French forces were invited in by the Danish authorities, after several earlier attempts by Danish and English forces had failed and been defeated. The French eventually defeated them unit by unit, as the rebels often had to flee after firing a single round, or used weapons other than firearms. In the end, many broke their muskets and killed themselves.[81]

We are rarely able to see quite so plainly the way in which the slave trade, by concentrating military captives and their former command elements in single colonies through the exportation of the defeated parties in battle in Africa, might make revolt possible. It is quite possible that some of the other revolts, about which we have fewer definite details, had similar histories, but we cannot be sure. However, the possibility is reinforced by the apparently "ethnic" character of so many American slave revolts: the "Amina" (Gold Coast) in the case of the St Jan's revolt, who actually planned to use the other slaves on the island as labourers on the estates they wanted to take over,[82] the many Coromantee revolts such as the Jamaican revolt of 1760–65, or the Kongo-led revolt at Stono in South Carolina in 1739.[83]

Contemporary observers often thought these revolts were the product of some sort of inherent militancy on the part of the rebels: this sort of thing was said in the Spanish Indies in the sixteenth century of the Jolof, and would be repeated many times with regard to the Coromantees as well. What is more likely, however, is that the circumstances of enslavement in these groups – a high percentage of ex-soldiers, perhaps the presence of former officers as well, and the rapid build-up and close proximity of former comrades in arms in American settings – made the revolts possible.

Even if the revolts were not simply led by former officers as the St Jan revolt was, certain features of military life are likely to encourage revolt. At the very least, the ex-soldier possessed certain important skills which plantation workers do not require and would not be provided by estate owners. These would include knowledge of anti-cavalry tactics, the ability to ride and use weapons from a horse, knowledge of firearms, and some tactical ideas such as the utilization of cover and setting ambushes. In this regard it is interesting to note that in the ethnically organized runaway communities that surrounded late-seventeenth-century Cartagena, the "Minas", who were drawn from the region around Dahomey, used guns, while the "Criollos", who were born in the colony, had only bows and arrows.[84] The Africans' familiarity with guns might just as well reflect the slow transformation taking place in African war at the time, a transformation which creoles, born in the colony or more likely born in the runaway communities themselves, could not benefit from.

Equally important, perhaps, the military veteran might be inclined to think of military solutions to problems, and having faced the terror of warfare was sufficiently seasoned to face it again bravely in the course of revolt. Having become accustomed to the comradeship born of hardship and mutually faced fear, soldiers, even if they had served in different and perhaps even opposing armies in Africa, might find it easier than those who had never fought, to co-operate, follow orders and risk their own lives to accomplish their mission.

These complexities came to a head in the Haitian Revolution, the largest and most complex slave revolt in history. The African military background of some of the participants cannot explain all the events of the revolt, nor account for its leadership even from the earliest times. But certainly African soldiers also played a role in this revolt. The original revolt in 1791 was largely organized by creole slaves who probably had no military experience at all, but was given its strength by Africans, who, according to early leaders, had served in African armies. These ex-soldiers did most of the fighting in the early weeks and were organized in ethnic-based units. This background is one of the easiest ways to explain how the rebels, in a matter of two weeks, were able to co-ordinate large-scale operations, hold their own against soldiers sent against them, manage artillery, raise their own cavalry and acquit themselves well against colonial cavalry.

In a general way as well, their tactics resembled those of African wars, in particular their penchant for skirmishing rather than mass attacks, though mass attacks could be organized when the situation called for it.[85] On the other hand, the conduct of war in the first year did not entirely resemble African wars. For the most part rebel units, some ethnic, some mixed, some creole and some mulatto or free black, formed and developed bases, typically on plantations, such as Gallifet, Tanyard, L'Acul or Limbé, which were then fortified as well as they could be under the circumstances (but often included considerable artillery), and this in turn was countered by the development of a series of government fortified camps. The war resolved itself into a series of sieges and assaults on these positions whether they were held by rebels or by government forces, interspersed with smaller actions and raids.[86]

The Africans' greatest weakness, however, would ultimately be their ethnic particularism, small scale of organization, and willingness to accept partial victories that could not be sustained. For the longer fight, and especially for taking and seizing power, it was ultimately creoles who predominated. They did so by seeking foreign military advice and by organizing their own armies, loyal to them and following European conventions of discipline and tactics.[87] This, in turn, gave them the edge in attacking fortified camps, still the main course of operations in the Revolution. The Africans bought them the time and opportunity to do this in the first year of the Revolution, and saved them in their darkest hour, when the French forces of General Leclerc sought to reconquer the island in 1802.

The drama of revolt was also probably the clearest example of a direct influence of African military ideas and organization in America. But outright revolts were fairly rare in American history; it was far more common for slaves who wished to change their lot to run away, sometimes secretly, often in small groups to someone or somewhere where they could be sheltered and establish some degree of autonomy. Indeed, many of the revolts ultimately resulted in the establishment of a runaway or rebel community in the mountains or forests, or among allied Native Americans. Since runaway communities developed slowly and were less likely to be mono-ethnic and draw from people with very similar backgrounds in Africa, the idea of direct transfer is less significant. But at the same time, runaway communities were usually created and maintained by African-born people, and their background and assumptions cannot be ignored. The remarkable use of a firing drill of the Surinam maroons described for John Gabriel Stedman in 1775 by his slave Hanibal was supposed to be the way that "Negroe Engaged Against Negroe". In it both parties were divided into small companies commanded by a captain who was able to give commands on his horn. They fired and then withdrew to reload in such a way that continuous fire was maintained, a system which seems to have fitted fairly well into Akan means of fighting in forests – and indeed, Akans were well represented among the maroons.[88] At the same time, however, it was probably a combination of Akan and European tactics and drill, evolved for this particular type of fighting.

Runaway communities, known as "maniels", were well developed in Santo Domingo by the 1540s, just two decades after the first large group of slaves had been imported for the growing sugar industry.[89] Many of the early settlements were fortified, as for example another early runaway community in Panama led by a certain King Bayamo, attacked by the Spanish in 1548.[90] By the 1570s the early Panama runaways had "grown into a nation" with two kings and dozens of settlements, when English visitors left details about them as they sought to enlist their help to attack the Spanish in 1573. Their town was built at the base of a hill, and enclosed with a "dike of eight foot broad and a thicke mud wall of ten foot high, sufficient to stop a sudden surprizer".[91] Interestingly enough, although many of these runaways must have been born in America, no doubt the constant influx of African-born continued to influence their warfare, for an English witness noted that they "leap and sing after manner of their own Country warres".[92] Indeed, fortifications were common in the larger runaway settlements; Spanish attacking one in the Mariscal Castellanos section of Venezuela in 1586 described it as a "New Troy".[93] In the early seventeenth century the settlement of King Diogo Bioho in what would become the Palenque de San Basilio above Cartagena was very strongly protected by a thick hedge and stockade.[94] A century later, runaways in the same area used fortifications, which were very well made in the opinion of their Spanish opponents, to their advantage in dealing with another attempt to dislodge them.[95]

Such fortification was also found in seventeenth-century Brazilian runaway settlements. When a Dutch military expedition visited an abandoned runaway settlement in the Palmares region in 1644, they admired its fortifications of two interconnected ranks of stockades, while a second one, which was a half-mile in circumference and included 220 houses, a palace for the ruler, a church and a council house, had a ditch full of anti-personnel traps as well. Similar anti-personnel devices were also scattered about on all the approaches.[96] Similar fortifications surrounded the very large settlement of Ganga Zumbi, the Palmares leader of the 1670s, although his palisade enclosed some 1,500 houses as well as a number of public buildings.[97]

Although one does not see as much in Caribbean documentation about fortifications for runaways, at least in one instance rebels did construct forts in the rocks in Martinique at the orders of the leader Fabulé in 1665.[98] Similarly, Padrejean, a rebel in Saint Domingue in 1679, also built a stronghold using trees.[99]

Conclusion

African warfare had an important Atlantic dimension in that wars and the slave trade were inseparable. This dimension not only includes the problematic relationship between war and the slave trade, but the fact that so many Africans who had served in these wars took this experience with them to the Americas. Africa was far too independent and complex to be simply a source of slaves that Europe could draw on at will. Wars and related struggles produced the slaves, though not without changes in organization and tactics that the possibilities of the slave trade opened up.

The fact that wars produced slaves had as an unintended consequence that these slaves might also make good rebels if conditions permitted. While the situation in America did not allow African armies to re-form, and local conditions changed the military possibilities considerably, Africans often found revolt a possibility and sometimes drew on African roots to drive them.

Conclusion

The study of warfare in precolonial Africa is still in its infancy; this study perhaps will push it on towards its childhood. In part, this is because for many regions the relevant primary sources have yet to be tapped, but a larger reason is that the relevant analysis remains to be done. War in Africa, as this survey shows, was quite different from that in other regions, even though some universal elements of warfare abide. The challenge of precolonial African warfare is above all to integrate its characteristics in the general study of war.

For many years this work was not done because African warfare was deemed to be primitive, and anthropologists whose purview included the study of primitives strove to understand the root causes of war, and usually left operations, organization and other important aspects of war unstudied. In any case, the possibility of conducting fieldwork of the sort that anthropologists rely upon among primitive warriors in Africa was cut off long ago – modern African wars are quite a different matter to those of the precolonial era, and nowhere have modern technology and organization made greater progress than in African armies.

The fact that no one imagines that, for example, the operations of the Angolan and South African forces during the Angolan civil war can provide much insight into the fighting conducted between Africans two centuries earlier, means that we are forced to rely on a conventional documentary record to reconstruct war in the past. Yet this record is not wholly satisfactory. This gap is clearly visible in the work above. We have very few operational descriptions of campaigns or battles, and while we know when and where these were waged, the military details are elusive. It is enough to allow us to see that warfare was radically different from today, but not enough to outline its details at the level available for many other world regions. This shortage of knowledge is doubly frustrating because, for most New World societies,

African wars are the ultimate source of much of their population. For it is abundantly clear that, while to understand lower- and middle-class European migration to the Americas one needs to know the social history of Europe, to understand African migration one needs to know the political, diplomatic, and above all military, history of Africa.

Nevertheless some general conclusions are in order. The most obvious one is that Africans were not primitive under virtually any definition that one can conjure up of primitive (or its cognate tribal). Although news media and even educational texts continue to refer to African military operations in this period as tribal wars, our study shows the presence of state structures, often elaborate ones, in all military organization, and wars of a much greater subtlety and complexity than this label implies. I have tried throughout to reflect this understanding in my own choice of terminology, preferring "state" to "tribe", "soldier" to "warrior", "unit" to "band", for example, or in general to apply the specific terminology of early modern European warfare to the African cases. Armies conducted "operations" and had "logistics" and leaders might be "generals" or at least "commanders". It is interesting to note, as a sideline, that this sort of terminology was widely used by the Europeans who observed African war at first hand in the sixteenth to eighteenth centuries.

Beyond this, it is obvious that there is not one African way of war but many. Each African region had a different mix of geography and thus of potentials. Political configurations varied widely as well. The different combinations of cavalry, infantry and marine elements in a regional art of war spelled radically different outcomes in various parts of Africa. This survey identifies five regions, but one could easily imagine other configurations, some even more local, others perhaps more overarching. General principles may be possible but at present they elude us.

In addition, it is also apparent that the European impact on Africa in this period has probably been exaggerated by many scholars, and is not as great as one might think. Europeans fought relatively little themselves in Africa outside of Angola, and they rarely even played an advisory role. European mercenaries, or African mercenaries under European command and guidance, were rarely over a few dozen in forces of a few thousand, and then mostly in the sixteenth and seventeenth centuries. Even in Angola the European role was in leadership and a small percentage of the soldiers, and the armies of Portuguese Angola resembled those of their opponents in many things. The shortage of written documentation of organizational and operational detail for African armies is testimony to this. In many places, where literate Europeans were the only witnesses to leave a relevant record, their concerns were with trade, and only peripherally with military affairs.

Therefore by extension, it is also obvious that the role of Europeans in the slave trade which grew out of African wars has been frequently exaggerated. Not only is the widespread folklore of direct capture of Africans by European marines (or African collaborators under European leadership) misleading, but the related ideas that Europeans were able to broker control over key items of technology (especially guns) – the "gun–slave cycle" – to force unwilling Africans to make war on their behalf is also overdrawn. The history of firearms in African warfare, as we have seen, is sufficiently complex that, even if European merchants and trading companies were able to operate in concert (which they were not) on weapons sales, they might not have been able to use this to force Africans to make wars. Similarly, Africans viewed firearms as one more of a range of missile weapons, and while many leaders came to recognize their value and to re-arm their troops with them, the process need not be seen as irreversible or permanent. The failure of Africans to develop a local firearms industry, despite having a ferrous metal-using culture and fairly high levels of skill throughout the time, is an interesting issue that needs more exploration.

Understanding how Europeans and Africans became involved in the slave trade and how it reached the proportions that it did clearly involves more than weapons blackmail. But at the same time, it is also clear that the existence of a slave trade and the potential to sell people in it in larger and larger numbers did have an impact on the way war was waged. The relationship between the desire to import weapons and munitions and the fact that participation in the slave trade was a crucial means of obtaining foreign exchange is fairly straight-forward. It is hard to imagine that African leaders did not consider the potential profits to be made from the sale of their opponents in deciding to make war, even if other interests also played an important role. The possibility, as we have seen in many examples, of selling off the demographic assets of an opponent, thus weakening them and strengthening the victors, must have changed the way war was waged at the lowest level.

Finally, it must be said that one of the most frustrating lacunae in the source material of African war is the absence of good materials illustrating the African end of slave capture. In part, this is because we lack good operational descriptions of most African wars. But even where we have good ones, such as Cadornega's descriptions of Angolan wars in the seventeenth century, or Isert's account of his travels with an army in the Volta region in the late eighteenth century, the crucial details are lacking. We do not have any description known to me, even exemplary, of precisely how prisoners were obtained in a war, how they were secured (aside from the types of bindings employed), how they were managed in the immediate aftermath of battle or war. We do not have a good knowledge of the commercial bargaining that went on between commanders and merchants, or how and when captives were taken from the point of capture to the coast or elsewhere. We are even woefully ignorant, save for a handful of cases, of the numbers of people captured in most operations, or from where they came (soldiers, camp followers and supply train, unprotected civilian population). This is as true of Portuguese operations in Angola, where a fiscally conscious government had the right to charge duties on the captives, as it is in areas where there were no literate observers. Yet no register of duty collected now exists, though occasionally one learns about this from anecdotal evidence.

There is much work that remains to be done. Of course, the search for source material needs to continue, and the processing of that already known must go on. Much more work on individual wars and campaigns, especially those which are well documented, needs to be done. The more we understand these local details, the better our knowledge of the larger picture will be. Finally, there is a great deal that can be done in understanding the regional politics that formed the background to war. Historical archaeology and fieldwork may allow battlefields to be located and manoeuvres to be reconstructed, something that traditionally has been done by modern armies themselves. Indeed, my final hope is that today's African military leaders will take a greater and more active interest in their own countries' military past and seek to study and document it.

Notes

The following abbreviations and short titles are used in the notes:

ACL	Academia das Cienças de Lisboa (Lisbon)
AEB	Arquivo do Estado de Bahia (Salvador)
AN: DAOM	Archives Nationales de France, Département des Archives d'Outre-mer
ANF	Archives Nationales de France (Paris)
ANTT	Arquivo Nacional de Torre do Tombo (Lisbon)
APF	Archivio "De Propaganda Fide" (Rome)
ARA	Algemeen Rijksarchief
BIFAN	*Bulletin, Institut Fondamentale de l'Afrique Noire* (Dakar)
BNP	Bibliothèque Nationale de Paris
Brandenburg Sources	Adam Jones, *Brandenburg Sources for West African History, 1680–1700* (Stuttgart: Steiner, 1985)
BSGL	*Bibliotera Sociedade de Geographia de Lisboa*, Lisbon
German Sources	Adam Jones (ed. and trans.), *German Sources for West African History, 1599–1699* (Stuttgart: Steiner, 1983)
IHGB	Instituto Histórico e Geografico Brasileiro
MMA	António Brásio (ed.), *Monumenta Missionaria Africana* 1st series, 15 volumes, Lisbon: Agência Geral do Ultramar, 1952–88; 2nd series, 5 volumes, Lisbon: Agência Geral do Ultramar, 1958–85
MSS Araldi	Manuscripts in the possession of the Araldi family, Modena
NBKG	Nederlands Bezittungen ter Kust Guinea (The Hague) (part of ARA)
PRO	Public Records Office (Kew), London
SRC	Scritture Riferite nel Congresso
T	Treasury series (of PRO)
VGK	Vest-India Guineisk Kompagnie (Copenhagen)
WIC	West Indische Compagnier

153

Introduction

1. John Keegan, *A History of Warfare* (New York: Alfred Knopf, 1993), p. 69.
2. On central Africa in general, John Thornton, "The Art of War in Angola, 1575–1680," *Comparative Studies in Society and History* **30** (1988), pp. 360–78; for an excellent contemporary account, "Relação da mais gloriosa e admirável victoria que alançarão as armas de elRey D. Affonso VI . . . *MMA* **12**, pp. 582–91.
3. Karl Maier, *Angola: Promises and Lies* (London: Serif, 1996), pp. 25–30.
4. Keegan, *History of Warfare*, pp. 28–32, and the Boer War figures on the map, p. 69.
5. Harry Turney-High, *Primitive Warfare: Its Practice and Concepts* (1st edn 1949, 2nd edn, Columbia SC: University of South Carolina Press, 1971).
6. "Introduction" and Robin Law, "Warfare on the West African Slave Coast, 1650–1850", in R. Brian Ferguson and Neil L. Whitehead (eds) *War in the Tribal Zone: Expanding States and Indigenous Warfare* (Santa Fe: School of American Research Press, 1992), especially pp. 124–5.
7. For a more up-to-date survey of anthropological scholarship on African war see Jean Bazin and Emmanuel Terray (eds), *Guerres de lignages, guerres d'état en Afrique* (Paris: Editions des Archives Contemporaines, 1982).
8. Ray Kea, "Firearms and Warfare on the Gold and Slave Coasts from the Sixteenth to the Nineteenth Centuries", *Journal of African History* **12**, 2 (1971), pp. 185–213; Ray Kea, *Settlements, Trade, and Polities on the Seventeenth Century Gold Coast* (Baltimore: Johns Hopkins University Press, 1982); Robin Law, "Horses, Firearms and Political Power in Pre-Colonial West Africa", *Past and Present* **72** (1976), pp. 112–32; Robin Law, " 'Here there is no Resisting the Country': The Realities of Power in Afro-European Relations on the West African 'Slave Coast' ", *Itinerario* **18** (1994); Robert S. Smith, *Warfare and Diplomacy in Pre-Colonial West Africa* (2nd edn, Madison: University of Wisconsin Press, 1989); see also Thornton, "Art of War".
9. Christian Georg Andreas Oldendorp, *Geschichte der Mission der evangelischen Brüder auf den Caraibischen Inseln St Thomas, St Croix und St Jan* (ed. Johann Jakob Bossart, Barby: Laux and Leipzig: Weidmann Erdman & Reich, 1777), p. 350.
10. Henry Gemery and Jan Hogendorn, "Technological Change, Slavery, and the Slave Trade", in Clive J. Dewey and A. G. Hopkins (eds), *The Imperial Impact: Studies in the Economic History of Africa and India* (London: Athlone Press for Institute of Commonwealth Studies, 1978), pp. 243–58.
11. Patrick Manning, *Slavery and African Life: Occidental, Oriental, and African Slave Trades* (Cambridge: CUP, 1990), pp. 39–44; 48–50.
12. Philip Curtin, *Economic Change in Precolonial Africa: Senegambia in the Era of the Slave Trade* (2 vols, Madison: University of Wisconsin Press, 1975) vol. **1**, pp. 156–68.
13. Boubacar Barry, *Senegambia and the Atlantic Slave Trade* (tr. Ayi Kwei Armah, Cambridge: CUP, 1998, French original: L'Harmattan, 1988), pp. 68–80.
14. Paul Lovejoy, *Transformations in Slavery: A History of Slavery in Africa* (Cambridge: CUP, 1983), p. 61.
15. Robin Law, "Dahomey and the Slave Trade: Reflections on the Historiography of the Rise of Dahomey", *Journal of African History* **27** (1986), pp. 237–67 for an overview of these issues in the classic case, the Kingdom of Dahomey.
16. Law, "Horses, Firearms". For discussion on these concepts, see James Webb, *Desert Frontier: Ecological and Economic Change along the Western Sahel, 1600–1850* (Madison: University of

Wisconsin Press, 1995), pp. 68–96; Ivana Elbl, "The Horse in Fifteenth Century Senegambia", *International Journal of African Historical Studies* **24** (1991), pp. 85–110.

17. Jack Goody, *Technology, Tradition and the State in Pre-Colonial Africa* (Cambridge: CUP, 1971), pp. 34–56. While Goody mentions the technology of spear and sword as well in his analytical statements, his argument scarcely takes them into consideration.

18. Smith, *Warfare and Diplomacy*.

19. Law, "Horses, Firearms"; and *The Horse in West African History* (Oxford: OUP, 1980).

20. Michael Roberts, *The Military Revolution, 1550–1660* (Dublin: M. Boyd, 1956); Geoffrey Parker, *The Military Revolution. Military Innovation and the Rise of the West, 1500–1800* (2nd edn, Cambridge: CUP, 1996); for a criticism see Jeremy Black, *European Warfare, 1660–1815* (New Haven and London: Yale University Press, 1994).

21. Similar arguments, with variations, can be found in William MacNeil, *The Pursuit of Power* (Oxford: OUP, 1983); and Keegan, *History of Warfare*.

22. Keegan, *History of Warfare*, pp. 16–24.

23. Geoffrey Parker, "Introduction", in *The Cambridge Illustrated History of Warfare* (Cambridge: CUP, 1995), pp. 2–9; see also David Ralston, *Importing the European Army* (Chicago: University of Chicago Press, 1990).

24. Keegan, *History of Warfare*, p. 399.

25. Thornton, "Art of War".

26. A classic statement of the idea of underdevelopment through the slave trade is Walter Rodney, *How Europe Underdeveloped Africa* (London: Bogle L'Ouverture Press, 1972); for a more recent version, see Barry, *Senegambia*, especially pp. 81–125.

27. For a debate on these issues in African economic history, see John Thornton, "Pre-Colonial African Industry and the Atlantic Trade, 1500–1800", responses by Ralph A. Austen, Patrick Manning, J. S. Hogendorn and H. A. Gemery, and Ann McDougall, and Thornton's rejoinder in *African Economic History Review* **9** (1992), pp. 1–54. Some issues have been revisited by a number of scholars, including those in this discussion in an Internet debate on H-Africa, "Development in Africa at the Start of the Sixteenth Century" (http://h-net2.msu.edu/logs/mlogs.cgi), December 1996–January 1997.

28. See John A. Lynn, "The Evolution of Army Style in the Modern West, 800–2000", *International History Review* **18** (1996), pp. 505–45.

29. Keegan, *History of Warfare*, pp. 222–34, updating, revising and modifying a theoretical scheme of Stanislav Andreski, *Military Organization and Society* (Berkeley: University of California Press, 1968).

30. For the success of Dahomey, see below and Werner Peukert, *Der Atlantische Sklavenhandel von Dahomey, 1740–1797. Wirtschaftsanthropologie und Sozialgeschichte* (Wiesbaden: Steiner, 1977).

31. P. M. Malone, *The Skulking Way of War: Technology and Tactics Among the Indians of New England* (Baltimore: Johns Hopkins University Press, 1991).

32. Thornton, "Art of War".

33. Some of these dimensions are explored in contact situations in D. M. Peers (ed.), *Warfare and Empires: Contact and Conflict between European and Non-European Military and Maritime Forces and Cultures* (Aldershot: Variorum, 1997).

34. John Thornton, *Africa and Africans in the Making of the Atlantic World, 1400–1800* (1st edn, 1992, 2nd edn, Cambridge: CUP, 1998), pp. xvii–xxxviii (including gazetteer).

35. Smith, *Warfare and Diplomacy*.

36. Alonso de Sandoval, *De Instauranda Etiope salute: El mundo de esclavitud negra en Colombia* (ed. Angel Valtierra, Bogotá: Emprensa Nacional de Publicaciones, 1957; 1st edn, 1627).

37. Oldendorp, *Geschichte*.
38. Also see Thornton, *Africa and Africans*, pp. 17–21 for a similar definition of the region by waterways.
39. Thornton, *Africa and Africans*, pp. 103–7.
40. Thornton, *Africa and Africans*, pp. 74–97.
41. John Thornton, "Mbanza Kongo/São Salvador, Kongo's Holy City", in Richard Rathbone and David Anderson (eds), *Africa's Urban Past* (London: James Currey, in press), and John Thornton, "As guerras civeis no Congo e o tráfico de escravos: a história e a demografia de 1718 a 1844 revisitadas", *Estudos Afro-Asiáticos* 32 (1997), pp. 55–74.

Chapter One

1. For an ecological overview with historical content, see George Brooks, *Landlords and Strangers: A History of Western Africa, 1000–1630* (Boulder CO: Westview, 1992). For the desert–Sahel–savannah regions, see James L. A. Webb, *Desert Frontier: Ecological and Economic Change along the Western Sahel, 1600–1850* (Madison: University of Wisconsin Press, 1995), pp. 3–26.
2. Antonio Malafante, "Copia cujusdam littere per Antonium Malafante a Tueto scrip[t]e, Janue Johanni Mariono. 1447", in Charles de Roncière, *La découverte de l'Afrique au Moyen Âge* (3 vols, Cairo Société royale de géographie d'Egypte, 1925–7) vol. 1, p. 154.
3. Alvise da Mosto, "Mondo Novo" in Tullia Gasparrini Leporace (ed.), *Le Navigazioni atlantiche del Veneziano Alvise da Mosto* (Milan: Instituto Poligrafico dello Stato, Liberia dello Stato, 1966), p. 37.
4. The traditions tend to deal with heroes as founders of lineages, reinforcing the formal nature of leadership. See Webb, *Desert Frontier*, pp. 27–67.
5. Michel Jajolet de la Courbe, *Premier Voyage du Sieur de la Courbe fait à la coste d'Afrique en 1685* (composite edition from three copies, P. Cultru, in BNP Paris, 1913), p. 147.
6. Mungo Park, *Travels in the Interior Districts of Africa in the Years 1795, 1796, and 1797* (London, 1799; facsimile New York: Arno Press, 1971), pp. 119–20.
7. Malafante, "Copia", p. 154; da Mosto, "Mondo Novo", p. 29.
8. de la Courbe, *Premier Voyage*, p. 147.
9. Gomes Eanes de Zurara, *Chrónica do descobremento e conquista de Guiné* (ed. Torquato de Sousa Soares, 2 vols, Lisbon: Academia Portuguesa da História, 1978), cap. 77. The date of Fernandes's visit is established in João de Barros, *De Asia* (Lisbon, 1552, facsimile Lisbon: Imprensa Nacional/Casa de Moeda), Decada I, Book 1, cap. 13.
10. Malafante, "Copia", p. 153.
11. For example, da Mosto observed that in the Jolof empire of the mid-fifteenth century there were no "walled cities" and the kings lived in mobile camps: da Mosto, "Mondo Novo", p. 42.
12. For a basic history, see the still standard Nehemia Levtzion, *Ancient Ghana and Mali* (London: Methuen, 1973); for Mali see M. Ly-Tall, *Contribution à la histoire de l'empire du Mali (13e–16e siècles): limites, principales provinces, institutions politiques* (Dakar: Nouvelles Éditions Africaines, 1977).

13. Malafante, "Copia", p. 154.

14. Songhay's rise is described in Sékéné Mody Cissoko, *Tombouctou et l'empire Songhay* (Dakar: L'Harmattan, 1975), pp. 44–96; Levtzion, *Ancient Ghana*, pp. 84–93. On Great Jolof, see Jean Boulègue, *Le grand Jolof (XIIIe–XVIe siècle)* (Paris: Karthala, 1987).

15. John Ralph Willis, "The western Sudan from the Moroccan invasion (1591) to the death of al-Mukhtar al-Kunti (1811)", in J. F. A. Ajayi and Michael Crowder (eds), *History of West Africa* (3rd edn, London: Longman, 1985), pp. 531–76; Michel Abitbol, "The end of the Songhay Empire", in B. A. Ogot (ed.), *UNESCO General History of Africa* (8 vols, London: Heinemann and Berkeley: University of California Press, 1982–92) vol. 5, pp. 300–26.

16. Jean Suret-Canale and Jean Boulègue, "The western Atlantic coast", in Ajayi and Crowder, *History of West Africa*, pp. 518–19; Avelino Teixeira da Mota, "Un document nouveau pour l'histoire des Peuls au Sénégal pendant les XVème et XVIème siècles", *Separata de Agrupamento de Estudos de Cartografia Antiga*, 56 (1969).

17. The best summaries are Boubacar Barry, "Senegambia from the sixteenth to the eighteenth century: evolution of the Wolof, Sereer, and the 'Tukulor' " in Ogot, *UNESCO General History* vol. 5, pp. 262–99; and Suret-Canale and Boulègue, "Western Atlantic Coast".

18. Willis, "Western Sudan" and Abitbol, "End of Songhay". See also Michel Abitbol, *Tombouctou et les Arma de la conquête marocaine du Soudan nigérien en 1591 à l'hégémonie de l'Empire du Maçina en 1833* (Paris: Maisonneuve et Larose, 1979).

19. Sékéné Mody Cissoko, *Contribution à l'histoire politique du Khasso dans le Haut-Sénégal des origines à 1854* (Paris: L'Harmattan, 1986); on the empire of Segu, see Sundiata A. Djata, *The Bamana Empire by the Niger: Kingdom, Jihad and Colonization, 1712–1920* (Princeton: Marcus Wiener, 1997) and Richard Roberts, *Warriors, Merchants and Slaves: The State and the Economy in the Middle Niger Valley, 1700–1914* (Stanford: Stanford University Press, 1987).

20. Boulègue, *Grand Jolof*, pp. 150–54.

21. Boubacar Barry, *Le royaume du Waalo: Le Sénégal avant la conquête* (Paris: François Maspero, 1972).

22. James F. Searing, *West African slavery and Atlantic commerce: The Senegal river valley, 1700–1860* (Cambridge: CUP, 1993).

23. Malafante, "Copia", p. 153; Robin Law, *The Horse in West African History* (Oxford: OUP, 1980), p. 91.

24. Valentim Fernandes, "Descriçã de Çepta e sua costa", in António Baião (ed.), *O Manuscrito 'Valentim Fernandes'* (Lisbon, 1940, revised reading in *MMA* 2nd series, 5 vols, Lisbon, 1958–80) vol. 1, fol. 110v. (citing foliation of original MS).

25. Abd al-Rahman al-Sa'di, *Tarikh al-Sudan* [c. 1655] (modern edn and French translation, Olivier Houdas, Paris, 1911), Ar. p. 119.

26. Mahmud al-Kati [ibn al-Mukhtar, c. 1665], *Tarikh al-Fettash* (modern edn and French translation Olivier Houdas and Maurice Delafosse, Paris, 1913), Ar. pp. 127/Fr. 233; al-Sa'di, *Tarikh al-Sudan*, Ar. p. 127.

27. al-Sa'di, *Tarikh al-Sudan*, Ar. p. 103.

28. Giovanni Lorenzo Anania, *L'Universale Fabrica del Mondo* (Naples, 1573, 2nd edn 1576, 3rd edn Venice, 1582) p. 332; variorum edition of Dierk Lange and Silvio Berthoud, "L'intérieur de l'Afrique Occidentale d'après Giovanni Lorenzo Anania (XVIe siècle)", *Cahiers d'histoire mondiale* **14**, 2 (1972), p. 324 (based on apparently independent testimony of Agostino Centorione); André Donelha, "Descrição da Serraleoa e dos Rios de Guiné do Cabo Verde", fol. 18v, in Avelino Teixeira da Mota and P. E. H. Hair (eds and trans.)

An Account of Sierra Leone and the Rivers of Guinea of Cape Verde (1625) (bilingual edition, Lisbon: Junta de Investigações Ciéntificas do Ultramar, 1977; marks the original pagination, which is cited hereafter). On their original lack of body armour, see the explicit statement of da Mosto, "Mondo Novo", p. 47, from 1455.

29. Malafante, "Copia", p. 153; da Mosto, "Mondo Novo", p. 38.
30. On mounted archers in Jolof, see André Alvares de Almada, "Tratado Breve dos Rios de Guiné . . ." in *MMA* 2nd series vol. 3 , p. 243; in the Fulbe, see Donelha, "Descrição", fol. 29v.
31. Fernandes, "Descriçã", in *MMA* fol. 92; the musket ball analogy is in Francisco Lemos Coelho, "Descrição da Costa de Guiné", 1667 and 1684, Portuguese text in Damião Peres (ed.), *Duas Descrições da Costa de Guiné* (Lisbon: Academia Portuguesa da História, 1953), pagination from the 1684 MS given in P. E. H. Hair's translation, fol. 6v.
32. al-Sa'di, *Tarikh al-Sudan*, Ar. p. 82; al-Kati, *Tarikh al-Fettash*, p. Ar. 117/211.
33. al-Kati, *Tarikh al-Fettash*, Ar. pp. 128/235.
34. Lemos Coelho, "Descrição", fol. 6v.
35. Anania, *Fabrica* (ed. Lange and Berthoud), p. 324; Alvares de Almada, "Tratado Breve", pp. 241–2; Biblioteca da Sociedade de Geografia de Lisboa, MS, Manuel Alvares, "Etiopia Menor e descrição geográfica da provincia da Serra Leoa", fol. 6.
36. See Law, *Horse*, for an exhaustive study of horses in west Africa.
37. Duarte Pacheco Pereira, *Esmeraldo de Situ Orbis* (modern variorum edn Augusto Epiphânio da Silva Dias, [1905] Lisbon: Academia Portuguesa da História), pp. 81, 89; Fernandes, "Descriçã" fols. 90v–93, revised reading in *MMA* 2nd series, vol. 1, pp. 672–739 with original foliation marked. For later, more modest ratios, *BSGL*, Alvares, "Etiopia Menor", fols 3v, 4, 7v.
38. Fernandes, "Descriçã", fol. 90v; Pacheco Pereira, *Esmeraldo*, pp. 81, 87; Giovan Leone Africano, "Descrizione dell'Africa", in Giovanni Battista Ramusio, *Delle Navigazioni e Viaggi raccolte da M. Gio. Battista Ramusio* (modern edn, 6 volumes, Turin: M. Milanesi, 1978) 1, p. 378; al-Kati, *Ta'rikh al-Fettash*, p. 70.
39. al-Kati, *Ta'rikh al-Fettash*, p. 264 (from "trustworthy sources"), but the Moroccan account gives Songhay only 8,000 horsemen, but 80,000 infantry: "Relacion de la Jornada que el Rey de Marruecos ha heco a la Conquista del Reyno de Gago . . ." in Henri de Castries, "La conquête du Soudan par el-Mansour (1591)," *Hésperis* **3** (1923), p. 461.
40. BNP, Fonds Français, MS 9557, "Mémoire sur les mines de Bambouc", 30 November 1762; M. Jacques Doumet de Siblas, "Mémoire historique sur les différentes parties de l'Afrique . . . 1769", (modern edn C. Becker and V. Martin, "Mémoire inédit de Doumet (1769)" *BIFAN* B, 36/1 (1974), p. 39.
41. Jean, comte d'Estrées, "Mémoire, tant sur l'arrivée des vaisseaux du roy au Cap Vert . . ." in G. Thilmans and N. I. de Moraes, "Le passage à la Petite Côte du vice-amiral d'Estrées (1670)", *BIFAN* B **39**, 1 (1977), p. 60.
42. Zurara, *Chrónica*, caps 60 and 63; for a continuation of the same weapons, see Estrées, "Description", p. 60.
43. Zurara, *Chrónica*, cap. 86–8, where Portuguese, in spite of their armour, saw their slightly wounded compatriots die after engagements.
44. al-Kati, *Ta'rikh al-Fettash*, Ar. pp. 50/Fr. 96–7.
45. Donelha, "Descrição", fol. 18v.
46. al-Sa'di, *Tarikh al-Sudan*, Ar. p. 127.
47. "Relacion" p. 460.

48. [Barbot, Jean] *Barbot on Guinea: The Writings of Jean Barbot on West Africa, 1678–1712* (eds P. E. H. Hair, Adam Jones and Robin Law, 2 vols, London: The Hakluyt Society, vols 175–76, 1992), p. 132.

49. al-Sa'di, *Tarikh al-Sudan*, Ar. p. 89.

50. Alvares de Almada, "Tratado breve", pp. 242–3.

51. This reconstruction combines "Relacion" (the Moroccan version), pp. 461–2 with al-Kati, *Tarikh al-Fettash*, pp. 134–39/263–66 (the Songhay version), seeking to reconcile their sometimes differing accounts. The date is given variously in *Tarikh al-Fettash* as 1 March [5 Jumada I], 12 March [16 Jumada I] or 13 March [17 Jumada I] 1591 [AH 999] (the latter in al-Sa'di, *Tarikh al-Sudan*, Ar. 140, who gives virtually no tactical details).

52. Joseph Alexandre le Brasseur, "Détails historiques et politiques sur la religion, les mœurs et le commerce des peuples qui habitent la côte occidentale d'Afrique . . ." [1778] variorium edn from three texts in Charles Becker and Victor Martin, "Détails historiques et politiques, mémoire inédit de J. A. le Brasseur", *BIFAN* B **39**, 1 (1977), p. 109 (author's note C).

53. [Anonymous], *Tedzkiret en-Nisian fi Akhbar Molouk es-Soudan* (2 vols ed. and trans. O. Houdas, Paris, 1899–1901, facsimile reprint Paris, 1966), p. 210.

54. *Tedzkiret*, p. 84.

55. La Courbe, *Premier Voyage*, pp. 108–9, 111.

56. da Mosto, "Mondo Novo", p. 42 (1455); Agostin Manuel y Vasconcelos, *Vida y Acciones del Rey Don Juan el Segundo* (Lisbon, 1639), extract in Avelino Teixeira da Mota, "D. João Bemoim e a Expedição Portuguesa ao Senegal em 1489", Separata de Agrupamento de Estudos de Cartografia Antiga, 63 (1971), p. 36 (c. 1624); Louis Moreau de Chambonneau, "Traité de l'origine des nègres du Sénégal, coste d'Affrique, de leurs pays, religion, coutoumes et mœurs", in Carson I. A. Ritchie, "Deux textes sur le Sénégal (1673–77)", *BIFAN* B **30**, 1 (1968), p. 324 (c. 1680).

57. Charles Boucard, "Relation du Voyage (1729)" ed. with introduction Philip Curtin and Jean Boulègue, *BIFAN* B **36** (1974), p. 272.

58. Claude Jannequin, Sieur de Rochefort, *Voyage de Lybie au royaume de Senega le long du Niger* (Editions Slatkine, Paris, 1643, facsimile reprint, Geneva, 1980), p. 59.

59. ANF C6/6, André Brüe, 6 April 1720; on the invasion, which was recalled by the Sultan, ANF C6/5 André Brüe, 31 December 1719.

60. Boucard, "Relation", p. 292.

61. ANF C6/11, Mémoire sur la Concession du Sénégal, 8 October 1734.

62. Pierre-Félix Barthélemy David, *Journal d'un voiage fait en Bambouc en 1744* (ed. André Delcourt, Paris: Société Française d'Histoire d'Outre-mer, 1974 with original foliation marked), fols 19, 79v–80.

63. La Brasseur, "Détails historiques", p. 97.

64. al-Kati, *Tarikh al-Fettash*, Ar. pp. 50/Fr. 97.

65. *Tedzkiret*, pp. 17–18.

66. *Tedzkiret*, p. 72.

67. *Tedzkiret*, p. 129.

68. Park, *Travels*, pp. 54, 64, 107, 111.

69. Park, *Travels*, pp. 226–7.

70. *Barbot*, Hair, Jones and Law edn, p. 91. It is not easy to assign a date to this passage, since it might have come from 1682 or as late as 1732.

71. ANF C6/11, Mémoire; Doumet de Siblas, "Mémoire", p. 39 (for 1769).

72. Park, *Travels*, pp. 101, 116–17.
73. *Tedzkiret*, p. 38.
74. de la Courbe, *Premier Voyage*, pp. 86, 156.
75. Park, *Travels*, pp. 119–20.
76. Park, *Travels*, pp. 139.
77. *Tedzkiret*, p. 93.
78. *Tedzkiret*, pp. 176–7.
79. ANF C6/6 Saint-Robert, 28 March 1721; ANF C6/6 Brüe, 28 March 1721.
80. Boucard, "Relation", p. 272.
81. Doumet de Siblas, "Mémoire", p. 39.
82. ANF C69 Charpentier, Mémoire du 1 April 1725, chapt III, p. 24; Boucard, "Relation", p. 272.
83. Mirabeau to Clarkson, 21 December 1789 in François Thesée, "Au Sénégal, en 1789. Traite des nègres et société africaine dans les royaumes de Sallum, de Sin et de Cayor", in Serge Daget (ed.), *De la traite à l'esclavage du Ve au XVIIIe siècle* (2 vols, Nantes and Paris: Société Française d'Histoire d'Outre-mer, 1988) vol. 1, pp. 227–8.
84. Park, *Travels*, pp. 107, 291–5.
85. *Tedzkiret*, pp. 71–3.
86. ANF C6/7 Fleury, 16 July 1722.
87. ANF C6/8 Charpentier to Director, 20 June 1724.
88. Park, *Travels*, pp. 108–10.
89. al-Sa'di, *Tarikh al-Sudan*, Ar., p. 72.
90. al-Sa'di, *Tarikh al-Sudan*, Ar., p. 76.
91. Appointments to this rank are detailed in al-Sa'di, *Tarikh al-Sudan*, Ar. pp. 80, 81, 93, 100 and *passim*.
92. al-Sa'di, *Tarikh al-Sudan*, Ar. p. 93. This source only gives the number of troops, but the context of this source suggests that cavalry are mentioned in most troop strength counts.
93. al-Sa'di, *Tarikh al-Sudan*, Ar. pp. 122–3, 127–9; al-Kati, *Tarikh al-Fettash*, Ar. pp. 125–8, 131. The latter suggests that the rebel force was 6,000, while one of his sources counted 4,600 cavalry and "infantry without number", suggesting that both forces counted cavalry only. The presence of Tuareg cavalry, who were not regular army soldiers, among the rebels may account for the discrepancy between the two witnesses.
94. *Tarikh al-Fettash* Ar. 117/Fr. 211.
95. al-Sa'di, *Tarikh al-Sudan*, pp. 133, 136, 185–6, 190–96, 197–9; al-Kati, *Tarikh al-Fettash*, pp. 231, 236, 258.
96. al-Sa'di, *Tarikh al-Sudan*, pp. Ar. 109, 124.
97. al-Sa'di, *Tarikh al-Sudan*, Ar. p. 10.
98. *Tedzkiret*, p. 107.
99. *Tedzkiret*, pp. 29–33 (his use of *legha*), 33–34 (his inability to appoint Lieutenant-Generals).
100. In 1743, for example, Oulad "Ali el Mobarek, a local commander, refused to render slaves accused of a murder to the Pasha, and mobilized his own *legha*: *Tedzkiret*, p. 123.
101. *Tedzkiret*, pp. 70–2.
102. *Tedzkiret*, pp. 91–3.
103. *Tedzkiret*, p. 43.
104. *Tedzkiret*, p. 25.
105. *Tedzkiret*, p. 81, (20 musketeers) in 1723.
106. *Tedzkiret*, p. 210.

107. Fernandes, "Descriçã", fol. 346. See also da Mosto, "Mondo Novo", p. 50.
108. Vasconcelos, *Vida*, pp. 36–7; Alvares de Almada, "Tratado breve", p. 261.
109. Alexis de Saint Lô, c. 1635 in G. Thilmans and N. I. de Moraes, "Dencha Four, souverain du Baol (XVIIe siècle)", *BIFAN* B **36**, 4 (1974), p. 702.
110. Rochefort, *Voyage*, p. 97.
111. Estrées, *Description*, p. 60; Sieur François Froger, *Relation du voyage de Mr. de Gennes au detroit de Magellan* (Paris, 1698), p. 16.
112. de Chambonneau, "Traité," p. 324.
113. Doumet de Siblas, "Mémoire", p. 39.
114. *Barbot*, Hair, Jones, and Law edn, p. 132.
115. ANF C6/8, Letter of Saint Louis, 28 March 1724.
116. ANF C6/29 undated document, cited and criticized in Barry, *Waalo*, p. 195 n. 6 (I was unable to locate this document myself).
117. Doumet de Siblas, "Mémoire", p. 44.
118. René-Claude Geoffroy de Villeneuve, *L'Afrique, ou historie, moeurs, usages et coutumes des Africains: Le Sénégal* (4 vols, Paris, 1814) vol. 4, pp. 27–30 cit. Barry, *Waalo*, p. 214, nn. 56–7.
119. le Brasseur, "Détails", p. 97.
120. ANF C6/9 Charpentier, Mémoire du 1 April 1725, chapt III. See also BNP MS 9339, fols 24–5.
121. ANF C6/9 Levens, 18 July 1725; ANF C6/10, Le Begue, Fort St. Joseph, 7 March 1731; Boucard, "Relation", p. 272.
122. David, *Journal*, fols 84, 85v.
123. Park, *Travels*, pp. 105–6.

Chapter Two

1. Duarte Pacheco Pereira, *Esmeraldo de Situ Orbis* (mod. variorum edn Augusto Epiphânio da Silva Dias, [1905] Lisbon: Academia Portuguesa da História, 1975), p. 102.
2. John Thornton, *Africa and Africans in the Making of the Atlantic World, 1400–1800* (2nd edn Cambridge: CUP, 1998), pp. 36–40.
3. Donald Wright, *The World in a Very Small Place in Africa* (Armonk, NY and London: M. E. Sharpe, 1997).
4. There are no contemporary accounts, but Gordon Laing, *Travels in the Timannee, Kooranko and Soolima countries in western Africa* (London, 1822), provides a chronology of events, which local oral tradition, collected and set in writing in Fulbe and Arabic in the nineteenth century, supplements.
5. André Alvares de Almada, "Tratado breve dos Rios de Guiné . . ." in *MMA* 2nd series, vol. 3, p. 360.
6. "The travailes of Job Hortop, which Sir John Hawkins set on land within the Bay of Mexico", in Richard Hakluyt, *The Principal Voyages Traffiques and Discoveries of the English Nation* (mod. edn, 12 vols, Glasgow: MacLehose, 1903), pp. 337–8.
7. André Thevet, *Les singularitez de la France antarctique* (Paris: Ambroise de la Porte, 1558, mod. edn with original pagination, P. Gaffarel, Paris: Maisonneuve, 1878), fol. 17;

Francisco Lemos Coelho, "Descripção da Costa de Guiné", 1667 and 1684, Portuguese text in Damião Peres (ed.), *Duas Descrições da Costa de Guiné* (Lisbon: Academia Portuguesa da História, 1953), pagination from the 1684 MS given in P. E. H. Hair's translation, fol. 21.

8. Valentim Fernandes, "Descriçã de Çepta e sua costa", in António Baião (ed.), *O Manuscrito 'Valentim Fernandes'* (Lisbon, 1940, revised reading in *MMA* 2nd series, 5 vols, Lisbon, 1958–80) vol. 1, fol. 110v. (citing foliation of original MS) fol. 122, 135.

9. Alvares de Almada, "Tratado breve", pp. 316–17, 325, 360; on the Sumbas, Clements Markham (ed.), *The Hawkins Voyages during the reigns of Henry VIII, Queen Elizabeth, and James I* (London: Hakluyt Society, 1878, original 1589, p. 18; André Donelha, "Descrição da Serraleoa e dos Rios de Guiné do Cabo Verde", fol. 18v, in Avelino Teixeira da Mota and P. E. H. Hair (eds and trans.) *An Account of Sierra Leone and the Rivers of Guinea of Cape Verde (1625)* (bilingual edition, Lisbon: Junta de Investigações Ciéntificas do Ultramar, 1977; fol. 13v, 14v.

10. "Travailes of Job Hortop", p. 338 (one English on one side, five Portuguese on the other); Markham, *Hawkins Voyages*, p. 71 (120 ground troops as well as naval bombardment); Alvares de Almada, "Tratado breve", pp. 369, 375; Biblioteca da Sociedade de Geografia de Lisboa, MS, Manuel Alvares, "Etiopia Menor e descrição geográfica da provincia da Serra Leoa", fol. 78.

11. Jean, comte d'Estrées, "Mémoire, tant sur l'arrivée des vaisseaux du roy au Cap Vert . . ." in G. Thilmans and N. I. de Moraes, "Le passage à la Petite Côte du vice-amiral d'Estrées (1670)", *BIFAN* B **39**, 1 (1977), p. 60; Louis Moreau de Chambonneau, "Traité de l'origine des nègres du Sénégal, coste d'Affrique, de leurs pays, religion, coutoumes et mœurs," in Carson I. A. Ritchie, "Deux textes sur le Sénégal (1673–77)", *BIFAN* B **30**, 1 (1968), p. 324.

12. François de Paris, "Voyage à la coste d'Affrique dite de Guiné et aux isles de l'Amerique fait ez années 1682 et 1683" in Guy Thilmans, "Le Relation de François de Paris (1682–83)", *BIFAN* B **38**, 1 (1976), pp. 1–51 (marks original foliation of text), fol. 31; Michel Jajolet de la Courbe, *Premier Voyage du Sieur de la Courbe fait à la coste d'Afrique en 1685* (composite edition from three copies, P. Cultru, in BNP Paris, 1913), p. 193 (but here referring to African Christian residents of Gambia region), 207 (Casamance, then well supplied), 208 (English defeat).

13. PRO T70/7, fol. 80, Anthony Rogers and Richard Hull, 26 June 1726.

14. Francis Moore, *Travels into the Inland Parts of Africa: Containing a Description of the Several Nations for the space of six hundred miles up the River GAMBIA: . . .* (London: Edward Cave, 1738), pp. 32, 121.

15. Moore, *Travels*, p. 68.

16. Abbé Demanet, *Nouvelle histoire de l'Afrique françoise* (2 vols, Paris, 1767) vol. 1, p. 249.

17. Nicholas Villault, Sieur de Bellefond, *A Relation of the Coasts of Africk called Guinée* (Paris, 1669, 2nd edn, London: John Starkey, 1670), p. 42; Johann Friedrich von der Gröben, *Guineische Reisebeschreibung, nebst einem Anhang der Expedition in Morea* (Mariewerder, 1694, Eng. trans. in *Brandenburg Sources*, original pagination), p. 42.

18. PRO T70/6, Johnson to Royal Africa Company, 15 April 1718.

19. Nicholas Owen, *Journal of a Slave-Dealer. "A View of Some Remarkable Axcedents in the Life of Nic. Owen on the Coast of Africa and America from the Year 1746 to the Year 1757"* (ed. Eveline Martin, London: Routledge and Sons, 1930), p. 24.

20. Owen, *Journal*, pp. 92–3.

21. John Matthews, *A Voyage to the River Sierra-Leone containing an account of the trade and*

productions of the country also of the civil and religious customs and manners of the people (London: B. White, 1788, facsimile reprint, London: Cass, 1966), Letter V (undated, c. 1786, between 29 July and 20 Nov 1786), p. 88; Thomas Winterbottom, *An Account of the Native Africans in the Neighbourhood of Sierra Leone* (London, 1803, facsimile reprint, ed. with new intro. John Hargreaves and E. Maurice Backett, London: Barnes and Noble, 1969) vol. 1, p. 158.

22. "Journal of Mr. James Watt, in his Expedition to and From Teembo in the year 1794 . . .", ed. Bruce Mouser in *Journal of James Watt: Expedition to Timbo Capital of the Fula Empire in 1794* (Madison: African Studies Program, University of Wisconsin, 1994 with original foliation), fols 9, 14, 84, 109 (Susus with many guns).

23. Watt, "Journal", fols 59v–63v, 77v (artillery).

24. Markham, *Hawkins Voyages*, p. 18.

25. Alvares de Almada, "Tratado breve", p. 372; BSGL, Alvares, "Etiopia Menor", fols 87–8v.

26. Matthews, *Voyage*, Letter V, p. 86–7; Winterbottom, *Account*, vol. 1, p. 154.

27. The authenticity of the account has been questioned, particularly because these ethnic names are not known from this region (although they may be archaic and local names), and because his elaborate account of his voyage defies geographical reconstruction. (See J. D. Fage, "Hawkins' Hoax? A sequel to Drake's fake", *History in Africa* **18** (1991), pp. 83–91.) However, it is possible that he did hear an account from an eyewitness of a war in the region, as there is certainly no other account of a battle in this detail.

28. Joseph Hawkins, *A history of A Voyage of the Coast of Africa* (Philadelphia: Ustick, 1797), pp. 79–84.

29. Gomes Eanes de Zurara, *Chrónica do descobremento e conquista de Guiné* (ed. Torquato de Sousa Soares, 2 vols, Lisbon: Academia Portuguesa da História, 1978), caps 75, 86; Alvise da Mosto, "Mondo Novo" in Tullia Gasparrini Leporace (ed.), *Le Navigazioni atlantiche del Veneziano Alvise da Mosto* (Milan: Instituto Poligrafico dello Stato, Liberia dello Stato, 1966), pp. 48, 112; Gomes, "Prima Inuentione", fol. 278 in Fernandes "Descriçã".

30. Fernandes, "Descriçã", fols 117v, 135; Pereira, *Esmeraldo*, p. 102.

31. Alvares de Almada, "Tratado breve", p. 284.

32. Fernandes, "Descriçã", fol. 102v.

33. Markham, *Hawkins Voyages*, p. 23.

34. Alvares de Almada, "Tratado breve", pp. 292–3.

35. Alvares de Almada, "Tratado breve", p. 289.

36. Alvares de Almada, "Tratado breve", pp. 304, 307, 313–14, 316, 337.

37. BSGL, Alvares, "Etiopia Menor", fol. 30.

38. Lemos Coelho, "Descripção", fols 31–7.

39. Markham, *Hawkins Voyages*, p. 71.

40. BSGL, Alvares, "Etiopia Menor", fols 78–78v.

41. de la Courbe, *Voyage*, p. 208.

42. PRO T70/7, fols 63–63v and 68v–69v, various letters of Plunkett, Drummond and Roders, 20 September, 27 October 1724.

43. Fernandes, "Descriçã", fol. 113v (Gambian region); Markham, *Hawkins Voyages*, p. 71; "Travailes of Job Hortop" p. 337.

44. Donelha, "Descripção", fol. 10v.

45. de Paris, "Voyage", fol. 23. On the general role of plants and trees in defence, see Christian Seignobos, "Pre-colonial plant systems of defense", in James Hughes (ed.), *The*

World Atlas of Archaeology (Cambridge and New York: Portland House, 1988), pp. 322–3, and sources cited in bibliography, p. 401.

46. Olifert Dapper, *Naukeurige Beschrijvinge der Afrikaensche Gewesten* (Amsterdam: Jacob van Meurs, 1668), p. 397.

47. Adam Jones, *From Slaves to Palm Kernels: A History of the Galinhas Country (West Africa), 1730–1890*, Stuttgart: Steiner, pp. 169–73.

48. Alvares de Almada, "Tratado breve", p. 356.

49. Alvares de Almada, "Tratado breve", p. 273.

50. Richard Iobson, *The Golden Trade: or a Discovery of the River Gambra* (London: Nicholas Oakes, 1623), pp. 42, 44.

51. de la Courbe, *Voyage*, p. 252.

52. PRO CO 267/14, Debat to O'Hara, 3 September 1768; Captain Tonyn to Lords of Admiralty, 28 August 1768; O'Hara to Lords of Treasury, 15 September 1768, cit. John M. Gray, *A History of the Gambia*, London: Frank Cass, 1940, p. 242.

53. Donelha, "Descripção", fols 11, 13v.

54. Alvares de Almada, "Tratado breve", pp. 364, 374; Donelha, "Descripção", fol. 13v.

55. Fernandes, "Descripçã", fol. 118.

56. BSGL, Alvares, "Etiopia Menor", fols 30–30v.

57. Moore, *Travels*, p. 36.

58. Mungo Park, *Travels in the Interior Districts of Africa in the Years 1795, 1796, and 1797* (London, 1799; facsimile New York, 1971), p. 36.

59. Matthews, *Voyage*, Letter VI, 20 November 1786, pp. 112–13.

60. Matthews, *Voyage*, Letter VII, 15 February 1787, pp. 154–5, describes the early stages of the revolt.

61. Winterbottom, *Account*, vol. 1, pp. 155–8.

62. Watt, "Journal", fols 113–113v.

63. Watt, "Journal", fols 33v, 67v, 77v.

64. Moore, *Travels*, p. 24.

65. ANF C6/17, Details sur l'Etablissement des français dans la rivière de Gambie et sur le Caractère de quelques Rois de ce pays. c. 1776, n. p.

66. Lemos Coelho, "Descrição", p. 41.

67. Fernandes, "Descriçã", fols 129, 135.

68. Markham, *Hawkins Voyages*, p. 16.

69. BSGL, Alvares, "Etiopia Menor", fol. 79v.

70. Matthews, *Voyage*, Letter V, pp. 85–90.

71. Winterbottom, *Account*, vol. 1, p. 153.

72. Jones, *Slaves to Palm Kernels*, pp. 18–19, 179–82.

73. Moore, *Travels*, pp. 33, 36.

Chapter Three

1. On the Akan/Twi language and the lack of language-based ethnic identity in this area, see John Thornton, *Africa and Africans in the Making of the Atlantic World, 1400–1800* (2nd edn Cambridge: CUP, 1998), pp. 321–2.

2. For a detailed study of the settlement pattern and its political manifestations, see Ray Kea, *Settlements, Trade, and Polities on the Seventeenth Century Gold Coast* (Baltimore: Johns Hopkins University Press, 1982), pp. 11–94, with complete cartography.

3. P. E. H. Hair, *The Founding of the Castelo de São Jorge da Mina: An Analysis of the Sources* (Madison: African Studies Program, University of Wisconsin, 1994).

4. A general introduction: Albert van Dantzig, *Forts and Castles of Ghana* (Accra: SEDCO, 1980).

5. William Towerson's voyage of 1556, in Richard Hakluyt, *The Principall Navigations, Voiages and Discoveries of the English Nation* (London, 1589) II, ii, pp. 30–31.

6. Pieter de Marees, *Beschryvinghe ende historische verhael, vant Gout Koninckrijck van Gunea . . .* (Amsterdam, 1602) mod. edn S. P. L'Honoré Naber: Linschoten Vereeniging (The Hague, 1912), English translation, Albert van Dantzig and Adam Jones, *Description and Historical Account of the Gold Kingdom of Guinea (1602)* (Oxford: OUP, 1987; both Dutch and translation mark original pagination), pp. 46–46a and plate 6; Samuel Brun, *Samuel Brun, des Wundartzt und Burgers zu Basel, Schiffarten* (Basel, 1624, mod. edn S. P. L'Honoré Naber, Hague, 1913, with pagination of original marked; facsimile ed. Eduard Sieber, Basel, 1945, and Graz, 1969) English translation, with original pagination marked in *German Sources*, pp. 82–3; Wilhelm Johann Müller, *Die Afrikansche auf der Guineischen Guld Cust gelegene Landschafft Fetu* (Hamburg, 1673, 3rd edn 1676, reprinted Graz, 1968, translation of 3rd edn in *German Sources* with pagination marked), pp. 126–35.

7. Nicholas Villault, Sieur de Bellefond, *A Relation of the Coasts of Africk called Guinée* (Paris, 1669, London: John Starkey, 1670) p. 242. Also see Kea, *Settlements*, pp. 151–4.

8. Müller, *Afrikansche*, p. 127. The primary source material at first seems contradictory, and I have sought to resolve it by seeing two levels of warfare with appropriate tactics, as presented here. For a different conclusion, and an idea of the varying possible interpretations found in sources see Kea, *Settlements*, pp. 151–4.

9. For a lengthy discussion of forest and its role in the Akan-speaking region, see Ivor Wilks, "Land, Labor, Gold, and the Forest Kingdom of Asante: A Model of Early Change", in Ivor Wilks, *Forests of Gold: Essays on the Akan and the Kingdom of Asante* (Athens, Ohio: Ohio University Press, 1993), pp. 41–66.

10. Michael Hemmersham, *Guineische und West-Indianische Reißbeschreibung de An. 1639 biß 1645 von Amsterdam nach St. Joris de Mina* (Nuremburg, 1663, mod. edn with original pagination marked S. P. l'Honoré Naber, Hague, 1930, English trans. with original pages marked, *German Sources*), pp. 27–8.

11. de Marees, *Beschryvinghe*, p. 39b.

12. Towerson in Hakluyt, *Principall Navigations*, II, ii, pp. 32, 42.

13. Brun, *Schiffarten*, p. 71.

14. Labadi is mentioned in an early sixteenth-century account as very powerful, and had, moreover, direct diplomatic relations with Portugal. It was noted in 1539, however, to be dependent on Benin, and perhaps declined as a result of this; see Avelino Teixeira da Mota, "Novidades náuticas e ultramarinas numa informação dada em Veneza em 1517", Separata de Centro de Estudos de Cartografia Antiga, no. 99 (Lisbon, 1977), p. 59 n. 18. Benin influence must have been minimal in the later sixteenth century, however, but Labadi all but disappeared from view in the meanwhile, though perhaps retaining its walls and fortifications in memory of an earlier glory.

15. de Marees, *Beschryvinghe*, p. 43a.

16. Brun, *Schiffarten*, pp. 86–7.

17. Villault de Bellefond, *Relation*, Fr. 262–3 (quoted in Kea, *Settlements*, p. 151).

18. de Marees, *Beschryvinghe*, pp. 43a–43b; Müller, *Afrikansche*, pp. 126–7.

19. Brun, *Schiffarten*, p. 81.

20. Brun, *Schiffarten*, pp. 82–3. Kea, *Settlements*, p. 152, after citing this source, argues that there were only two battle lines, but he supports this with an early eighteenth-century source which might reflect the different tactics of that time, or might represent an interpretation of the two types of fighters rather than what was probably one rank acting as a close reserve for the rank in front of it.

21. Kea, *Settlements*, pp. 152–3. The third group is somewhat hypothetical as argued by Kea, but seems to be both possible and appropriate.

22. de Marees, *Beschryvinghe*, p. 45a; Brun, *Schiffarten*, p. 82.

23. Müller, *Afrikansche*, p. 137.

24. Willem Bosman, *Naauwkeurige beschryving van de Guinese Goud-, Tand- en Slave-Kust* ([Utrecht, 1704], English translation, *A New and Accurate Description of the Coast of Guinea* (London, 1705, reprint London: Frank Cass, 1967), p. 182.

25. Towerson in Hakluyt, *Principall Navigations* II, ii, pp. 32, 41. P. E. H. Hair has shown that the claim of John Vogt (*Portuguese Rule on the Gold Coast, 1479–1632*, Athens, GA, 1979, pp. 109–12, 125) that Portugal had established their rule over parts of the coastal area through deploying forces is exaggerated: Avelino Teixeira da Mota and P. E. H. Hair, *East of Mina: Afro-European Relations on the Gold Coast in the 1550s and 1560s* (Madison: African Studies Program, University of Wisconsin, 1988), pp. 9–14.

26. de Marees, *Beschryvinghe*, p. 46b; Kea has dated the origins of this movement more precisely in shipping records to the 1590s (*Settlements*, pp. 158–60), but his contention, p. 158, that there were no imports between 1607 and 1660 is contradicted by many references to their import and trade in the 1650s on the following page.

27. Brun, *Schiffarten*, pp. 84–6, 88.

28. Kea, *Settlements*, pp. 159–60.

29. Brun, *Schiffarten*, p. 88.

30. Kea, *Settlements*, pp. 158–64.

31. Villault de Bellefond, *Relation*, Eng. p. 242 (Fr. pp. 355–6).

32. [Barbot, Jean] *Barbot on Guinea: The Writings of Jean Barbot on West Africa, 1678–1712* (eds P. E. H. Hair, Adam Jones and Robin Law, 2 vols, London: The Hakluyt Society, vols 175–76, 1992), p. 607; also see Johan Nieman, 8 March 1684, in Jones, *Brandenburg Sources*, p. 89.

33. Bosman, *Description*, pp. 184–7; also *Barbot*, pp. 606–7.

34. Johann Friedrich von der Gröben, *Guineische Reisebeschreibung, nebst einem Anhang der Expedition in Morea* (Mariewerder, 1694, Eng. trans. in *Brandenburg Sources*, original pagination), pp. 60, 75, 88.

35. Bosman, *Description*, pp. 28, 33.

36. Erick Tilleman, *En Kort og Enfoldig Beretning om det Landskab Guinea og dets Beskaffenhed* (Copenhagen, 1697, English translation with pagination of original, Selena Axelrod Winsnes, *A Short and Simple Account of the Country Guinea and its Nature* Madison: African Studies Program, University of Wisconsin, 1994), p. 69.

37. Johannes Rask, *En kort og sandferdig Reise-Beskrivelse til og fra Guinea* (Trondheim, 1754), modern Norwegian edn, *Ferd til og frå Guinea, 1708–1713* (Fonna Forlag, 1969), pp. 61–2.

38. Bosman, *Description*, p. 182.

39. Ludvig Ferdinand Rømer, *Tilforladelig efterretning om Kysten Guinea* (Copenhagen, 1760, French trans., Mette Dige-Hesse, *Le Golfe de Guinée 1700–1750: Récit de L. F. Römer, marchand d'esclaves sur la côte ouest-africaine*, Paris: Karthala, 1989 [cited]), pp. 149–51.

40. Rømer, *Golfe de Guinée*, p. 134; the arrow-using people of the interior regions were also mentioned by slaves from the region in the West Indies, see Christian Georg Andreas Oldendorp, *Geschichte der Mission der evangelischen Brüder auf den Caraibischen Inseln St Thomas, St Croix und St Jan* (ed. Johann Jakob Bossart, Barby: Laux and Leipzig: Weidmann Erdman & Reid, 1777), p. 278.

41. de Marees, *Beschryvinghe*, pp. 44a–b; for general observations and more documentation, see Kea, *Settlements*, pp. 131–6.

42. Hakluyt, *Principall Navigations*, II, ii, p. 31.

43. *Barbot*, p. 606.

44. de Marees, *Beschryvinghe*, pp. 44b–45a; Brun, *Schiffarten*, p. 82.

45. *Barbot*, p. 606.

46. Brun, *Schiffarten*, pp. 82, 88.

47. Hemmersham, *Reißbeschreibung*, p. 27.

48. Kea, *Settlements*, pp. 146–9.

49. Nicolaas van Wassenaer, *Historisch verhael alder ghedenckweerdichste geschiedenissen* (21 vols, Amsterdam, 1622–35) 9 (May 1625), fol. 59, 59v.

50. van Wassenaer, *Historisch verhael*, 4 (December 1622), fols 87–87v.

51. K. Ratelband, *Vijf Dagregisters van het kasteel Sao Jorge da Mina (Elmina) aan de Goudkust (1645–1647)* (Hague: Martinus Nijhoff, 1953), pp. 165, 168, 170, 174, 190, 224, 226, 255, 260, 281.

52. Villault de Bellefond, *Relation*, pp. 245–6; Müller, *Afrikansche*, pp. 59–60, 125, 142–3.

53. Bosman, *Description*, p. 180.

54. Rømer, *Golfe de Guinée*, pp. 95–7; *Barbot*, p. 604.

55. WIC 124 Elmina council minutes, 10 March 1700, Albert van Dantzig (ed. and trans.), *The Dutch on the Guinea Coast 1674–1742: A Collection of Documents from the General State Archive at the Hague* (Accra: Ghana Academy of Arts and Science 1978), pp. 61–2.

56. Bosman, *Description*, pp. 65–71; WIC 97 van Sevenhuysen to X, 30 May 1701, van Dantzig, *Dutch on Guinea Coast*, p. 73.

57. Hakluyt, *Principall Navigations*, II, ii, pp. 32–3. 41. See also Vogt, *Portuguese Rule*, pp. 111–25, which however, exaggerates the extent of Portuguese influence, see da Mota and Hair, *East of Mina*, pp. 13–15.

58. de Marees, *Beschryvinghe*, p. 46.

59. Brun, *Schiffarten*, pp. 84–89.

60. van Wassenaer, *Historisch verhael*, Part 9, May 1625, fols 59, 59v.

61. van Wassenaer, *Historisch verhael*, Part 4, December 1622, fols 87–87v.

62. Kwame Daaku, *Trade and Politics on the Gold Coast* (Oxford: OUP, 1970), p. 110.

63. Rask, *Ferd*, p. 61.

64. Kea, *Settlements*, pp. 154–8.

65. von der Gröben, *Reisebeschreibung*, pp. 60, 75.

66. Rask, *Ferd*, pp. 61–2.

67. Oldendorp, *Geschichte*, pp. 277–8.

68. Tilleman, *Beretning*, pp. 56, 68–9, 74, 80.

69. Tilleman, *Beretning*, p. 106.

70. Rømer, *Golfe de Guinée*, p. 128.

71. PRO T70/376 CCC to RAC 21 December 1699 cited in Daaku, *Trade and Politics*, p. 98 n. 5.

72. Protest by Cuep and Schoonwitz on behalf of General Hendrik Lamey from Prussia

in WIC 124, Minutes of Council, Elmina, 16 September 1707, van Dantzig, *Dutch on Guinea Coast*, p. 132.

73. WIC 124, Minutes of Council Meetings, 15 February 1712, van Dantzig, *Dutch on Guinea Coast*, p. 164.

74. WIC 124 Minutes of Elmina Council, Report of W. Butler, 26 August 1717, van Dantzig, *Dutch on Guinea Coast*, pp. 195–6.

75. Ivor Wilks, "What Manner of Persons Were These? Generals of the Konti of Kumase", in *Forests of Gold*, pp. 241–92, and T. E. Bowditch, *Mission from Cape Coast Castle to Ashantee* (London: John Murray, 1819 facsimile London: Frank Cass, 1966), p. 322.

76. NBKG 82, From Hendricks at Apam to Elmina, 6 and 10 April 1716 cited in Daaku, *Trade and Politics*, p. 175, n. 2.

77. WIC 114, pp. 298–300, "Relaas gedaan door Djemoe Dienaar van wijlen de Directeur Generaal de Gietere, en Kofiandafor Dienaar van den Oud President Ulsen betreffende hun wedervaren, & Verrichtingen, Eerst Uijt ordere van voornoemde Generaal Van September 1754 tot dessele overlijdn op 24 Octob, 1755".

78. WIC 116, J. P. T. Huydecooper, 29 December 1764; T70/31, W. Mutter, 25 January 1765, cited in J. K. Fynn, *Asante and its Neighbours, 1700–1807*, (London and Evanston: Longmans, 1971) p. 95 n. 2.

79. VGK, Biorn to Dalzel, CCC 6 May 1792, cited in Fynn, *Asante*, pp. 131–2, n. 1.

80. Kea, *Settlements*, pp. 164–8.

81. Rømer, *Golfe de Guinée*, p. 91.

82. WIC, 120 Contracten met naturellem 1659–1792, cited in Fynn, *Asante*, p. 18, n. 2.

83. Rawlinson, C.746, ff 159v and 194v, Ralph Hassell, 22 May 1682, Robin Law, *Further Correspondence of the Royal African Company of England Relating to the "Slave Coast", 1681–1699* (Madison: African Studies Program), 13; *Barbot*, p. 620. For raiding in 1685, see Rawlinson C.745, fols 408–09; John Carter, 22 November 1686 in Law, *Further Correspondence*, p. 42. A source of 1688 makes it all the people of Alampo, Rawlinson C.747, fo. 172v, Mark Bedford Whiting, 25 January 1687/8, in Law, *Further Correspondence*, p. 49.

84. Rawlinson C.747, fols 43v–45, John Carter, 10 May 1687 in Law, *Further Correspondence*, p. 47.

85. Rømer, *Golfe de Guinée*, pp. 97, 101, 133.

86. Rømer, *Golf de Guinée*, p. 110.

87. Elmina Council Minutes 27 May 1737, van Dantzig, *Dutch on Guinea Coast*, p. 320.

88. Rømer, *Golfe de Guinée*, p. 120; VGK Wærœ and Council 28 December 1730; WIC 109 Pranger, 1 March 1731 cit. Fynn, *Asante*, p. 72, n. 2.

89. On the term and its implications, Rømer, *Golfe de Guinée*, p. 120.

90. Rømer, *Golfe de Guinée*, p. 98.

91. NBKG 190 Diary of Des Bordes Journey to Accra, entry 9 and 22 June 1737, van Dantzig, *Dutch on Guinea Coast*, p. 321; Rømer, *Golfe de Guinée*, pp. 187–9.

92. Oldendorp, *Geschichte*, p. 279.

93. Oldendorp, *Geschichte*, p. 279.

94. Rømer, *Golfe de Guinée*, pp. 132–4.

95. Rømer, *Golfe de Guinée*, pp. 116–117; on the initial Akwamu success, VGK A. P. Wærœ 24 December 1730 as cited in Fynn, *Asante*, p. 70, n. 4.

96. The course of the war can be followed in ARA: NBKG 93, pp. 371–2 and 384, Letters of Pieter Valcknier, Jacob Elet and J. Maes, 13–20 May 1726.

97. ARA: WIC 109, Jan Panger, 11 August 1731, as quoted and cited in Fynn, *Asante*, p. 66, n. 3.

98. Minutes of Elmina Council, 16 February 1731, van Dantzig, *Dutch on Guinea Coast*, p. 257.
99. Rømer, *Golfe de Guinée*, p. 133.
100. Rømer, *Golfe de Guinée*, p. 83.
101. ARA: NBKG 84, Elmina Diary, van Alzen to Butler, 30 October 1717, entered 7 November 1717.
102. PRO T70/31 William Mutter CCC 20 July 1765; Gilbert Petrie CCC 20 August 1764; ARA: WIC 116 Huydecooper 8 May 1765, cited in Fynn, *Asante*, p. 96, n. 6.
103. Rømer, *Golfe de Guinée*, pp. 155–6.
104. Fynn, *Asante*, pp. 77 et seq. passim.
105. For the great roads, see Ivor Wilks, *Asante in the Nineteenth Century: The structure and evolution of a political order* (Cambridge: CUP, 1975 and 2nd edn [same pagination], 1989), pp. 1–42. On the earlier period, it is quite difficult to distinguish the ordinary paths or trading paths from the larger strategic constructions of Asante that take up the later period in the sources. Rømer's quotation is, in my mind, critical for the timing of the construction. Closer examination of sources will eventually yield more on this.

Chapter Four

1. On the ecology and early history see especially Robin Law, "Trade and Politics behind the Slave Coast: The Lagoon Traffic and the Rise of Lagos, 1500–1800", *Journal of African History* **24** (1983), pp. 21–48; Robin Law, "Between the Sea and the Lagoons: The Interaction of Maritime and Inland Navigation on the Pre-Colonial Slave Coast, *Cahiers d'études africaines* **29** (1989), pp. 209–37; and Robin Law, *The Slave Coast of West Africa* (Oxford: OUP, 1992).
2. Oyo's history is reconstructed on the basis of tradition in Robin Law, *The Oyo Empire, c. 1600–c. 1836: A West African Imperialism in the Era of the Atlantic Slave Trade* (Oxford: OUP, 1977), pp. 33–44.
3. On Benin in this period, see A. F. C. Ryder, *Benin and the Europeans, 1485–1890* (New York: Humanities Press 1969); for the civil war, see Paula Gerschick and John Thornton, "Civil War in the Kingdom of Benin, 1689–1732: Social Change or Continuity", *Journal of African History* (in press).
4. Law, *Oyo Empire*, pp. 150–82; *Slave Coast*, pp. 225–344; older, but still valuable is I. A. Akinjogbin, *Dahomey and its Neighbours, 1708–1818* (Cambridge: CUP, 1967).
5. Pieter de Marees, *Beschryvinghe ende historische verhael, vant Gout Koninckrijck van Gunea . . .* (Amsterdam, 1602) mod. edn S. P. L'Honoré Naber: Linschoten Vereeniging (The Hague, 1912), English translation, Albert van Dantzig and Adam Jones, *Description and Historical Account of the Gold Kingdom of Guinea (1602)* (Oxford: OUP, 1987; both Dutch and translation mark original pagination), p. 117 (for Benin).
6. Jean-Baptiste Labat, *Voyage du Chevalier des Marchais en Guinée, isles voisines, et a Cayenne, fait en 1725, 1726, & 1727* (Amsterdam: Compagnie M.DCC.XXXI [1731]) 4 vols) vol. 2, pp. 194–5.
7. Willem Bosman, *Naauwkeurige beschryving van de Guinese Goud-, Tand- en Slave-Kust* [Utrecht, 1704], English translation, *A New and Accurate Description of the Coast of*

Guinea (London, 1705, reprint London: Frank Cass 1967), p. 396; Labat, *Voyage*, 2, p. 195.

8. Johann Peter Oettinger, *Unter Kurbrandenburgischer Flagge: Nach dem Tagebuch des Chirurgen Johann Peter Oettinger* (ed. Paul Oettinger, Berlin, 1886], original pagination plus new edition in Jones, *Brandenburg Sources*), p. 60.

9. Labat, *Voyage*, vol. 2, p. 154.

10. Labat, *Voyage*, vol. 2, p. 190.

11. ANF, Dépôt des archives d'outre mer, MS 104 "Relation du Royaume de Judas en Guinéé . . .", (c. 1712) fols 82–5.

12. Labat, *Voyage*, vol. 2, pp. 189–91, 196. Labat possibly based his account on the reports of the war between Allada and Whydah in 1725 when he was present in the country, see vol. 3, p. 1.

13. Duarte Pires, 20 October 1516, *MMA* 1, p. 370.

14. ANTT Corpo Cronologico II, 46/165.

15. Andrea Josua Ulsheimer, "Warhaffte Beschreibung ettlicher Raysen . . . in Europa, Africa, Ostindien, und America." (MS of c. 1616, ed. and trans. Adam Jones, in Jones, *German Sources* with original pagination), fols 32a–32b.

16. Bonaventura da Firenze, "Come entrò la fede di Giesu Christo nel regno d'Ouere per la prima uolta", in Vittorio Salvadorini (ed.), *Le missioni a Benin e Warri nel XVII secolo* (Milan: Giuffre, 1972) original foliation marked, fol. 16.

17. Biblioteca Provincial de Toledo, Coleción de MSS Borbón-Lorenzana, MS 244, Basilio de Zamora, "Cosmografia o descripcion del mvndo" (1675), fol. 59.

18. Sieur d'Elbée, "Journal du Voyage du Sieur Delbée . . . aux Isles, dans la coste de Guynée pour l'etablissment du commerce en ces pays, en l'année 1669 and la present", in Clodoré, *Relation de ce qui s'est passé dans les Isles et Terre-Ferme de l'Amerique* (Paris: Gervais Cleusier, 1671), p. 399.

19. Rawlinson C.745; John Thorne, Offra, 4 December 1681; Accounts of John Thorne, Offra, entries for 4 and 12 November 1681 (Bodleian Library, Oxford).

20. William Snelgrave, *A New Account of Some Parts of Guinea and the Slave Trade* (London, 1734, facsimile, London: Cass, 1971), unpaginated introduction, from 1713.

21. *The Parliamentary History of England, from the Earliest Period to the Year 1803* (vol. 23 [1789–91] (London, 1816), p. 85 published in facsimile in Robin Law, "Further Light on Bulfinch Lambe and the "Emperor of Pawpaw": King Agaja of Dahomey's Letter to King George I of England, 1726", *History in Africa* **17** (1990), pp. 211–26.

22. Snelgrave, *New Account*, pp. 77–8.

23. Snelgrave, *New Account*, pp. 56–7.

24. Domenico Bernardi da Cesena, "Viaggio al Brasile, all'isola di S. Tommaso e del Principe, et al Regno del Benin in Africa, fatto dal Capucino P. Domenico Bernardi (1713–1726)" in Salvatore Saccone, *Il viaggio di Padre Domenico Bernardi in Brasile ed in Africa nel quadro dell'attività missionaria dei Cappuccini agli inizi dell'età moderna. Con il testo della Relazione del "Viaggio"* (Bologna: Pàtron Editore, 1980), pp. 180–1.

25. Paul Erdmann Isert, *Reise nach Guinea und den Caribaischen Inseln in Columbien in Briefen as senne Frunde beschreiben* (Copenhagen, 1788), English trans. with pagination of original, tr. Selena Axelrod Winsnes, *Letters on West Africa and the Slave Trade. Paul Erdmann Isert's Journey to Guinea and the Caribbean Islands in Columbia (1788)* (Oxford: Oxford University Press, 1992), pp. 34–8.

26. Isert, *Reise*, pp. 83–95.

27. Duarte Pacheco Pereira, *Esmeraldo de Situ Orbis* (modern variorum edn Augusto

Epiphânio da Silva Dias, [1905] Lisbon: Academia Portuguesa da História, 1975) II, cap 9, pp. 121–2.

28. Olifert Dapper, *Naukeurige Beschrijvinge der Afrikaensche Gewesten* (Amsterdam: Jacob van Meurs, 1668), p. 136.

29. Biblioteca del Palacio (Madrid) MS 722, Juan de Santiago, "Brebe relacion delo sucedide a doce Religiosos Cappuchinos . . ." (MS of 1648), fols 143–5.

30. Moureau de St-Méry, "Observations sur le royaume de Ouaire à la Côte d'Or en Afrique" in Paul Rossier, "Documents sur les relations entre la France et le royaume de Ouaire à la Côte d'Afrique (1784–1787)", *Bulletin du Comité d'études historiques et scientifiques de l'Afrique occidentale française* **2** (1928), pp. 365–6.

31. "Extraits du Memoire adressé au Minister par Olivier Montaguerre, directeur du Comptoir de Juda", (1787) in Paul Roussier, *L'établissement d'Issiny 1697–1702*, Paris: Larose (1935), p. 380.

32. Robert Norris, *Memoirs of the Reign of Bossa Ahádee, King of Dahomey an Inland Country of Guiney.* (London, 1789, reprint London: Cass, 1968), pp. 55–6.

33. Archibald Dalzel, *History of Dahomy An Inland Kingdom of Africa* (London, 1793, 2nd edn, London: Frank Cass, 1967), p. 169.

34. Dalzel, *History*, p. 191.

35. John Adams, *Remarks on the Country extending from Cape Palmas to the River Congo* (London, 1822, reprint London: Frank Cass, 1966), p. 136.

36. Cartoon XIX Officiers Majors and mariners du Navire, "le Soleil" 3 March 1788, cited Akinjogbin, *Dahomey* p. 167, n. 3.

37. Bonaventura da Firenze, "Come entrò la fede", fol. 16.

38. Landolphe in J. S. Quesné (ed.), *Mémoires du Capitaine Landolphe contenant l'histoire de ses voyages . . . aux côtes d'Afrique* (2 volumes, Paris: A. Bertrand, 1823), vol. II, p. 7.

39. Labat, *Voyage*, vol. 2, p. 192.

40. Francisco Pereyra Mendes, 4 April 1727 quoted in Pierre Verger, *Fluxo e Refluxo do Tráfico de Esclavos entre o Gulfo de Benin e a Bahia de Todos os Santos dos Século XVII a XIX* (trans. Tasso Gadaanis, São Paulo: Editoria Corrupia, 1987), p. 122.

41. Thomas Wilson to Francklin, Reed, & Peake, 29 April 1728, Robin Law, *Correspondence of the Royal African Company's Chief Merchants at Cabo Corso Castle with William's Fort, Whydah, and the Little Popo Factory* (Madison: African Studies Program, 1991), pp. 25–6; Snelgrave, *New Account*, pp. 115–17; a French version, ANF C6/25 unsigned letter Whydah 22 May 1728.

42. Norris, *Memoirs*, pp. 58–9; PRO T.70/ 1159, Day Book, William's Fort, 12 July 1763.

43. Diary of des Bordes, entry of 28 July 1737, and Hertogh to C. Patakrie, 2 October 1737, enclosure, Declaration of Johan Joost Steinmark, 4 December 1737, in Albert van Dantzig (ed. and trans.), *The Dutch on the Guinea Coast, 1674–1742: A collection of Documents from the General State Archive at the Hague* (Accra: Ghana Academy of Arts and Sciences, 1978) pp. 326, 328.

44. Norris, *Memoirs*, pp. 31–33; ANF C6/25, Jacques Levet, Whydah, 20 August 1743; Relatório of 29 October 1744, Verger, *Fluxo*, p. 207.

45. João Basílio, 29 April 1730, quoted in Verger, *Fluxo*, p. 149.

46. Snelgrave, *New Account*, pp. 151–2; João Basilio letter, 8 September 1732 in Verger, *Fluxo*, p. 154 (this letter is translated in Robin Law, *Contemporary Source Material for the History of the Old Oyo Empire, 1627–1824*, Ibadan: Institute of African Studies, 1992, p. 32).

47. Rømer, *Golfe de Guinée*, pp. 187, 189, 210.

48. da Cesena, "Viaggio", p. 180.

49. Olaudah Equiano, *The Interesting Narrative of the life of Olaudah Equiano or Gustavus Vassa, the African* (2 vols, London, 1789, and eight other editions 1790–1814), extract annotated by G. I. Jones, "Olaudah Equiano of the Niger Ibo" in Philip Curtin (ed.), *Africa Remembered: Narratives of Africans from the Era of the Slave Trade* (Madison: University of Wisconsin Press, 1968), p. 74.

50. Mémoire contre le Sr Galot, 8 November 1730 cited in Robin Law, *The Slave Coast of West Africa, 1550–1750: The Impact of the Atlantic Slave Trade on an African Society* (Oxford: OUP, 1991), p. 288 n. 122

51. Hendrik Hertogh 16 February 1728 entered 23 March 1728, in van Dantzig, *Dutch on Guinea Coast*, p. 231.

52. Norris, *Memoirs*, pp. 12–15 (in his reprint of this text, Law, *Source Materials*, p. 36, dates the event to 1742, rather than 1738 as Norris stated in the text).

53. Letter of Dupetival, 20 May 1728 in Law, *Source Material*, pp. 20–2; Snelgrave, *New Account*, pp. 121–2.

54. Norris, *Memoirs*, pp. vi-vii, 92–3.

55. Dalzel, *History*, p. 191.

56. Adams, *Remarks*, p. 77.

57. Snelgrave, *New Account*, pp. 148–9.

58. Norris, *Memoirs*, pp. 20–22.

59. Norris, *Memoirs*, pp. 23–4.

60. Dalzel, *History*, pp. 176–7.

61. Snelgrave, *New Account*, p. 113.

62. For a general assessment, see Norris, *Memoirs*, pp. 26–7.

63. ANF C6/25, Sr. Levet, 29 November 1733; 17 January 1734.

64. Dalzel, *History*, p. 183.

65. Norris, *Memoirs*, pp. 131–2.

66. ANF C6/26 Dewarel to Minister of Colonies, Whydah, 1 November 1776.

67. de Marees, *Beschrijvinghe*, p. 117b.

68. Dapper, *Beschrijvinge*, p. 128.

69. [Barbot, Jean] *Barbot on Guinea: The Writings of Jean Barbot on West Africa, 1678–1712* (eds P. E. H. Hair, Adam Jones and Robin Law, 2 vols, London: The Hakluyt Society, vols 175–76, 1992), p. 641.

70. Oettinger, *Unter Kurbrandenburgischer Flagge*.

71. AN: DAOM, MS 104 "Relation du Royaume de Judas en Guinéé . . .", p. 27, 82; Bosman, *Description*, pp. 394–5.

72. Labat, *Voyage*, vol. 2, pp. 188, 189–90.

73. "Relation de la Guerre de Juda par le Sr. Ringard Captaine . . . ", p. 2 in Robin Law, "A Neglected Account of the Dahomian Conquest of Whydah (1727): The 'Relation de la Guerre de Juda' of the Sieur Ringard of Nantes", *History in Africa* **15** (1988), pp. 326–8.

74. AN: DAOM, MS 104 "Relation", pp. 35, 44–5; Barbot, p. 644.

75. Labat, *Voyage*, vol. 2, pp. 200–1.

76. AEB 20, doc. 61, Francisco Pereyra Mendes 22 May 1726 in P. Verger, *Fluxo e Refluxo do Tráfico de Esclavos entre o Golfo de Benin e a Bahia de Todos os Santos dos Século XVII a XIX* (São Paulo: Editoria Corrupio, 1987), p. 143–4, tr. Law, *Source Material*, p. 15.

77. "Guerre de Juda", fols 2–3, in Law, pp. 326–8.

78. AEB 21, doc. 58, Francisco Pereyra Mendes, 4 April 1727 in Verger (Port).

79. Snelgrave, *New Account*, pp. 112, 116, 127.

80. ANF C6/25, piece 38, 29 November 1733, Sr. Levet, Verger (Port), p. 166.

81. Dahl letter, 25 April 1769, and E. Quist letter, 4 May 1769, quoted in Sandra Greene, *Gender, Ethnicity, and Social Change on the Upper Slave Coast: A History of Anlo-Ewe* (Portsmouth, NH and London: Heinemann and James Currey, 1996), pp. 57–8.

82. Rey de Calabar to Francesco da Monteleone (22 September 1692), *MMA* vol. 14: p. 224; see also John Thornton, "The African Slaves of the 'Henrietta Marie'", forthcoming.

83. His career is highlighted in Ryder, *Benin*, pp. 154–71 *passim*.

84. Moreau de St-Méry, "Observations sur le Royaume de Ouaire à la Côte d'Or en Afrique" in Paul Roussier (ed.), "Documents sur les Relations entre la France et le Royaume d'Ouaire à la Côte d'Afrique (1784–1785)", *Bulletin du Comité d'Études Historiques et Scientifiques de l'Afrique Occidentale Française* **11** (1928), p. 366.

85. Norris, *Memoirs*, p. 24.

86. Norris, *Memoirs*, p. 85–6.

87. Snelgrave, *New Account*, p. 32.

88. Snelgrave, *New Account*, pp. 77–8.

89. Joseph Pruneau de Pommegorge, *Description de la Nigritie par M. P. D. P.* (Amsterdam and Paris, 1789), p. 164.

90. Norris, *Memoirs*, pp. 88–9.

91. Norris, *Memoirs*, pp. 94, 97; in 1797 Ferreira Pires gave the strength of the royal female bodyguard company at 80, along with 50 males (probably eunuchs): Vicente Ferreira Pires, *Viagem de África em o Reino de Dahomé* (ed. Claudo Ribeiro de Lessa, São Paulo: Companhia Editoa Nacional, 1957), p. 71.

92. Dalzel, *History*, p. 176.

93. Van Hoolwerff to Amsterdam Chamber, 10 February 1688, in van Dantzig, *Dutch on Guinea Coast*, p. 31.

94. Bosman, *Description*, pp. 332–3, 335; Letter 18 February 1692, van Dantzig, *Dutch on Guinea Coast*, p. 52; Rawlinson C.747, fols 312v–313v, John Bloome, Accra, 9 June 1692, in Law, *Further Correspondence*, p. 56; Rawlinson C.747, fols. 367 and 416, Josiah Pearson, Whydah, 3 April 1694, Law, *Further Correspondence*, p. 58.

95. Snelgrave, *New Account*, pp. 126, 128.

96. ANF C6/26 Gourg to Minister, 16 July 1788.

97. Snelgrave, *New Account*, p. 148.

98. Minutes of Mina Council, Jan de Heere, 9 May 1733; NBKG Elmina Journal 6 December 1733, J. Elet, 8 November 1733, van Dantzig, *Les Hollandais sur la Côte de Guinée à l'Époque de l'Essor de l'Ashanti et du Dahomey 1680–1740* (Paris: Société Française d'Histoire d'Outre-Mer, 1980), pp. 236–7.

99. Norris, *Memoirs*, pp. 7–9, mistakenly dates the events to 1735; on the likely date, see NBKG 105, Elmina Journal 1 February 1741, van Dantzig, *Dutch on Guinea Coast*, p. 353, which gives the title of the rebel as "Vordersaunee" and supplies the number of troops.

100. Norris, *Memoirs*, pp. 36–7.

101. Norris, *Memoirs*, pp. 41–8.

102. Norris, *Memoirs*, pp. 50–1.

103. ANF C6/25 Delisle, Dahomey, 15 September 1728 cited in Law, *Slave Coast*, p. 272, n. 45.

104. Ferreira Pires, *Viagem*, p. 106.

105. Dalzel, *History*, p. 200.

106. Norris, *Memoirs*, p. 59. The total size of the force is given by PRO T.70/ 1159, Day Book, William's Fort, 12 July 1763.

107. Isert, *Reise*, Letter of 8 April 1784, p. 50.

108. Isert, *Reise*, Letter of 18 May 1784, pp. 80, 84.

109. De Chenevert and Abbé Bullet, "Réflexions sur Juda" 1776, cited in Akinjogbin *Dahomey*, p. 131 n 3, and p. 147 n 1 also cites C6/26, O. Montaguere to Minister de Colonies, 6 October 1777.

110. Rawlinson C.747, fols 367 and 416, Josiah Pearson, Whydah, 3 April 1694, Law, *Further Correspondence*, p. 58.

111. AN: DAOM, MS de Chenevert and Bullet, "Réflexions", p. 7 cited in Law, *Slave Coast*, p. 270 n 39.

112. Norris, *Memoirs*, pp. 57–9, chronology given in a contemporary account, PRO T.70/ 1159, Day Book, William's Fort, 12 July 1763.

113. Snelgrave, *New Account*, pp. 121–2.

114. Snelgrave, *New Account*, pp. 126–8. Chronology is given in PRO T.70/7 Charles Testefolle 30 October 1729 cited in Law, *Slave Coast*, p. 292 n 131, who cites the date as 5 July, Old Style.

115. Dalzel, *History*, pp. 163–4.

116. Bosman, *Description*, p. 336.

117. ANF C/27bis, Abbé Bullet, (ca 1776).

118. Dalzel, *History*, pp. 167–9.

119. Dalzel, *History*, p. 180; T 70/1545 Lionel Abson, 4 December 1783, Verger, *Fluxo*, p. 219 (in Portuguese translation), which records the overall operation as a success with some 1,000 slaves captured.

120. Isert, *Reise*, pp. 46–65.

121. Outlined in Greene, *Gender*, pp. 85–6.

Chapter 5

1. The standard general source for this period is still David Birmingham, *Trade and Conquest in Angola: The Mbundu and their Neighbours and the Portuguese* (Oxford: OUP, 1966).

2. On the "Jaga" episode, see Joseph C. Miller, "Requiem for the Jagas", *Cahiers d'études africaines* **13** (1973), pp. 121–49 (including a summary of the earlier work). The article sparked a debate: see John Thornton, "A Resurrection for the Jagas" (and Miller's reply, "Thanatopsis"), *Cahier d'études africaines* **18** (1978), pp. 223–7 and 227–30; François Bontinck, "Une mausolée pour les Jagas", *Cahiers d'études africaines* **20** (1980), pp. 187–9, and Ann Hilton, "The Jaga Reconsidered", *Journal of African History* **22** (1981), pp. 191–202.

3. A detailed study of this period is found in Beatrix Heintze, "Das Ende des Unabhängigen Staates Ndongo (1617–1630)", *Studien zur Geschichte Angolas im 16. und 17. Jahrhundert* (Cologne: Rüdiger Köppe Verlag, 1996), pp. 111–68.

4. For eighteenth-century Portuguese activity and its commercial origins, see Joseph C. Miller, *Way of Death: Merchant Capitalism and the Angolan Slave Trade, 1730–1830* (Madison: University of Wisconsin Press, 1988).

5. Rui de Pina, *Cronica d'el Rei D. Joham* (ca. 1515), cap. 60, *MMA* 1, p. 113.
6. Baltasar Afonso letter, 9 October 1577, *MMA* 3, p. 157.
7. António de Oliveira de Cadornega, *História general das guerras angolanas (1680–81)* ed. José Matias Delgado and Manuel Alves da Cunha (3 vols, Lisbon 1940–42, reprinted Lisbon, 1972) vol. 2, pp. 277, 278.
8. Cadornega, *História*, vol. 2, pp. 283.
9. Pero Rodrigues, "História da residência dos Padres da Companhia de Jesus em Angola, e cousas tocantes ao reino, e Conquista", *MMA* vol. 4, p. 563 (a chronicle collected in 1594 from testimony of early Jesuit missionaries and veterans of the first campaigns).
10. MSS Araldi, Cavazzi, "Missione Evangelica", vol. A, book 1, pp. 103–4.
11. Johan Nieuhof, *Gedenkwaerdige Brasiliaense Zee- en Land-reize* (Amsterdam: Jacob van Meurs, 1682), p. 56.
12. Giovanni Antonio Cavazzi da Montecuccolo, *Istorica Descrizione de' tre regni Congo, Matamba ed Angola* (Bologna: Giacomo Monti, 1687), Book 6, para. 31.
13. Cadornega, *História*, vol. 1, facing p. 3 and vol. 3, facing pp. 109, 215.
14. MSS Araldi, Cavazzi, "Missione Evangelica," vol. B, p. 592.
15. Cadornega, *História*, vol. 1, pp. 86–7.
16. Rodrigues, "História", *MMA* vol. 4, p. 563.
17. "Relação do Alevamentamento de D. Affonso, Irmão del Rei do Congo D. Alvaro", 24 January 1622, *MMA* vol. 15, p. 531.
18. Rodrigues, "História", *MMA* vol. 4, p. 567.
19. Diogo da Costa, 31 May 1586, *MMA* vol. 3, pp. 336–7.
20. Rodrigues, "História", *MMA* vol. 4, p. 564.
21. Marcellino d'Atri, "Gionate apostoliche fatte da me Fra Marcellino d'Atri . . . 1690" [1702] in Carlo Toso (ed.) *L'anarchia congolese nel sec. XVII. La relazione inedita di Marcellino d'Atri* (Genoa: Bozzi, 1984), p. 519.
22. "Lembramça das coussas para Reino de Manicomguo", 1512, *MMA* vol. 1, pp. 250–1.
23. Afonso to Manuel, 5 October 1514, *MMA* vol. 1, p. 312.
24. Afonso to Manuel, 5 October 1514, *MMA* vol. 1, pp. 319–20.
25. Afonso to Manuel I, 5 October 1514, *MMA* vol. 1, p. 296.
26. "Lembramça das cousas para Reino de Manicomguo", 1512, *MMA* vol. 1, p. 248.
27. Rodrigues, "História", *MMA* vol. 4, pp. 565, 571.
28. Baltasar Barreira to Provincial do Brazil, 27 August 1585, *MMA* vol. 3, p. 324; Rodrigues, "História", *MMA* vol. 4, p. 569.
29. d'Atri, "Giornate apostoliche", fols 519–21.
30. d'Atri, "Giornate apostoliche", fol. 474; da Lucca, "Lettera Annua, 1703", trans. in Jean Cuvelier (ed. and trans.), *Relations sur le Congo du Pére Laurent de Lucques* (Brussels: Mémoires, Institute Royal Colonial Belge, **32**, 1954), p. 83.
31. Manoel Correia Leitão, "Relação e breve sumário da viagem que eu, o sargento-mor dos moradores do Dande, fiz às remotas partes de Cassange e Olos, por mandado do Il.mo e Ex.mo Sr Governador e capitão-general dêstes Reinos, D. António Alvares da Cunha" (1755–6) in Gastão Sousa Dias (ed.), "Uma viagem a Cassange nos meados do seculo XVIII", *Boletim da Sociedade de Geografia de Lisboa* **56** (1938), pp. 18–19.
32. Correia Leitão, "Viagem", p. 25.
33. Elias Alexandre da Silva Corrêa, *História de Angola* (2 volumes, Lisbon: Editorial Ática, 1937), vol. 1, pp. 350–51, 354–6.
34. Silva Corrêa, *História*, vol. 1, p. 361.

35. ACL, MS Vermelho 296, Raphael Castello de Vide, "Viagem do Congo do Missinoario Fr. Raphael de Castello de Vide, hoje Bispo de S. Thomé", p. 118.
36. Pinheiro de Lacerda, "Noticias da campanha e paiz do Mosul, que conquistou o Sargento Mor Paulo Martins Pinheiro de Lacerda, 1790–91", *Annaes Maritímos e Colonias* **6**, 3 (1845), pp. 130–1; AHU Cx 76, doc. 28, Paulo Martins Pinheiro de Lacerda letter 20 May 1791; AHU Cx 76 doc 73, Manuel d'Almeida e Vasconcelos, 7 August 1791, fols iv and 1.
37. Silva Corrêa, *História*, vol. 2, pp. 179–230 *passim*.
38. da Lucca, "Lettera annua, 1703", p. 83.
39. Pinheiro de Lacerda, "Noticias", p. 131.
40. Silva Corrêa, *História*, vol. 2, pp. 185, 187, 190–91, 200, 203–4.
41. João de Barros, *Decadas de Asia* (Lisbon, 1552), Decade 1, Book 3, cap. 10, *MMA* vol. 1, p. 144.
42. Diogo da Costa letter, 20 July 1585, *MMA* vol. 3, p. 320.
43. Rodrigues, "História", *MMA* vol. 4, p. 563.
44. Rodrigues, "História", *MMA* vol. 4, p. 576.
45. Silva Corrêa, *História*, vol. 1, p. 336.
46. Andrew Battell, *The Strange Adventures of Andrew Battell of Leigh, in Angola and the Adjoining Regions* (ed. E. G. Ravenstein, London: Hakluyt Society, 2nd series, no. 6, 1901; reprinted Nendeln, Liechtenstein: Kraus, 1967) pp. 20, 28–9.
47. Battell, *Strange Adventures*, pp. 30–1.
48. Pedro Mendes letter, 2 December 1710, in Levy-Jordão de Paiva Manso (ed.), *História do Congo (Documentos)* (Lisbon: Typographia da Academia, 1877, p. 355.
49. d'Atri, "Giornate apostoliche", p. 545; da Lucca, "Lettera Annua, 1702", p. 261.
50. da Lucca, "Lettera annua, 1707", pp. 325–6.
51. da Lucca, "Lettera annua, 1707", pp. 318–19.
52. Battell, *Strange Adventures*, pp. 13–15.
53. Cadornega, *História*, vol. 1, p. 347.
54. Silva Corrêa, *História*, vol. 2, pp. 202–6.
55. Silva Corrêa, *História*, vol. 2, pp. 58–60.
56. Silva Corrêa, *História*, vol. 1, pp. 306–7.
57. AHU Cx. 61, doc. 18 Antonio de Lemcastro, 1 July 1776.
58. Martin Fernandez de Enciso, *Suma de Geographia q[ue] trata largamente del arte del marear* (Seville: Jacobo Cröberger, 1519), fol. 110; similar estimates in Jean Fonteneau dit Alphonse de Saintogne, *La Cosmographie* in Georges Musset (ed.), *Recueil de Voyages et de Documents pour servir à la histoire de la Géographie . . .* (Paris: Larose, 1904), original foliation marked, fol. 126.
59. Afonso to João III, 25 August 1526, *MMA* vol. 1, pp. 475–6.
60. Jean Fonteneau dit Alphonse de Saintogne, *Voyages aventureax* (1547 2d ed. 1559), p. 55. written 1536 according to Georges Musset (ed.), *Recueil de Voyages et de Documents pour servir à la histoire de la Géographie . . .* (Paris: Larose, 1904), p. 21.
61. Cadornega, *História*, vol. 2, p. 281.
62. Rui de Pina, *Cronica d'el Rei D João Segundo* (ca. 1515) cap. 13, *MMA* vol. 1, p. 135.
63. Baltasar Afonso to Miguel de Sousa, 4 July 1581, *MMA* vol. 3, pp. 199–203; Rodrigues, "História", *MMA* vol. 4, p. 566 (different details, but perhaps describing the same operations).
64. Biblioteca Riccardiano, Codice 1910, fol. 94a, published with original pagination and Portuguese translation in Carmen M. Radulet, *O Cronista Rui de Pina e a "Relação do*

Reino do Congo" (Lisbon: Imprensa Nacional Casa de Moeda, 1992). The official chronicle, probably based on the same original sources, gave the numbers of follower per nobleman as 100,000: cap. 60, *MMA* vol. 1, p. 114.

65. Afonso I to Manuel I, 5 October 1514, *MMA* vol. 1, p. 297.

66. Afonso to Lords of the Country, 1512, *MMA* vol. 1, p. 257, probably based on a lost letter of 1509.

67. "Auto da inquirição . . . " (1550), *MMA* vol. 2, p. 251.

68. Afonso I to Manuel I, 5 October 1514, *MMA* vol. 1, p. 295.

69. "Auto da inquirição . . . " *MMA* vol. 2, pp. 255–60.

70. [Mateus Cardoso], *História do Reino de Congo (1624)* (ed. António Brásio, Lisbon: Centro de Estudos Históricos Ultra marinos, 1969), cap. 14, f. 15.

71. The text of one is preserved, "Manifesto da guerra de D. António", 13 July 1665, *MMA* vol. 12, pp. 549–50.

72. da Montecuccolo, *Descrizione*, Book 1, para 315.

73. "Relação do Alevamentamento de D. Affonso, Irmão del Rei do Congo D. Alvaro", 24 January 1622, *MMA* vol. 15, p. 531. "Mobatas" in this Portuguese letter is from Kikongo *muvata* or "village person" (*vata* in modern Kikongo is village), pluralized according to Portuguese rules. "Cabonzo" is not found in any dictionary of Kikongo known to me, including the seventeenth-century one of Joris van Gheel, but context clearly reveals it to be an arrow poison.

74. Jesuits to Lord Collector, 20 October 1623, *MMA* vol. 15, p. 517; for demographic estimates, see John Thornton, "Demography and History in the Kingdom of Kongo, 1550–1750", *Journal of African History* **18** (1977), p. 526.

75. John Thornton, *The Kingdom of Kongo: Civil War and Transition, 1641–1718* (Madison: University of Wisconsin Press, 1983), pp. 42–4.

76. "Relação do Alevamento", *MMA* vol. 15, pp. 530–1, 537.

77. Rodrigues, "História", *MMA* vol. 4, pp. 562–4; for a good overview of the institutions of Ndongo, Beatrix Heintze, "Unbekanntes Angola: Der Staat Ndongo im 16. Jahrhundert", *Anthropos* **72** (1977), pp. 776–8; 788–90.

78. Battell, *Strange Adventures*, p. 14.

79. Baltasar Barreira to Provincial do Brazil, 27 August 1585, *MMA* vol. 3, p. 324.

80. Diogo da Costa letter, 20 July 1585, *MMA* vol. 3, p. 320.

81. Battell, *Strange Adventures*, pp. 35–6.

82. Battell, *Strange Adventures*, pp. 64–5.

83. Representation of Manuel Cerveira Pereira, 3 July 1618, *MMA* vol. 6, pp. 315–16.

84. Battell, *Strange Adventures*, pp. 28–33, has the earliest account of their organization and mode of life.

85. Silva Corrêa, *História*, vol. 1, pp. 348–50.

86. Thornton, *Kingdom of Kongo*, pp. 88–93.

87. BN Madrid, MS 3165, fol. 94v, Andrea da Pavia, "Viaggio apostolico alle missioni", (1692); d'Atri, "Gionate apostoliche", p. 53 (original pagination); Luca da Caltanisetta, "Relatione della Missione fatta nel Regno di Congo per il Padre Fra Luca da Caltanisetta . . . sino alla fine del 1701", in Raimondo Rainero (ed.), *Il Congo agli inizi del setecento nella relazione del P. Luca da Caltanisetta* (Florence: La Nuova Italia, 1974), fols 8–9v (original foliation).

88. d'Atri, "Giornate apostoliche", pp. 546–53.

89. APF: SRC Congo I, fol. 14, Giuseppe Maria da Busseto, "Come io, Fra Giuseppe Maria da Busseto . . . lo stato delli Missioni di Congo . . ." 1675; Girolamo Merolla

da Sorrento, *Breve e succinta relatione del viaggio nel Congo* (Naples: F. Mollo, 1692), pp. 158–62.

90. d'Atri, "Giornate apostoliche", pp. 76–90.

91. John Thornton, *The Kongolese Saint Anthony: Dona Beatriz Kimpa Vita and the Antonian Movement, 1684–1706* (Cambridge: CUP, 1998), for this episode in Kongo history.

92. Academia das Ciênças de Lisboa, MS Vermelho 296, Raphael Castello de Vide, "Viagem do Congo do Missinoario Fr. Raphael de Castello de Vide, hoje Bispo de S. Thomé", pp. 260–2.

93. John Thornton, "Mbanza Kongo/São Salvador: Kongo's Holy City", in Richard Rathbone and Andrew Roberts (eds), *Africa's Urban Past* (London: James Currey, in press).

94. Certificate of Francisco de Sá e Silva, 11 December 1718, António de Almeida, "Relações com os Dembos das cartas do Dembado de Kakulu-Kahenda", in *I Congresso da História da Expansão Portugesa no mundo* (4th section, Lisbon, 1938), doc. 7, p. 32.

95. Silva Corrêa, *História*, vol. 2, pp. 49–52.

96. Cadornega, *História*, vol. 1, p. 135, 347, 403.

97. Cadornega, *História*, vol. 1, p. 403, 407.

98. Cadornega, *História*, vol. 2, p. 268.

99. IHGB, DL 106/15, "Relação que faço cormanamente assem da viagem como das Marchas, Sitios e Provincia donde passou o Exercito, que ele mandou ao Reyno de Beng[uel]a castigar aos Souvass Cabundas e seus aliaddos, por ordem do Mma Exmo Gov o Snr Dom Antonio Alz da Cunha no anno de 1755 tudo pasto comverdade de Succedido", fol. 2.

100. MSS Araldi, Cavazzi, "Missione Evangelica", MS B, p. 528.

101. Silva Corrêa, *História*, vol. 1, p. 349.

102. Silva Corrêa, *História*, vol. 2, pp. 54–5.

103. Baltasar Barreira to Provincial do Brazil, 27 August 1585, *MMA* vol. 3, p. 323–4; Rodrigues, "História", *MMA* vol. 4, p. 569.

104. Rodrigues, "História", *MMA* vol. 4, p. 574–5.

105. Cadornega, *História*, vol. 1, pp. 350–1.

106. Cadornega, *História*, vol. 2, p. 278.

107. "Relação da mais gloriosa e admirável victoria que alançarão as armas de elRey D. Affonso VI . . . " *MMA* vol. 12, pp. 582–91; Cadornega, *História*, vol. 2, pp. 208–13.

108. Silva Corrêa, *História*, vol. 1, pp. 338–9.

109. Silva Corrêa, *História*, vol. 2, pp. 52–7.

110. "Noticias . . . Pinheiro de Lacerda", pp. 129–32.

111. Raimondo da Dicomano, *L'Informazione sul Regno del Congo' di Raimondo da Dicomano* (Rome: L'Italia Franciscana, 1977), fol. 115.

112. Silva Corrêa, *História*, vol. 2, pp. 225–9.

113. ACL MS 296, Castello da Vide, "Viagem", p. 118–19.

114. Silva Corrêa, *História*, vol. 2, pp. 179–230, *passim*.

Chapter Six

1. The version in the book does not include the use of a net, see Alex Haley, *Roots: The Saga of an American Family* (Garden City, New York: Doubleday, 1976) (the television series aired in 1977), pp. 24, 44–54, 124–7.

2. PRO CO 268/2 fols 25 *et seq.*, "Instructions to the Superintendent of Trade in Senegambia", 6 December 1765 cited in John M. Gray, *A History of the Gambia* (1940), p. 234.

3. See how the term is used by Mungo Park, *Travels in the Interior Districts of Africa in the Years 1795, 1796, and 1797* (London, 1799; facsimile New York: Arno Press, 1971), p. 8.

4. Michael Gomez, *Exchanging Our Country Marks: The Transformation of African Identities in the Colonial and Antebellum South* (Cambridge: CUP, 1998), pp. 199–214.

5. Philip Curtin, *Economic Change in Precolonial Africa: Senegambia in the Era of the Slave Trade* (2 vols, Madison, 1975) vol. 1, pp. 156–9.

6. Boubacar Barry, *Senegambia and the Atlantic Slave Trade* (trans. Ayi Kwei Armah, Cambridge: CUP, 1998), pp. 61–80.

7. A good review of this literature is in Robin Law, "Dahomey and the Slave Trade: Reflections on the historiography of the rise of Dahomey", *Journal of African History* **27** (1986), pp. 237–67.

8. Valentim Fernandes, "Descriçã de Çepta a sua costa", in António Baião (ed.), *O Manuscrito "Valentim Fernandes"* (Lisbon, 1940, revised reading in *MMA* 2nd series, 5 vols, Lisbon, 1958–80) vol. 1, fol. 96v.

9. André Alvares de Almada, "Tratado Breve dos Rios de Guiné . . ." in *MMA* 2nd series vol. 3, p. 243.

10. Claude Jannequin, Sieur de Rochefort, *Voyage de Lybie au royaume de Senega le long du Niger* (Paris: Editions Slatkine, 1643, facsimile reprint, Geneva, 1980), pp. 86–7; Jean, comte d'Estrées, "Mémoire, tant sur l'arrivée des vaisseaux du roy au Cap Vert . . ." in G. Thilmans and N. I. de Moraes, "Le passage à la Petite Côte du vice-amiral d'Estrées (1670)", *BIFAN B* **39**, 1 (1977), p. 61.

11. ANF C6/5 André Bruë to Compagnie, 3 October and 31 December 1719.

12. ANF C6/11, Saint-Adon letter, 22 July 1737; Abdoulaye Bathily, Les *Portes de l'or: Le royaume de Galam (Sénégal) de l'ère musulmane au temps des négriers (VIIIIe–XVIIIe siècles)* (Paris: L'Harmattan, 1989), p. 326, no source given, but probably based on ANF C6/11, Extrait of Saint-Adan letter, 15 February 1738.

13. ANF C6/18, "Remarques Etat et aperçu des esclaves", 1783; the British perspective more or less confirms the French summary, see "Answers to questions posed in Lt. Col. Maxwell, January 1, 1811", *British Parliamentary Papers, Colonies, Africa* (Dublin: Irish Universities Press, 1977) vol. 1, p. 152. The incident has been much discussed in recent historiography, see Boubacar Barry, *Le royaume du Waalo: Le Sénégal avant la conquête* (Paris: François Maspero, 1972), p. 209 and James F. Searing, *West African slavery and Atlantic commerce: The Senegal river valley, 1700–1860* (Cambridge: CUP, 1993), p. 153.

14. ANF C6/14, letter of 20 June 1754.

15. Lamiral, *L'Afrique et le peuple Afriquaine.* (Paris: Dessenne, 1789), p. 171.

16. Mirabeau [quoting de Villeneuve] to Clarkson, 21 December 1789 in François Thesée, "Au Sénégal, en 1789. Traite des nègres et société africaine dans les royaumes de Sallum, de Sin et de Cayor", in Serge Daget (ed.), *De la traite à l'esclavage du Ve au XVIIIe siècle* (2 vols, Nantes and Paris: Société Française d'Histoire d'Outre-Mer, 1988), pp. 228, 230.

17. ANF C6/7, M de la Rigaudere, 3 May 1722.

18. ANF C6/29 undated document, cited and criticized in Boubacar Barry, *Waalo*, p. 195.

19. Park, *Travels*, pp. 293–4.

20. Alvares de Almada, "Tratado breve", p. 337.

21. Samuel Brun, *Samuel Brun, des Wundartzt und Burgers zu Basel, Schiffarten* (Basel, 1624, reprinted, ed. S. P. L'Honoré Naber, The Hague: Linschoten Vereeniging, 1913;

Facsimile, ed. Eduard Sieber, Basel, 1945, and Graz, 1969) pp. 84, 88. English translation, Jones, *German Sources* (with original pagination marked).

22. Michael Hemmersham, *Guineische und West-Indianische Reißbeschreibung de An. 1639 biß 1645 von Amsterdam nach St. Joris de Mina* (Nuremburg, 1663, mod. edn with original pagination marked S. P. l'Honoré Naber, The Hague, 1930, English trans., with original pages marked, Jones, *German Sources*), pp. 25–6.

23. For the Dutch perspective, West India Company Council Minutes, entries 1 May 1683, 3 August 1683, van Dantzig, *The Dutch on the Guinea Coast, 1674–1742: A Collection of Documents from the General State Archive at the Hague* (Accra: Ghana Academy of Arts and Sciences, 1978), pp. 39, 40; for the English, MS Rawlinson C 745, fol. 199v, Hugh Sears, Annamboe, 21 May 1683; fol. 228, Mark Whiting, Seccondee, 27 July 1683; fol. 218, Mark Whiting, Succondee, 18 August 1683.

24. Abramz to X, 23 Nov 1679 in van Dantzig, *The Dutch on the Guinea Coast, 1674–1742: A Collection of Documents from the General State Archive at the Hague* (Accra: Ghana Academy of Arts and Sciences, 1978), pp. 17–18.

25. West Indian Company Council Minutes, entry of 24 November 1693 in Albert van Dantzig (ed. and trans.), *The Dutch on the Guinea Coast, 1674–1742: A Collection of Documents from the General State Archive at the Hague* (Accra: Ghana Academy of Arts and Sciences, 1978), pp. 55–6.

26. Willem Bosman *Naauwkeurige beschryving van de Guinese Goud-, Tand- en Slave-Kust* ([Utrecht, 1704], English translation, *A New and Accurate Description of the Coast of Guinea* (London, 1705, reprint London: Frank Cass 1967), pp. 29–36; Kwame Daaku, *Trade and Politics on the Gold Coast* (Oxford: OUP, 1970), pp. 83–4 (which elaborates the basic account with more documents and chonology), sees the war as prime evidence of the nefarious effects of European rivalries and meddling in African affairs.

27. Enclosure in Minutes, Meeting of Zeeland Council, 7 February 1730, in van Dantzig, *The Dutch on the Guinea Coast, 1674–1742: A Collection of Documents from the General State Archive at the Hague* (Accra: Ghana Academy of Arts and Sciences, 1978), p. 240; the change to a "slave coast" and the exchange of the gold trade for the slave trade was noted earlier, in 1705, Provisional D-G Pieter Nuyts to X, 13 November 1705, van Dantzig, *The Dutch on the Guinea Coast, 1674–1742: A Collection of Documents from the General State Archive at the Hague* (Accra: Ghana Academy of Arts and Sciences, 1978), p. 122.

28. Ludvig F. Rømer, *Le Golfe de Guinée 1700–1750. Récit de L. F. Römer, marchannd d'escalves sur la côte ouest-africaine* (tr. Mette Dige-Hesse, Paris, 1989), pp. 43–4.

29. Ray Kea, *Settlements, Trade, and Polities on the Seventeenth Century Gold Coast* (Baltimore: Johns Hopkins University Press, 1982), pp. 164–8.

30. Bosman, *Description*, p. 178.

31. Bosman, *Description*, pp. 74–6.

32. Brun, *Schiffarten*, p. 86.

33. Rømer, *Golfe*, p. 120. The practice seems to have begun earlier, for example, Asante's plundering of Denkyira in 1701: Bosman, *Description*, pp. 74–5.

34. Rømer, *Golfe*, p. 98.

35. Rømer, *Golfe*, pp. 98–102, 110, 133.

36. Robin Law's scholarship has done a great deal to establish Dahomey in its regional context and to reduce, to some degree, the idea of its uniqueness; see especially *The Slave Coast of Africa, 1550–1750* (Oxford: OUP, 1992).

37. L. A. Akinjogbin, *Dahomey and its Neighbours, 1708–1818* (Cambridge, CUP 1967),

pp. 39–67; a much modified but similar argument appears in Law, *Slave Coast*, pp. 224–60.

38. [Barbot, Jean] *Barbot on Guinea: The Writings of Jean Barbot on West Africa, 1678–1712* (eds P. E. H. Hair, Adam Jones and Robin Law, 2 vols, London: The Hakluyt Society, vols 175–76, 1992), p. 644; AN: DAOM MS 104, "Relation du Royaume de Judas en Guinée . . . ", pp. 33–35.

39. Robin Law, "Dahomey and the Slave Trade: Reflections on the Historiography of the Rise of Dahomey", *Journal of African History* **27** (1986).

40. Robert Norris, *Memoirs of the Reign of Bossa Ahádee, King of Dahomey an Inland Country of Guiney*. (London, 1789, reprint London: Cass, 1968), pp. 17–19.

41. Archibald Dalzel, *History of Dahomy An Inland Kingdom of Africa* (London, 1793, 2nd edn, London: Cass, 1967), pp. 217–19.

42. For example, Dalzel, *History*, p. 226.

43. William Snelgrave, *A New Account of Some Parts of Guinea and the Slave Trade* (London, 1734, facsimile, London: Cass, 1971), p. 125.

44. Snelgrave, *New Account*, pp. 126, 128, 129.

45. Norris, *Memoirs*, p.135.

46. "Despacho de G[onçal]o Roïz pera se lhe fazer seu côtrauto por que asy o despachou elRey noso senhor," 1509, *MMA* vol. 4, p. 61.

47. For the relationship between concentrations of people in the region around Mbanza Kongo/São Salvador and the development of centralization in Kongo, see John Thornton, "The Kingdom of Kongo, c. 1390–1678: History of an African Social Formation", *Cahiers d'études africaines* (1982), vol. 22, pp. 325–42.

48. Afonso to Manuel, 5 October 1514, *MMA* vol. 1, pp. 314–15.

49. Afonso to João III, 6 July 1526, *MMA* vol. 1, pp. 470–1. This letter has had many interpretations, since it also orders that no more slaves be sold from Kongo, and no merchants come. It was correlated with the end of the first Portuguese mission to Ndongo.

50. These events are outlined in the chronicle of Pero Rodrigues, "História da residência dos Padres da Companhia de Jesus em Angola, e cousas tocantes ao reino, e Conquista" (1 May 1594) *MMA* vol. 4, pp. 546–81.

51. Rodrigues, "História", p. 561–2.

52. On this aspect of the Portuguese rule see Beatrix Heintze, "Das Ende des unabhängigen Staates Ndongo (1617–1630)", *Studien zur Geschichte Angolas im 16. und 17. Jahrhundert. Ein Lesebuch* (Cologne: Rüdiger Köppe Verlag, 1996), pp. 111–14, 117–20, 122–6, 137–44, 156–68.

53. "Copia dos excessos que se cometem no gouerno de Angola que o bispo deu a V. Magestade pedindo remedio delles de presente, e de futuro", 7 September 1619, *MMA* vol. 6, pp. 368–71; Jesuits to Lord Collector, 20 October 1623, *MMA* vol. 15, pp. 512–22.

54. Bartholomeu Paes Bulhão, 16 May 1664, cited in David Birmingham, *Trade and Conquest in Angola: The Mbundu and their Neighbours and the Portuguese* (Oxford: OUP, 1966), p. 120.

55. António de Oliveira de Cadornega, *História general das guerras angolanas (1680–81)* ed. José Matias Delgado and Manuel Alves da Cunha (3 vols, Lisbon 1940–42, reprinted Lisbon, 1972).

56. Elias Alexandre da Silva Corrêa, *História de Angola* (2 volumes, Lisbon: Editorial Ática, 1937), vol. 2, p. 50.

57. Silva Corrêa, *História*, vol. 2, pp. 54–5, 60–61.
58. Andrew Battell, *The Strange Adventures of Andrew Battell of Leigh, in Angola and the Adjoining Regions* (ed. E. G. Ravenstein, London: Hakluyt Society, 2nd series, no. 6, 1901; reprinted Nendeln, Liechtenstein: Kraus, 1967), pp. 20–23 (see p. 30 for their manner of making palm wine).
59. Luis Mendes de Vasconçelos to King, 28 August 1617, *MMA* vol. 6, pp. 283–5.
60. Battell, *Strange Adventures*, pp. 32–3.
61. Manoel Correia Leitão, "Relação e breve sumário da viagem que eu, o sargento-mor dos moradores do Dande, fiz às remotas partes de Cassange e Olos, por mandado do Il.mo e Ex.mo Sr Governador e capitão-general dêstes Reinos, D. António Alvares da Cunha" (1755–6) in Gastão Sousa Dias (ed.), "Uma viagem a Cassange nos meados do seculo XVIII", *Boletim da Sociedade de Geografia de Lisboa* **56** (1938), pp. 19–20.
62. Alexander Falconbridge, *An Account of the Slave Trade on the Coast of Africa* (London: J. Phillips, 1788), p. 9.
63. On the rivalry and the sources of supply of slaves in that period, see John Thornton, "As guerras civis no Congo e o tráfico de escravos: a história e a demografia de 1718 a 1844 revisitadas", *Estudos Afro-Asiáticos* **32** (1997), pp. 55–74.
64. Marcellino d'Atri, "Giornate apostoliche fatte da me Fra Marcellino d'Atri . . . 1690" [1702] in Carlo Toso (ed.), *L'anarchia congolese nel sec. XVII. La relazione inedita di Marcellino d'Atri* (Genoa: Bozzi, 1984)(original pagination marked), pp. 76, 86.
65. Luca da Caltanisetta, "Relatione della Missione fatta nel Regno di Congo per il Padre Fra Luca da Caltanisetta . . . sino alla fine del 1701", in Raimondo Rainero (ed.), *Il Congo agli inizi del setecento nella relazione del P. Luca da Caltanisetta* (Florence: La Nuova Italia, 1974) (original foliation marked), fol. 99v.
66. Raimondo da Dicomano, "Informação sobre o Reino de Congo" (1798) in "Informação do Reino do Congo de Frei Raimundo de Dicomano", *Stvdia* **34** (1972), pp. 19–34 (with original foliation marked), fol. 115.
67. IHGB, DL 106/15, "Relação que faço cormanamente assem da viagem como das Marchas, Sitios e Provincia donde passou o Exercito . . . no anno de 1755", fol. 1v.
68. D. António de Lencastre, 25 November 1772, and 1773 in António de Almeida, "Relações com os Dembos das cartas do Dembado de Kakulu-Kahenda", in *I Congresso da História da Expansão Portugesa no mundo* (4th section, Lisbon, 1938), docs 30 and 32, pp. 40–1.
69. A pioneering work in this regard is Daniel Littlefield, *Rice and Slaves: Ethnicity and the Slave Trade in Colonial South Carolina* (Baton Rouge: Louisiana State University Press, 1981); see also John Thornton, *Africa and Africans in the Making of the Atlantic World, 1400–1800* (2nd edn, Cambridge: CUP, 1998), pp. 135–6.
70. Large selections from his diaries are published in Douglas Hall, *In Miserable Slavery: Thomas Thistlewood in Jamaica, 1750–86* (London: Macmillan, 1989).
71. Gonzalo Fernández de Oviedo y Valdés, *Historia general y natural de las Indias* (ca. 1532, several modern editions), Lib IV, cap IV.
72. Crucial documentation on these two has been printed in Cipriano de Utrera, *Historia Militar de Santo Domingo (Documentos y Noticias)* (3 vols, Ciudad Trujillo, n.d. [1950]) vol. 1, pp. 383–400.
73. For example, one surviving inventory of an early estate, the Gorjón estate, probated in 1547, shows all the cattlemen to be Senegambians: Escripta de Licenciado Cerrato, 17 December 1547, Incháustegui Cabral, *Reales cédulas* vol. 1, pp. 236–9.
74. Grájeda to King, 28 June 1546, Utrera, *Historia Militar* vol. 1, p. 389.

75. Juan de Castellanos, *Elegías de Varones illustres de Indias* (Caracas; Academia de la Historia, 1962), elegy 5, canto 2.

76. Gov. Jonathan Atkins to Sec. Joseph Williamsom 3/13 October 1675, *Calendar of State Papers, Colonial*, vol. 9, #690, p. 294.

77. Lt Gov Molesworth to William Blathwayt, 29 August 1685, *Calendar*, vol. 12, #339, p. 82–3.

78. Pierre J. Pannet, *Report on the Execrable Conspiracy Carried Out by the Amina Negroes on the Danish Island of St. Jan in America 1733* (ed. and trans. Aimery P. Caron and Arnold R. Highfield, Christiansted: Artilles Press, 1984), pp. 12–14, 17.

79. Ray Kea, " 'When I die, I shall return to my own land': An 'Amina' Slave Rebellion in the Danish West Indies, 1733–34", in John Hunwick and Nancy Lawler (eds), *The Cloth of Many Colored Silks: Papers on History and Society Ghanaian and Islamic in Honor of Ivor Wilks* (Evanston IL: Northwestern University Press, 1996), pp. 174–80.

80. Pannet, *Report*, p. 18.

81. Champigny to Gardelin, 12 April 1734, and Longueville to Minister, 21 June 1734, and Orgueville to the Minister, 1 July 1734, in Aimery P. Caron and Arnold R. Highfield (ed. and trans.) *The French Intervention in the St. John Slave Revolt of 1733–34* (Christiansted, 1981), pp. 34, 41–49.

82. Pannet, *Report*, p. 17.

83. J. Thornton, "The African dimensions of the Stono Robellion", *American Historical Review* 96 (1991): 1101–13.

84. Maria del Carmen Borrego Pla, *Los Palenques de Cartagena de Indias a finales del siglo XVII* (Seville, 1971), p. 27.

85. This argument is presented in detail in John Thornton, "African Soldiers in the Haitian Revolution", *Journal of Caribbean History* 25 (1991), pp. 58–72.

86. "St Domingo Disturbances: A journal kept there and given to Correspondent", *Philadelphia General Advertiser* 10 November 1791, n. 348, 11 November 1791, n. 349 (events of September); Jean-Phillippe Garran, *Rapport sur les troubles de Saint Domingue* (4 volumes, Paris, vol. 1, An V, vol. 2 An VI) vol. 1, p. 260; Mr. Gros, *An Historick Recital of the Different Occurrences in the Camps of Grande-Riviere, Dondon, Sainte Suzanne and others from the 26th of October 1791 to the 24th of December of the same year* (Baltimore: Samuel and John Adams, nd [1793]) pp. 64, 95–7.

87. Thornton, "African Soldiers", pp. 73–4.

88. John Gabriel Stedman, *Narrative of a Five Years Expedition against the Revolted Negroes of Surinam* (mod. edn Richard and Sally Price, Baltimore and London: Johns Hopkins University Press, 1988), pp. 397–9, see also pp. 404–6, 408 (for an actual engagement).

89. Carlos Esteban Dieve, *La Esclavatud del negro en Santo Domingo, 1492–1844* (2 volumes, Santo Domingo: Museo del Hombre, 1980), pp. 446–7, 451.

90. Aguado, *Recopilación Historial de Venezuela* (Caracas: Academia Nacional de la Historia, 1963) Book 3, cap. 11.

91. Philip Nichols, *Sir Francis Drake Revived* (London, 1628), p. 51 (modern edition in Irene Wright (ed.) *Documents concerning English Voyages to the Spanish Main, 1569–80*, London: Hakluyt Society, 2nd series, vol. 71, 1932).

92. Nichols, *Drake*, p. 63. The leader of this section of the runaways was one Anton Mandinga (according to Diego de Frias Trejo to Crown, 15 May 1578 in Wright, *English Voyages*, p. 217), and if they had organized themselves by nation, as runaways sometimes did, then perhaps the country in question would have been in Senegambia.

93. Luis de Rojas to King, 16 April 1586, in Ermila Troconis de Veracoechea, *Documentos*

para el estudio de los esclavos negros en Venezuela (Caracas: Academia Nacional de Historia, 1969), p. 79.

94. Jeronimo de Suazo to King, 16 February 1603 and 25 January 1604, published in Roberto Arrazola, *Palenque, Primer Pueblo Libre de America* (Cartagena: Hernandez, 1970), pp. 35, 41.
95. Juan Pando de Estrada to King, 24 May 1686 in Arrazola, *Palenque*, p. 85.
96. Jan Blaer, "Diario da viagem do capitão João Blaer aos Palmares em 1645" (trans. Alfredo de Carvalho), *Revista do Instituto Archaeologico e Geograhico Pernambucano* **10**, 56 (March 1902), pp. 91–2.
97. "Relação das guerras feitas aos Palmares de Pernambuco no tempo do governador D. Pedro de Almeida de 1675 a 1678", (ed. Drummond) *Revista do Instituto de Historia e Geographia do Brasil* **22** (1859), pp. 306–7.
98. R. P. du Tertre, *Historie générale des Antilles habitées par les François* (4 vols, Paris: Thomas Sully, 1667) vol. 3, p. 202.
99. Pierre François Xavier de Charlevoix, *Historie de l'Isle Espagnole ou de S. Domingue* (2 vols, Paris: F. Barrois, 1730–31) vol. 1, p. 123.

Index

185